Fighting for Liberty and Virtue

OTHER BOOKS BY MARVIN OLASKY

Loving Your Neighbor, editor
(1995)

Philanthropically Correct
(1993)

Abortion Rites: A Social History of Abortion in America
(1992)

The Tragedy of American Compassion
(1992)

Patterns of Corporate Philanthropy: The Progressive Deception,
co-author (1992)

Central Ideas in the Development of American Journalism
(1991)

Patterns of Corporate Philanthropy: Funding False Compassion,
co-author (1991)

More Than Kindness, co-author
(1990)

The Press and Abortion, 1838-1988
(1988)

Freedom, Justice, and Hope, editor
(1988)

Prodigal Press
(1988)

Patterns of Corporate Philanthropy
(1987)

Turning Point, co-author
(1987)

Corporate Public Relations: A New Historical Perspective
(1987)

Fighting for Liberty and Virtue

Political and Cultural Wars in Eighteenth-Century America

Marvin Olasky

REGNERY PUBLISHING, INC.
Washington D.C.

This book was originally published in 1995 by Crossway Books, a division of Good News Publishers. It is reprinted by arrangement with Crossway Books.

First Regnery edition published 1996.

Library of Congress Cataloging-in-Publication Data

Olasky, Marvin N.
Fighting for liberty and virtue : political and cultural wars in eighteenth-century America / Marvin Olasky.
p. cm.
Includes bibliographical references and index.
Originally published : Wheaton, Ill. : Crossway Books, 1995.
ISBN 0-89526-712-8
1. United States—Politics and government—To 1775. 2. United States—Politics and government—1775–1783. 3. United States—Politics and government—1783–1809. I. Title.
[E195.043 1996]
973.3—dc20 96-7004
CIP

Published in the United States by
Regnery Publishing, Inc.
An Eagle Publishing Company
422 First Street, SE, Suite 300
Washington, DC 20003

Distributed to the trade by
National Book Network
4720-A Boston Way
Lanham, MD 20706

Printed on acid-free paper.
Manufactured in the United States of America

10 9 8 7 6 5 4 3 2 1

For my grandparents,

Mr. and Mrs. Louis Olasky
and
Mr. and Mrs. Robert Green

"We have fled from the political Sodom;
let us not look back, lest we perish and become a
monument of infamy and derision to the world."

—Samuel Adams

An Oration Delivered at the State House in Philadelphia,
to a very Numerous Audience,
on Thursday the 1st of August, 1776

Acknowledgments

Fighting for Liberty and Virtue owes its existence to the passion and generosity of Howard and Roberta Ahmanson, whose friendship over nearly a decade I enormously value. The book was improved by the discerning critiques of Herbert Schlossberg and Jay Budziszewski; they are not responsible for the errors that remain. The five people who are humanly most responsible for what good I do are my four children—Pete, David, Daniel, and Benjamin—and my wife, Susan, who was writing a novel for children about Patrick Henry's daughter, Annie, as I was writing this history. A marriage in which husband and wife not only enjoy each other's company but share the same historical heroes is blessed indeed. Love for and pride in our four sons, all becoming men of character, motivates me to leave them a legacy.

Another debt I owe is to my grandparents, now all deceased; it is to them and their generation of immigrants that I dedicate this book. They courageously came to this country early in this century from thousands of miles away, leaving behind family and familiar environs. They came from lands where they had little liberty to a country whose streets were paved, or at least coated, with virtue. Much that was unholy went on in the back alleys, but at least publicly the nation's leaders were committed to upholding liberty without license. When my grandparents became citizens they committed themselves to upholding a constitution that was ambiguously worded in places but had not been stood on its head. They worked very hard to make a better life for their descendants.

I also thank Lane Dennis, Len Goss, Steve Hawkins, Jan Ortiz, and others at Crossway who are devoted to publishing good books.

Most of all, I am grateful to Jesus Christ, the Lord of history, who brought the world out of nothingness and me out of darkness.

Table of Contents

Preface

BY CAL THOMAS

The English poet Samuel Taylor Coleridge (1772-1834) said of the past, "If men could learn from history, what lessons it might teach us! But passion and party blind our eyes, and the light which experience gives is a lantern on the stern, which shines only on the waves behind us!"

Sadly, the closest we get to history today is the instant replay. A generation of baby boomers, who mostly discarded the past as morally inferior to the present, has mired us in a cultural goo from which it is extremely difficult to extricate ourselves.

If we are to be liberated from this mire of our own making and find true freedom, I am convinced our emancipation will not come by external means—that is, by government, no matter which party or philosophy is in power, or by "values" imposed from the top-down. "Trickle-down" morality won't work. We must pursue "bubble-up" morality—that which flows from the people, upward. Historically, the quality of leadership has reflected the quality of followership. When ancient Israel was obedient to the law and the will of God, they generally enjoyed righteous leadership. But when they pursued their own ways and turned their backs on God, they got terrible leadership, not only to punish them, but to bring them to repentance and restoration.

In our day, we have confused the words "values" and "virtue." In her book, *The Demoralization of Society*, Gertrude Himmelfarb properly defines the words. Values, she says, are external. Virtue is internal. We have values, she argues, when sufficient numbers of citizens exhibit virtue in their own lives. Government cannot give us virtue. We must fight for it against the condition that is in each of us, a condition diagnosed in scripture as "sin." If we win the battle over vice, and virtue prevails, only then will society accept the values which shared virtue produces.

I am disturbed by the values movement and other activities which seek to impose, through political power alone, a code of morals and ethics that many in the camp advancing such a code do not sufficiently practice in their own lives. Whether it is prayer in government schools, stable families, or sexual purity (the list is much longer), one wishes those desiring the culture to reflect such things would, themselves, become virtue's mirror. Instead, too many are asking government to cheerlead these virtues as if we were engaged in a contest to vanquish the forces of darkness on the cultural playing field, rather than first conquering such things in our own hearts.

Professor Marvin Olasky offers us a rearview mirror and a compass. In this book, he looks back at previous battles between vice and virtue and the political conditions that resulted when one prevailed and the other was in remission. He first focuses on our relationship with Mother England. It is important for us to consider what virtues in most of our forebears and what vices in most of the English authorities preceded the American Revolution. We fought against tyranny, yes, but we fought for something far greater. Our revolution was an enormous personal and corporate battle to gain independence from Britain while declaring our dependence on God.

I am proud to say I knew of (and was quoting) Marvin Olasky before his discovery by conservative think tanks and Speaker of the House Newt Gingerich. That the Speaker now uses every opportunity to extol Professor Olasky's ideas is not only a testimony to his sound scholarship but an affirmation from one history professor (the Speaker) to another (Olasky) that history is something we shall repeat if we learn nothing from it.

Virtue—"Conformity to a standard of right"—produces liberty. But liberty, uncontrolled by virtue, quickly becomes license, and license produces a climate of licentiousness. It is that condition in which we presently find ourselves. No power on earth can free a people from this vice grip. Remaining in such a condition is the greatest threat to our liberties.

Two old hymns come to mind when I think of history. One is "Oh God our help in ages past, our hope for years to come; Be Thou our guide while life shall last and our eternal home."

And the other offers a challenge to us, just as it did to those who passed this way before: "Once to every man and nation comes the moment to decide; In the strife of truth with falsehood, for the good or evil side. Some great cause, some great decision, offering each the bloom or blight; And the choice goes by forever, 'twixt that darkness and that light."

This is our moment to decide. The memory of what those who have gone before stood for is fading. Only those fifty and older can remember a time before the present moral crisis—a time when *Ozzie and Harriet*, though an ideal, was worthy of emulation. Now we have *Beavis and Butt-Head.*

The personal knowledge and experience of a nation that once enshrined virtue and resisted sin, at least in its public attitudes, is nearly history. We are embarrassed by that history when we should be embarrassed by the history we are creating for the future to see. The former virtues will not be easily restored, but they must be if we are to hand to our children what was faithfully delivered to us. Those who preceded us were willing to sacrifice their lives, jeopardize their fortunes but, having done so, managed to preserve their sacred honor.

If we do not fight for a restoration of the virtue that has departed from us in the education of our children and grandchildren, and maintain our own marriages and family relationships, we will be overwhelmed by our vices and our very liberty will be crushed by totalitarian elites who will have little to restrain them.

Marvin Olasky's book looks to the past, but his book can illuminate the future. Unfortunately the time is growing short, and the light is growing dim.

Introduction

John Brown, an eighteenth-century English dramatist, poet, composer, and essayist, saw his country in danger and the American colonies as Britain's hope. Many people today argue that every lifestyle is valid and that private actions are of no concern to anyone but the individuals directly involved. Brown thought differently; in *An Estimate of the Manners and Principles of the Times* (1757), he examined whether "the present ruling Manners and Principles of this Nation may tend to its Continuance or Destruction."[1]

Brown was not optimistic. Leaders of England, he observed, were promiscuous self-pleasers. "We all wish to continue free, tho' we have not the Virtue to secure our Freedom," Brown wrote.[2] "The Spirit of Liberty is now struggling with the *Manners and Principles*, as formerly it struggled with the *Tyrants* of the Time. But the Danger is now greater, because the Enemy is *within*. . . ."[3] British colonists in America would have to fight for liberty and virtue: they would have to fight their own natures, and they might have to fight others within the empire.

Brown's book was an extended essay; this book is a history that spotlights the intersection of politics and morality. For example, the Great Awakening was a mighty revival, yes, but it did not stop there: Christians risen from slumber pushed on for governmental and moral reformation. The French and Indian War ended with Canada changing hands, yes, but there was more to come: Defeat of one evil empire led to criticism of another. Debates over the Constitution emphasized the need for checks and balances within the federal system, yes, but the larger discussion emerged from concern about the ravages of original sin and centered on whether to trust factions within a nation's capital or to promote countervailing forces outside.

This book, in the Brownian tradition, examines the interplay of politics, religion, sex, and revolution. It is a book for those who have read a conventional early-American history text or have some vague memories from high school or college courses; I have assumed a basic knowledge of the major developments and attempted to go deeper without descending into academic trivia. It is a serious work for thoughtful readers, but I have tried to keep the action moving. It is a book with eight long chapters, but each is divided into five sections and includes human interest and specific detail.

The first two chapters of this history examine the cultural and political divide between America and England. Chapter 1 tells of the transvestite governor dispatched by London to America in 1701 and notes the problems of other prize administrators with whom the colonies were favored. It delineates two competing visions of governance and shows how the colonists often frustrated ruling authorities. Chapter 2 describes the attractions of empire—economic, cultural, and social—that forestalled potential movement to independence.

Chapter 3 shows how the spirit of reformation that came with the Great Awakening empowered colonists to burst the golden chains that London was all too willing to provide: Colonists slowly came to oppose official faith in a human king's handing out boons. Chapter 4 describes how the French and Indian War gave more Americans a close-up view of the growing cultural divide. By 1760, propelled by victories for the small government ideal and the renewed interest in holy government that arose out of the Great Awakening, colonists were wondering whether they needed the centralized administration that London favored.

Chapter 5 shows how the independence movement involved two very different groups: Enlightenment-influenced politicians who demanded small government, and Awakening-energized Christians who pushed for holy government. To coalesce against the forces of big government and cultural decadence, leaders of those groups had to hammer together a platform of common principles and agree to disagree on others.

Chapter 6 shows how the British effort in the Revolutionary War, led in London by cabinet members who were promiscuously

Here is a second historical presupposition: This book is written out of a strong belief in God's providence, but an understanding as well that we see through a glass darkly and should not make assumptions about God's particular work in America. For example, unusual weather conditions at crucial junctures during the Revolutionary War often aided the patriotic cause, sometimes by preventing ill-considered American offensives and sometimes by forestalling British attacks; at other times, however, the British received the benefit of supposedly chance occurrences. I know full well that nothing happens by chance, but I do not know exactly why God acted in particular ways at particular times. If I am patient, I hope to find out some day.

And here is my request: I ask readers also to be patient. Overall, eighteenth-century American history has an essential drama, but it is not that of today's television shows, with murders every few minutes to keep viewers from turning channels. The first half of this book might contain more detail than some readers would prefer, but that information helps the drama build, decade by decade, as a corrupt father, instead of granting his growing son more independence, adds layers of control and entices him with vicious lures. The son eventually gains his independence and resolves not to repeat his father's mistakes—but worries whether he is to spend the rest of his life doing what he had pledged to avoid.

heterosexual and homosexual, faltered in the confrontation with Americans who still valued virtue. Colonists who had developed their own governmental structures realized that all of the ruling authorities could not be obeyed; most chose those close at hand and closer to them in philosophy, rather than those across the ocean.[4]

The final two chapters analyze the continuing debate as Americans moved from war with the old order to debates about establishing a new one. Chapter 7 describes the constitutional battle and the continued emphasis of the debaters on the precautions needed to prevent political vice; both Federalists and anti-Federalists worried about the slide that would be inevitable if private corruption grew and sapped public performance. Chapter 8 describes the battle that emerged in the last decade of the century when radical doctrines from France gained support, and when issues of church and state came to the forefront once more.

Parallels to today's debate are inevitable. The preponderance of power has shifted, but today's battling political emphases—small government, big government and/or holy government—would be familiar to our forebears. So would current discussions of term limits, restrictions on judicial power, and other means of leashing leaders. American history displays a regularity in debates over governmental control of the economy, with many of today's ideas similar to those that animated London courtiers and their opponents during the 1760s and 1770s. Nevertheless, I have deliberately refrained in these pages from equating current political leaders and parties with those of the past; readers may draw their own conclusions.

A decent respect to the opinions of readers requires that historians should declare their views of how history proceeds—so here I confess my belief in the importance of individuals. Notable leaders run through these pages: Benjamin Franklin and Patrick Henry, Samuel Adams and the Earl of Sandwich, and many more. Deterministic impersonality has been popular among historians in recent years, but the Bible emphasizes the role of individual leaders who (whether they know it or not) are God's agents for liberation or destruction. Throughout the eighteenth century, the ABCs of decay in high places—adultery, bribery, coverup—were on display. These personal tendencies had a political impact that changed the course of the empire.

CHAPTER ONE

Dual Governments

Like other cities and towns of the British empire, New York City in the early eighteenth century was no Eden. Absent agreement on sanitary procedures, some residents emptied tubs of filth into city streets. Over fifty taverns encouraged hard drinking and fast riding by offering partakers a parting shot: "One Spur in the head is worth two in the heel."[5] Not trusting to conciliators or courts, men fought duels, and even women scuffled with each other: one record shows that a Joan Atkins "with staves swords Clubbs and other weapons, did beat wound and evill treat" Isabelle Maynard.[6] North of the city, other parts of the colony also had problems; the New York legislative assembly recognized that "prophaneness and licentiousness have of late overspread this province."[7]

Along with domestic disharmony came the threat of foreign invasion. In 1700 French officers in Canada proposed to Paris an extravagant invasion plan featuring regular soldiers plus six thousand Indian warriors who would destroy all the towns and villages along the way to Boston, then devastate the city itself and march for New York. Five French warships were to follow along the coast. "Nothing could be easier," a French military theorist argued, "for the road is good, and there are plenty of horses and carriages. The troops would ruin everything as they advanced, and New York would quickly be destroyed and burned."[8]

The French invasion never materialized, but the threat of it concentrated New York minds wonderfully. Demands grew for a law-and-order governor capable of overcoming natural disorder and providing the minimal government needed to protect person and property.[9] Robert Livingston, a prominent New York merchant, sent London an impassioned plea for the appointment of a man who feared God, possessed incorruptible morality, and could win respect from all of New York's factions. He did not want a transvestite liar with aspirations to dictatorship—but that is what New York received in 1701 in the person of Edward Hyde, Lord Cornbury, a cousin of Queen Anne.[10]

Some New Yorkers suspected that the new governor might not be the right man for a difficult job. Cornbury was a heavy drinker. He was delayed in arriving when an English merchant obtained a warrant for his arrest for failing to pay a debt of £600 (almost $50,000 today, estimating from precious metal and commodity prices that a pound then was roughly equivalent to about $70 or $80 now).[11] Cornbury stayed out of jail only by claiming immunity as a member of Parliament. Nevertheless, leading New Yorkers hoped that Cornbury's contacts with the ruling elite could gain the struggling colony favor in important eyes. Moreover, profligacy among British appointees was not unusual; Cornbury's gubernatorial predecessors had incurred for the colony debts of at least £12,000, or roughly $1,000,000 today.

Cornbury's political honeymooon lasted throughout 1702. When he submitted sky-high charges for firewood and candles for the military garrison, and for the expenses of a conference with Iroquois leaders in Albany, the colony's legislative assembly paid him: Defense was essential.[12] In 1703, Cornbury demanded and the assembly voted a doubling of his salary from £600 to £1,200 (close to $100,000 today).

But the governor started to act strangely, in several ways. First—this would attract little attention in New York City now, but was remarkable three centuries ago—Cornbury sometimes became, after drinking heavily, a cross-dresser. William Smith, an eighteenth-century New Yorker, reported that "It was not uncommon for him to dress himself in a woman's habit, and then to patrol the fort. . . ."[13] One account noted "general dismay after the queen's kinsman arrived and began marching upon the ramparts in women's clothes . . . [He drew] a world of spectators about him and consequently as many censures for exposing himself in such a manner on all the great Holidays and even in an hour or two after going to the 'Communion.'"[14] Manhattanites even then could tolerate some weirdness, but a transvestite governor was too much.

By the end of 1703, therefore, New York assemblymen began to look more critically at Cornbury's spending policy that began to resemble one of tax, spend, and steal. The assembly did not go along with Cornbury's request for additional taxes to eliminate the colony's debt but suggested that he bring expenses under control. When Cornbury declared that the assembly had a responsibility to support him, legislators insisted that they were willing to pay taxes but that they were also responsible to protect private property from official theft: "the people of this colony think they have an undoubted . . . property in their goods and estates, of which they ought not to be divested but by their free consent, in such manner, to such ends and purposes, as they shall think fit, and not otherwise."[15]

Cornbury's followers tried to amend the legislators' revenue bill, but they refused to give in and adjourned in 1703 without passing a new tax bill. The next year Cornbury again demanded higher taxes (an additional duty of 10 percent on many imported goods) and said they were necessary for defense, but assembly members suspected that money recently raised for such needs had been "prodigally expended or embezzled."[16] Some said that £1500 raised for cannon to protect New York City may have been spent by Cornbury in the erection of a "pleasure house." As William Smith wrote, legislators "prudently declined any further aids, till they were satisfied that no misapplication had been made."[17]

Cornbury got back at the assembly first by refusing to pay the salaries of its clerk and doorkeeper and then by dissolving it. Since he still needed money, he ordered new elections but was chagrined to find that voters generally returned to office the same men.[18] Cornbury's political effectiveness fell further in 1705 when a French privateer entered the defenseless New York harbor and "put the inhabitants into great consternation." Assemblymen then voted funds for the defense of the frontiers and harbor, but only on condition that they could also nominate a treasurer responsible to them. The assembly was explicit on how and when the money should be spent, and also raised questions about the use of funds previously appropriated for defense, and the payment of taxpayer money to Cornbury's friends for "services never rendered."

Cornbury huffed and puffed about what today is called legislative gridlock, then dissolved the assembly again.[19] He took his revenge by giving away huge amounts of the colony's land to those who flattered him; as William Smith put it, Cornbury "beggared half the province by the extortions of his favorites."[20] Furious assemblymen did what they could to limit Cornbury's authority by setting up an independent board of commissioners to oversee special appropriations.[21]

HUGE GOGGLE EYES AND A SOFT, FAWNING GRIN

New Yorkers, in going outside the established authority, were taking their first small step toward the American Revolution. So were leaders in other colonies when they forced concessions from officials like Cornbury. Appointments like his were not unusual. Royal governors owed their posts to political connections in England; most apparently valued the assignments as opportunities for private enrichment rather than public service. Money-making dreams often did not become reality: salaries often were small, and economic perquisites of office meager. But government's economic power created opportunities, and those who were willing to take bribes and cheat had the opportunity to garner large tracts of land or conspire with pirates and privateers. Let's examine the nature of colonial government during the first half of the century.

One initially obvious problem is that honor in graft-friendly offices was rare. Nomination of governors was in the hands of Britain's secretary of state for the southern department, and positions in the colonial bureaucracy often went to "pimps, valets de chambre, electioneering scoundrels . . . decayed courtiers and abandoned, worn-out dependents," in the words of one disgusted American observer. "Whenever we find ourselves encumbered with a needy Court-Dangler whom, on Account of Connections, we must not kick down Stairs, we kick him up into an American Government," an Englishman would comment.[22] Other appointees also gained their positions not because of superior ability but through patronage; a chief justice of a province received appointment after "publically prostituting his honour and conscience in an election," and a tax collector received his reward after "prostituting his handsome wife."[23]

Repeatedly, colonial governorships were factors in British economic transactions.[24] New Hampshire's Benning Wentworth, the colonial governor who set the record for longest continuous service (twenty-five years), achieved his position because he failed in business. In 1733, Wentworth delivered a large shipment of timber to the Spanish government, but relations between Spain and England worsened, Spain refused to pay, and Wentworth could not pay his debts. Wentworth's London creditors saw that Wentworth would be able to repay them only if he became a colonial governor with a good salary, so they used their political ties with the Duke of Newcastle to get Wentworth the job in 1741.[25]

Gubernatorial appointments were so important and so potentially lucrative because the governor, unless stopped by the colonial assembly, could combine major portions of legislative, judicial, and executive power. A skillful governor could have considerable influence over legislation in that he could summon and dissolve the assembly as he chose, and could also wield his absolute veto (which he was instructed to use energetically to protect royal prerogatives) whenever he chose. A governor had judicial power not only through his power to make judicial appointments (with assistance from the governor's council that he appointed) but also because, with the council, he was the provincial appeals court. Only in major cases could appeals go past him to the Privy Council in Great Britain.

Colonial assemblymen often commented on this concentration of influence. They came to believe it vital to restrict the influence of government whenever possible, and to separate powers within government. As they tried to develop honest political institutions from the 1720s through the 1750s, they could not look to British government for guidance: British subjects on both sides of the Atlantic were aware of the degree of corruption in London.[26] Widely known ballads accurately depicted Robert Walpole, prime minister for two decades during that period, as a corrupt politician with "Belly not small . . . huge goggle Eyes, and a soft fawning Grin."[27] Walpole debauched public morals both through bribery and draining the treasury; when investigations and audits were inescapable, Walpole delayed them for months or even years, with crucial records lost in the shuffle.[28]

Walpole was not able, however, to stop publication in London (and republication in America) of the articles known as Cato's Letters. From 1720 to 1723 authors John Trenchard and Thomas Gordon reported that "Public corruption and abuses have grown upon us," with offices handed to "worthless and wicked men" whose motto could be "luxury, idleness, and expense."[29] Later in the decade and continuing into the 1730s, another critical newspaper, the *Craftsman*, ran contributions by Henry St. John, Viscount Bolingbroke, a former prime minister who knew from his own experience the dangers of dissolute living, and thus had the background to evaluate political corruption and its consequences. Bolingbroke complained that the "Corruption and Contrivances of evil Ministers" had produced an unrepresentative Parliament where bribery so ran the show that Britain was subject to "the arbitrary Will and fantastical Government of *such Prostitutes*. . . ."[30]

The willingness to be bribed was also a weak point in British colonial administration, and subjects west of the Atlantic paid attention. Perceiving early in the century London's desire to have colonies pay for their own governance, colonists gained leverage and used it to determine salaries and approve fees for appointed officials. This in turn enabled them to gain a share in the administration and achieve power "even beyond that of the British House of Commons."[31] One New Jersey assemblyman, noting that the governor could not compel the assembly to appropriate even a shilling, said of the London-appointed officials, "let us keep the dogs poore and we'll make them do what we please."[32]

The cynicism of colonial appointments had an unanticipated long-term effect. Many appointees were ready to accept bribe-accompanied legislative initiatives (that would then become precedents) if they could do so with little risk of reprimand from London. Virginia and Pennsylvania forced the governors to choose sheriffs from among local nominees. New Jersey and Maryland required all appointees to have local residence. Pennsylvania required that all militia officers be chosen by election rather than through appointment. In South Carolina, the legislature appointed the treasurer, comptrollers, and all tax gatherers. Everywhere, even early in the century, the colonists were challenging British procedures and establishing their own rules.

Legislators did not typically list permanent salaries for royal officials, so the officials knew that the performance reviews done by those they nominally ruled deeply affected their livelihoods. Colonial assemblymen also pushed for highly specific appropriations, and demanded—on grounds that later would be summarized as "no taxation without representation"—the exclusive right to lay taxes, make appropriations, and audit accounts of public officials.[33] Governors generally retained some authority over the method of tax gathering, but in most colonies legislators over the first half of the century gained the power to choose the colony's treasurer, and often other revenue officers as well.[34]

Sometimes colonial legislatures preferred bureaucratic positions to be left unfilled, except in times of military crisis, so that more damage would not be done. Colonists in this regard saw the breadth of the Atlantic Ocean, for once, as an advantage: A crossing of the ocean might require two months, and pirates might seize governors for ransom.[35] Virginians enjoyed a six-year period early in the century when they were without a governor or lieutenant governor in Williamsburg: one chose to collect his salary as an absentee, another died soon after his arrival, and a third was captured by French marauders on his way to Virginia. During the six years, the colony not only survived very well, but Virginians revised and codified their laws and completed other large tasks with alacrity.

The Revolutionary War thus had its roots in the political battles of the first half of the century as a dual governmental authority emerged: The royal governor had executive authority, as well as considerable legislative and judicial influence, but the assembly could see his bids for power and raise them through its control over appropriations. Legislative leaders fought the growth of an executive bureaucracy funded well enough to exist independently of legislative approval. Each colony used its assembly to check the power of royal governors. Local officials and representatives—"lesser magistrates," to use John Calvin's term, in relation to the greater officials sent over by London—fought defensive political wars against attempts by London and royal governors to extort additional money and power.

As they were building an alternative ruling authority, colonial leaders thought about ways to make it work well. They knew the enemy was not just London. The experience of colonial leaders in bribing governors helped them realize that legislators also could be bribed and could conspire with each other against the public good. Colonists typically proposed that legislators serve for only short periods of time, for prolonged power tempted a representative to join with other representatives in conniving against the public. Legislators who enjoyed life in the capital more than simpler countryside pleasures also became easy prey for royal governors.[36]

The inoculation against such corruption was what colonists called "rotation of offices." After one or two terms, a representative was replaced, but could come back later. Rotation also was accomplished unofficially by keeping legislative pay low; thus membership was unattractive. Henry Beekman of New York hoped to leave the New York assembly in 1745: "If other good men Can be fixed on, I had rather be out than in."[37] Edward Shippen of Pennsylvania, when asked to run for the assembly there, was "not anxious to be in the House. A seat there would give me much trouble, take up a great deal of my time and yield no advantage."[38]

Legislators received no regular salaries and had to make do with a stipend for attendance that often barely covered expenses. Since legislative posts brought with them only a pint of power and a dollop of money, John Adams' feelings on being chosen a representative for the first time were apparently not unusual: "Many Congratulations were offered, which I received civilly, but they gave no Joy to me," Adams wrote. "At this time I had more Business at the Bar, than any Man in the Province: My health was feeble; I was throwing away as bright prospects [as] any Man ever had before him. . . ."[39]

Americans recognized a staggering contrast between the potentially enriching life of a member of Parliament in London and that of an assemblyman in the colonies, where public service generally was service. Colonial assemblymen could not obtain peerages, unlike their major-league counterparts; most of the lucrative positions as tax collectors or judges were reserved for Englishmen who were well-connected in London (but not well-enough connected to get the same or any position in London). Since the colonies did not have standing armies or huge bureaucracies, political connections did not lead to lucrative contracts for supplying soldiers, except during the French and Indian War. In the colonial lands of opportunity, a political career was not the best way to make a fortune.

Even without a formal rotation of offices, therefore, colonial one-termers were common. Massachusetts averaged about a 45 percent turnover per session from 1700 through the Revolution; New York averaged 33 percent, and New Jersey slightly over 50 percent. In Virginia and South Carolina over half the legislators elected stayed just one term.[40] The contrast between a close-to-the-people assembly and a distant royal government could not have been clearer.

How Dare You Preach in My Government

Now, back to Lord Cornbury's experience, and how it displayed religion as the wild card in all these serious games of governance. For three-fourths of the century leaders of the Church of England (supported by mandatory tithes) often provided a moral cover for London appointees; dissenting ministers—Presbyterians, Congregationalists, Baptists—sometimes challenged corruption. For example, as Cornbury became unpopular he wrapped himself in Anglican robes: Support from the state-established church could make it seem that opposition to him was rebellion against God.[41] Cornbury won influential support by pushing the colonial assembly to give Trinity Church, an Anglican stronghold, a lucrative corporate charter with an ample supply of real estate. He also jailed dissenting preachers so that he could fill vacant parishes with Anglican clerics.

The governor's imprisoning highhandedness was a declaration of war on Presbyterian and Dutch Reformed ministers. Cornbury declared that they had no right to preach without his gubernatorial license, which he could provide or withhold at his discretion. Some tame ministers submitted and trilled niceties about Cornbury. In 1707, Francis Makemie, just elected moderator (chairman) of the first American presbytery, did not.[42] He had been traveling to Boston from the presbytery's first meeting in Philadelphia; when local Dutch Reformed and French Reformed church members invited Makemie to preach in their buildings, he followed protocol by requesting permission from the governor. When Cornbury refused, Makemie resolved to preach anyway.

On Sunday, January 19, 1707, Makemie conducted a service,

including the baptism of an infant, at a private home with about ten persons present. Not wanting to seem secretive, Makemie preached "in as publick a manner as possible," with the doors open. Makemie's sermon about grace and character was of use to his listeners that day, but some of his specifics might also have applied to the life of their governor: Makemie spoke of "Irregularities of Life and Conversation," and noted that "To whom much is given, of them much is required . . . the higher our Station or Calling is, the more shining and exemplary should our lives be."[43]

Makemie also said that "as it is profitable to our Bodies, to lead orderly lives, so it would be highly advantageous to our Estates; for how expensive a darling Sin and Vice has proved to many families, and particular persons, who have been brought, by irregular & riotous living, to want & Poverty."[44] Particular persons, Makemie noted, should understand

> the great reproach, and manifest scandal, that an irregular life, and disorderly Conversation brings on the Christian Religion, and our holy Profession. What a shame is it to own a God, whom we neither honour, adore, nor obey, but daily dishonour, and offend, by our words and actions . . . to profess his Ways & Service, & in our lives to fulfill our divers lusts, rebel against our God, and act the works of the Devil. What a scandal and reproach is it to see those who boast and value themselves as Christians, yet acting and speaking what Pagans would be ashamed of.[45]

Cornbury reacted quickly to the pointed preaching of Makemie and his fellow Presbyterian pastor, John Hampton, who preached that day at Newtown on Long Island. He issued a warrant for their arrest: The warrant stated that the two men were preaching "without having obtained My License for so doing . . . they are gone into Long-Island, with Intent there to spread their Pernicious Doctrine and Principles." Cornbury's men seized Makemie and Hampton and brought them before Cornbury, who accused them of preaching without a license, but Makemie produced his license from Virginia, and Hampton his from Maryland.[46]

Cornbury then asked (according to a Makemie supporter), "How dare you take upon you to Preach in my Government, without my License?" Makemie responded, "We have Liberty from an Act of

Parliament made the first year of the reign of King William and Queen Mary, which gave us Liberty, with which Law we have complied." Makemie went on to explain that even though he was not a minister settled in New York he was operating within the law, and Cornbury concluded the discussion by giving up his legal pretensions and stressing pure power: "You shall not spread your Pernicious Doctrines here! . . . None shall Preach in my Government, without my License . . . you must go to Gaol!"[47]

And go Makemie and Hampton did, for forty-six days, from January until March 11. At that point the two were released. For a reason still unknown, charges against Hampton were dropped, but Makemie was remanded for a June 3 trial. By that time his sermon had been published, with two biblical texts on the frontispiece: Matthew 5:11—"Blessed are ye when men shall revile you, and persecute you, and shall say all manner of evil against you falsely, for my Name's sake"; and Acts 5:29—"Then Peter, and the other Apostles answered, and said, We ought to obey God, rather than men."

At the trial, the prosecuting attorney stressed statutes dating back to the time of Henry VIII. Then it was the turn of Makemie's attorney William Nicoll, who stated that the prosecutor "has been entertaining us with some History from the Reign of K. Henry 8. And it is fit we should entertain him with some History also, more ancient, and from better Authors, and that is from the Acts of the Apostles." Nicoll argued that "Teaching, or Preaching, or Speaking, in itself, or by the Common Law, was never found a Crime; for the Apostle Paul Preached a very new Doctrine to the Athenians, which was an ancient Commonwealth, and was not Condemned or Imprisoned for it, but they were curious to hear again, Acts 17."

Nicoll implied that Cornbury's standards were lower than those of the Athenians, who thought of themselves as lovers of truth; Cornbury's refusal to allow preaching was related to a lust for money similar to that of the Ephesians who refused in Acts 18 to tolerate "any Doctrine which tended to infringe the gain of the Silver-Smiths. . . ." Nicoll was equating Cornbury's persecution with mob action, which meant that Cornbury was not fulfilling his gubernatorial mandate to maintain order. The jury accepted Nicoll's conclusions and brought in a verdict of not guilty, one that told everyone that Cornbury was guilty not only of venality but also of persecution. Makemie was released, but Cornbury had one more recourse: The judge stayed in the governor's good graces by imposing on the innocent Makemie the cost of his trial and imprisonment, £83 (the equivalent of perhaps $6,000 today). That last insult so enraged New York citizens that in the following year, 1708, the assembly passed an act making it illegal to assess an innocent party for expenses.[48]

Cornbury's reach for religious tyranny led to his dismissal from office. Eighteenth-century New Yorker William Smith described how Cornbury's "persecution of the Presbyterians . . . increased the number of his enemies. The Dutch too were frightful of his religious rage against them, as he disputed their right to call and settle ministers, or even schoolmasters, without his special license." When these factors were combined with Cornbury's "excessive avarice, his embezzlement of the publick money, and his sordid refusal to pay his private debts," Cornbury's reputation fell so low "that it was impossible for his adherents, either to support him, or themselves, against the general opposition."[49]

New Yorkers, detailing the governor's outbursts and tyrannical inclinations, sent letters of protest to London. The most significant came from Robert Livingston, whose letter at the turn of the century had been instrumental in bringing Cornbury. Livingston complained that the governor was "wholly addicted to pleasure," that the colony's public debt had grown so large that it would take at least a decade to clear it, and that Cornbury's reputation for taking public money for his own use was hurting the reputation of the crown.[50]

When the new assembly met in August 1708, William Nicoll, Makemie's lawyer, was elected speaker. Nicoll moved quickly. A committee of grievances took up the problem of Cornbury and condemned his tax-spend-and-steal philosophy, with particular emphasis on the collection of extravagant fees not established by law, and the imposition and levying of taxes and port charges without the assembly's consent. The assembly unanimously adopted the committee's report and sent its resolution to London along with a clear message: Given the volatility of New York politics, Cornbury's continuance in office could provoke rebellion and French invasion.[51]

Even though English monarchs in the 1700s no longer ruled

autocratically, it still took gumption for London officials to remove the cousin of the queen. But the cumulative impact of the complaints, and the threat of civil war at a time when hostilities with France and Canada were likely, was too much to overlook. London sent a new governor in 1709.

Cornbury tried to make a quick getaway—but he was not allowed to leave immediately. During his last several years as governor he had continued to buy huge amounts of liquor, and some dresses and other items as well, from ten merchants of New York. Cornbury went into debt because he was unable to steal as much as previously, but as long as he had the political power to destroy them, the merchants were unwilling to bring suit. The day after the new governor arrived, however, one of the merchants, Stephen Delancey, initiated legal action to have Cornbury jailed for not paying debts that amounted to £10,000, and other creditors immediately joined in.

The displaced governor desperately pulled strings in London, where political connections outweighed justice; Cornbury lugubriously complained to his father, the Earl of Clarendon, that he had exhausted his fortune in public service, only to learn that "a Porter in the streets of London is a happier man than a governour in America."[52] Eventually the faithful cousin, Queen Anne, ordered Cornbury freed and shipped across the Atlantic. New York was finally rid of him.[53]

The New York Assembly sealed the victory with a declaration in 1711: the "Right of the Assembly to dispose of the money of the Freemen of this Colony does not come from any Commission, Letters Patent or other Grant from the Crown, but from the free Choice and Election of the People, who ought not to be divested of their Property (nor justly can) without their Consent."[54] In colonial eyes, two sets of ruling authorities were emerging: the assembly, representing property holders, and the governor, representing only the king. Colonists continued to want help from England, but they wondered whether governors like Cornbury—a man "bent upon getting as much money as he could squeeze out of the purses of an impoverished people," a man set upon persecution of dissenters—was all they could expect. If so, they could not be at ease in dependence.

The Power of the Crown Shall Be Clipt

New York was not the only colony to have rough times early in the eighteenth century. Massachusetts residents quarreled so often that a frustrated Cotton Mather was driven to call Boston "a Hell upon Earth."[55] Litigation of all kinds increased; Connecticut leaders called court battles involving property and debt "Rhode Islandism," but that was like calling venereal diseases the Spanish or French plague, when they were just as prevalent elsewhere.[56]

New York's middle-state neighbors also were troubled. In Pennsylvania, William Penn had lost hope that "Men of universal Spirits" would build in Pennsylvania a society of "Primitive Christianity Revived."[57] When a provincial judge was impeached for abusing witnesses who appeared before him; when a member of the ruling council called his associates "pestiferous apostates and runagadors"; when "scurvy Quarrels" broke out in the legislature, Penn had to conclude that his colony would not be a place where citizens naturally would "love, forgive, help and serve one another."[58]

Further south, the hospitality that would become famous was already in evidence by 1705. One sojourner wrote, "A Stranger has no more to do, but to inquire upon the Road, where any Gentleman or good House-keeper Lives . . . and the poor Planters, who have but one Bed, will very often sit up, or lie upon a Form or Couch all Night, to make room for a weary Traveller."[59] But the governing process brought with it little rest for the weary: Reliable accounts stressed frequent drunkenness and brutality in high places and the royal governor's cursing with "Billingsgate Language" as he pledged to "hang up those that should presume to oppose him with Magna Carta about their necks."[60]

Nor were the disputes Cornbury inspired unusual. Many colonies were encumbered decade after decade with lordly executives whose financial and sexual lusts were all too evident. Legislatures and crown appointees faced off in colony after colony. For example, Alexander Spotswood became lieutenant governor of Virginia in 1710—he was essentially the colony's chief executive, since the appointed governor took his pay but never showed up—and waded into controversy in 1713 by proposing a measure supposedly designed to benefit all.

Spotswood's bill called for improving the shipment of tobacco by providing warehouses at convenient locations for loading. Spotswood's argument was that (1) some inferior tobacco was being exported, (2) such exports reduced the price and reputation of Virginia leaf, and (3) government agents were needed to inspect tobacco, pay for that leaf of sufficiently good quality, and then ship it. The state monopoly supposedly would lower freight charges, since carriers could pick up tobacco at warehouses rather than at scattered individual plantations. Planters who used their own wharves for loading and shipping, however, opposed the requirement to transport their barrels to the warehouses.

Beneath the public justification lay a clever plan by Spotswood to increase not only governmental economic power but his own power over the government. Spotswood believed that he did not have sufficient patronage for purposes of corruption; under the act he had power to appoint forty tobacco inspectors.[61] Spotswood said colonial legislatures were an annoyance; twenty-five of the inspector jobs went to seat holders in the forty-seven-member House of Burgesses, and sons or brothers of four others also received jobs. Bribed burgesses passed his legislation, and Spotswood relished the legislative majority's dependence on him.[62]

Several developments frustrated Spotswood's corrupting plan, however. First, a drought reduced the tobacco crop by half, which meant that the rationale of the act—to make sure that inferior tobacco was not sent over—no longer held. In a bad year, even inferior tobacco had value. When tobacco inspectors still planned to destroy the inferior tobacco and in the process bring many small planters virtually to ruin, some planters complained that the inspection plan was an arrogant extension of governmental power and Spotswood's personal reign.

Facing voter unrest, Virginia's House of Burgesses passed a bill deferring implementation of the law for another year—but that change was not enough to save the seats of some who had voted for the original plan and had accepted Spotswood's thinly disguised bribes. In new elections, only one-third of the representatives were reelected; most of those had opposed Spotswood. A reform-minded majority passed bills repealing the inspection and warehouse laws and also barring members of the assembly from holding bureaucratic positions.

Spotswood then received more criticism for another patronage deal he engineered, one giving a monopoly of the Indian trade south of Virginia to a company that pledged to provide forts for the colony's protection. Spotswood successfully promoted the agreement as a way to relieve Virginia taxpayers of a fort-building burden, but he and his friends purchased many shares of the company. Soon the measure was seen not as tax reduction but as the creation of a state monopoly for private benefit.

Burgesses in 1715 complained of these matters, and Spotswood replied with full-bore declaration of the London perspective: Virginia's elected representatives, Spotswood complained, were demanding that

> the notions of the people shall be rather followed than the judgment of the king's governor; that the power of the crown shall be clipt by . . . excluding all officers in places of profit or trust from sitting in the assembly . . . not to mention all the ridiculous propositions and grievances which the seditious or ignorant vulgar have set their marks to. . . .[63]

With a colonial legislature and a London-appointed chief executive again at an impasse, the controversy dragged on for years, as the House of Burgesses petitioned King George I for a redress of grievances. One message to the king showed that Spotswood had perverted laws, especially those involving land grants, and had used public funds for private gain by spending more on his house than was appropriated.[64] London officials finally dismissed Spotswood in 1722, exhibiting in that way a willingness to give in to avoid a fight.[65]

The number of London courtiers eager to head west swelled in the 1720s as many sought to recoup their fortunes following the London stock-market collapse known as the South Sea Bubble. William Burnet, controller of the customs in London and one of the big losers, successfully schemed to have himself transferred to Massachusetts. There he found both more and less than he had bargained for.

The *more* lay in extravagant tributes from those who wished a governor's favor: "What the tall cedar shows to different woods/Is Burnet's comely stature mongst the gods," one welcomer said.[66] An ode printed in the *Boston Weekly News-Letter* began, "Great BURNET's name,/Swells big the Sails of Hope as well as Fame!" The new governor was expected to increase exports: "Perhaps the Trading Medium will Demand/Some Master stroke from your Superior Hand." Following that obvious sycophancy came an expression of hope and expectation concerning the new governor's influence at court: "The KING's high Favours bless the prosperous State;/While the KING's Friend's our powerful Advocate." It was even hoped that he could stop Indian raids: "Perhaps a fixed Frontier Barrier too,/If possible, may be atchiev'd [sic] by You." And the praise ascended: "Great Sir! our Hope, and Crown and Joy!/ Whilst you, your mighty Powers for us employ,/A tyde of Love, in every Breast shall spring;/And each glad Tongue your grateful Praises sing:/The joyous Land with every Blessing crown'd/The Fields & Floods shall our blest Name resound."[67]

Burnet also received *less* than he expected in one crucial area: money. Massachusetts legislators, not wanting Burnet to become a Cornbury or a Spotswood, tried to place him under their influence by voting the new governor not an annual salary, but a gift of £1,700—a typical tactic of colonial assemblies attempting to make governors dependent. Burnet sweetly responded that he could not accept, because a system of temporary grants might pressure him to give consent to laws against the crown's interest.[68] That was exactly the point, so the assembly tried to sweeten the deal by almost doubling the grant. Burnet, holding out for more so as to retire his debts rapidly, said that he would not be bribed.

Gridlock arrived. The assembly declared that it would never vote a fixed salary, and a Boston town meeting supported that position. Both sides sent letters to London, and the Board of Trade publicly backed Burnet.[69] The assembly then upped its offer to a grant of £6,000: Burnet's persistence had more than tripled his "gift." Once again, however, he demanded a commitment to that amount for years to come. It is not clear what would have happened because those years did not come for him. Burnet's coach was upset at the Boston ferry, and Burnet, thrown in the water, became ill, developed a fever, and died in a week.[70]

The battle was not yet over. Jonathan Belcher, Burnet's successor, began his tenure by criticizing the assembly for its refusal to authorize a salary. The Boston town meeting once again instructed its representatives to stand firm: "We enjoin you to oppose any bill . . . that may in the least bear upon our natural rights and charter privileges, which we apprehend the giving in to the King's instructions would certainly do."[71] Belcher argued that legislators were attempting to "weaken, if not cast off, the obedience they owe to the Crown and the dependence which all colonies ought to have on their mother country."[72] And yet, Belcher, hungry for money, took the bait, with London's authorization—and a precedent was set that a future generation of Massachusetts partisans would remember.[73]

Not only in New York, Virginia, and Massachusetts but also in other colonies as well, legislators during the first half of the century often took a stand against arbitrary royal government and frequently won limited victories.[74] From the perspective of London, the battles were skirmishes; London's winks and nods were temporary peacekeeping measures, and in time, more aggressive administrations could take steps to bring the colonists to heel.[75]

We Must Not Chuse the Covetous Man

Here's what is crucial: From the beginning of the eighteenth century, two visions of America's political future were in competition. The Board of Trade, set up in London to advise the king on colonial matters, suggested putting all of the colonies under martial law, with a "Military Head or Captain General" serving as dictator. Radical centralizing action was needed, board officials argued in 1701, because colonial privileges were harming "the king's revenue."[76] That same year, however, a book by a Virginian (probably Robert Beverly) who chose to remain anonymous suggested establishment of a colonial general assembly with representation roughly proportional to population: Virginia would have four votes, Maryland and Massachusetts three each, New York, Connecticut, and Rhode Island two each, and Pennsylvania, Carolina, and the Jerseys, one each.[77] The colonial assembly would legislate for America as Parliament did for England.[78]

Neither proposal was adopted, and neither dictatorship nor representative government won out. The threat of one and the hope for another remained in contention for the next seventy-five years, but top London officials enjoyed the power that a muddled system of political payoff accorded them.[79] British politicians emphasized the power of bribery; colonial voters who wanted to fight back learned to emphasize not only the political positions of various candidates, but their character. One New Englander urged election of "Men of Probity," and another wanted "Men of establish'd Characters for Honesty and Integrity. . . ."[80] The *New York Weekly Journal* editorialized, "We must not chuse . . . the Covetous Man; he that is fond of high Places, grasps at Power, or is greedy at Gain, is unfit to be trusted."[81]

Furthermore, legislators who coveted more legislation also were not to be trusted. The colonists typically were legal minimalists: They quoted writers who declared that "it were better to have fewer Lawes, with better Execution, than more Lawes, with more trouble and lesse use."[82] At a time when doctors' remedies were as likely as not to kill their customers, another much-quoted author noted that "as wiser Physicians tamper not excessively with their Patients," so laws should be "complying with the motions of nature, than contradicting it with vehement Administrations. . . ."[83]

Colonists compared their simpler situation with that of England, where (as Henry Robinson wrote) laws were "so numerous and intricate . . . that it is not possible to know them all, much lesse keep them in memory, and avoyd being entangled by them." Robinson asked "Whether the Multiplicity of Courts of Justice do not cause a more mischievous Confusion in the World, than the Babilonian of Languages"; colonists hoped to avoid the Babylon of English justice. The laws then were simple compared to our own, but even then, because of "Meanders, Quirks and subtilties" it was easy for "the very best Lawes wee have to be evaded and frustrated, and the whole Formality and proceedings to be avoyded and deluded by legall fallacies and tricks."[84]

Many colonists, in short, tried to learn from English mistakes by moving consistently toward a small-government approach: they built up an authority that would provide an alternative to royal government, but they did not want that alternative to aggrandize itself. Rotation of offices and limitations on legislation and on the ability of those in office to bribe poor voters were crucial in the battle to reduce corruption.[85]

In the colonists' vision of limited government, taxation without representation was a problem, but so was representation without taxation—that is, voting by those who were at the mercy of the wealthy and thus easy to bribe. Colonial leaders quoted the English jurist Blackstone's accepted view that if those "in so mean a situation as to be esteemed to have no will of their own" were given the vote, they would be tools of the powerful.[86] Colonists discussed the right level of property qualification, one that would exclude the dependent while encouraging voting by all those with a "stake in society." Rural areas of England for three centuries had maintained a property qualification that severely restricted suffrage, but that same requirement would extend it broadly in America, where most white settlers owned land.

The franchise in America extended far more broadly than it did in England. In Virginia, voters needed to own twenty-five settled acres or one hundred unsettled, with lifetime leases as good as ownership. In Massachusetts, almost any farm with a house, barn, and five acres of land sufficed. In Pennsylvania, Delaware, Maryland, Georgia, and the Carolinas, fifty acres were needed. There were other variations, but the overall result was striking: Only about one out of seven male voters in Britain could vote early in the century, but half to three-fourths of the adult, male, white population in America had the franchise. Servants, however, did not vote.[87]

The goal was to include all independent men in community decision-making, and to exclude all who were economically dependent. Property-holding requirements are often seen today as attempts to make government a plaything of the rich, but for the colonists, modest voting restrictions primarily restrained the rich. As one Virginian noted, the goal was "to prevent the undue & over-whelming influence of great landholders in elections" by disfranchising the landless "tenants & retainers" who depended "on the breath & varying will" of their masters.[88]

Along these lines, voting regulations of Essex County, Massachusetts, noted that "all the members of the state are qualified to make the election, unless they have not sufficient discretion, or are so situated as to have no wills of their own."[89] The voting age of twenty-one became standard not because that was seen as the beginning of wisdom but because it was the standard age of independence. Exceptions proved that rule: An eighteen-year-old voted in a Sheffield, Massachusets, election in 1751 after his father had died and he had become head of his family; the town's elected representative explained that the eighteen-year-old "had a good right to vote, for his estate rested in him. . . ."[90]

Since men were family leaders, women generally were dependent. Records from several Massachusetts towns show widows who owned substantial property given voting rights, and the *New York Gazette* reported in 1737 that at a Queens county election "two old Widdows tendered and were admitted to vote."[91] On the other hand, a woman who tried to vote in South Carolina in 1733 was prevented from doing so—and voting by women clearly was rare.[92] In part, the rationale was one family, one vote—but the principle also reflected the emphasis on independence, and on reducing the ability of the rich few to plunder the people in the name of the masses.[93]

At one time even patterns of restriction by race showed that emphasis. Indians who settled down were offered the franchise: All thirty-seven Indian male adults in Stockbridge, Massachusetts, in 1763 were qualified voters, and twenty-nine of them that year actually voted.[94] Slaves were not allowed to vote, but early-American slavery was sometimes a variant of indentured servitude, and it had an exit: Some blacks became free, bought land and property, and had rights similar to those of whites. North Carolina and Virginia documents show voting by blacks, and Berkeley County, South Carolina, records of 1703 and 1704 show that "free Negroes were received and taken as good Electors as the best Freeholders in the Province."[95]

Sadly, such color-blind enfranchisement soon disappeared. Carolina rice cultivation that became highly profitable around 1700 demanded a high concentration of back-breaking labor; white servants bowed out, blacks were forced in, and in the course of a generation, the South Carolina economy became dependent on African slave labor. By 1710, in South Carolina, blacks outnumbered whites; by 1720, the ratio was two to one, and in some agricultural areas five to one. Once whites were outnumbered, their desire to put up defenses grew, and one of those defenses was a deprivation of voting rights even for those blacks who were free.

Virginia rules changed similarly during the 1720s, after several slaves were imprisoned for planning revolts. The royal governor demanded that the House of Burgesses establish the death penalty for conspiracy to revolt, and legislators complied. Amid general hysteria, since free blacks were suspected of aiding slaves, all blacks were disenfranchised. Racial restrictions on voting violated the stake-in-society argument and were a step into the sea of contradictions that engulfed slaveholders who prized their own liberty.[96] Increasingly, as the century wore on, Virginians, such as Richard Henry Lee, who demanded liberty for themselves, attacked the enslavement of others.[97] The visions of small and expansive government also clashed in their view of judicial fiat. Through the first three-fourths of the century colonists were exposed, in John Dickinson's blunt summarizing words, to "the arbitrary decision of bad judges" who extended laws in accordance with their own judgment.[98] Justices appointed by royal governors often used their authority arbitrarily, and the Privy Council was an arrogant supreme court, with final appellate jurisdiction over colonial court decisions. That council, along with the Board of Trade, had authority to eliminate all acts of colonial legislation contrary to imperial policy.[99] London enjoyed such power; colonists objected.

The fundamental problem of British justice went beyond issues of imperial oversight, however. Since the British constitution was an unwritten one, judges had to interpret, and sometimes juggle, Acts of Parliament, laws passed by colonial assemblies, and application of the legal precedents that went into common law, without having a single supreme document. That left judges with broad discretion: "our COURTS EXERCISE A SOVEREIGN AUTHORITY, in determining what parts of the common and statute law ought to be extended."[100] Colonists began to contemplate the usefulness of a written constitution designed to bind judges. They also discussed other means; John Dickinson, for example, proposed that colonial assemblies have the freedom to withhold salaries of judges, so that "there will be some check upon their conduct."[101]

All of these experiences would figure prominently in the debates concerning the Articles of Confederation and the Constitution during the 1770s and 1780s. They also had an impact earlier: From the American perspective each successful assertion of authority by the colonists created a precedent, and kings or courtiers who violated precedent did so at their own peril. The American understanding was that London officials and royal governors were to levy taxes only by agreement with colonial legislatures, and that governors were to tolerate theological dissenters.

Throughout the first half of the century, colonists successfully fought to have salaries of governors and appointees determined by colonial assemblies, so that legislators could withhold or lower pay when local prerogatives were not heeded. Colonial assemblies extended their authority by demanding successfully that peacetime military matters be under their control; in wartime, legislators insisted on being consulted, not ordered around. In other ways as well, they fought to limit royal power and to keep government small. Decade by decade, as such duels concluded with slight but significant colonial victories, royal governors, on paper, retained all their power, but in reality a system of dual governments—one appointed by London, one elected by taxpayers—emerged.

CHAPTER TWO

Golden Chains

As colonists gained political authority, some faced the question of whether they would be content with "rural entertainments," and with becoming bigger fish in what remained a small pond. Boston, for example, grew throughout the eighteenth century and at the time of the Revolution was the third-largest city in North America, with enough shops and townhouses, offices and wharves, to make it a social, cultural, and economic center. But the streets were alternately muddy or dusty, and often clogged with animals and garbage. The Boston Common sported defecating cattle and the Back Bay, a tidal basin of the Charles River, had its celebrated stinking mud flats.[102] By the standards of the European elite Boston, like other large American cities, was a stinking hole.

London, on the other hand, seemed thoroughly modern. America and England displayed a political contrast; they also differed morally. The rise of dual governments paralleled the rise in dual standards of social conduct. It is hard to get a clear look at sexual conduct during an era when reticence was the rule; intimate diaries are the stuff of which historians' dreams are made. The diary of William Byrd II of Virginia, kept in code to forestall prying, is the best extant indication of the less glorious fascinations of some colonial leaders. The economic chains with which London bound its colonies have often been analyzed, and we will get to them shortly—but sexual lures also were significant, and Byrd's diary illuminates the pattern.

Byrd, in 1710, had it all, by colonial standards of the time: birth into a prosperous family, the best English education in business and law, a seat on the governor's council, marriage to the daughter of a colonial governor, children, slaves, and 26,231 acres left to him on his father's death in 1704. But he was not happy. His secret diaries record a daily routine: food eaten, ailments suffered through, medicine taken, people met, books read, work performed, lusts experienced, sexual acts completed. When his Virginia and London diaries are compared, they also display his frustration with the isolation of Virginia plantation life and his relishing of life in the imperial capital.[103]

Byrd's earliest known entries, made in 1709 when he was thirty-five, record frequent arguments with Lucy, his wife of three years. In one period of ten days he noted, "My wife was out of humor for nothing. . . . I was ill treated by my wife, at whom I was out of humor. . . . My wife and I disagreed about employing a gardener. . . . My wife and I continued very cool. . . . My wife came and begged my pardon and we were friends again. . . . My wife and I had another foolish quarrel. . . . My wife and I had another scold about mending my shoes. . . ."[104] Problems continued into 1710: "In the afternoon I played at cards with my wife but we quarrelled and she cried. . . . I had a great quarrel with my wife. . . . After we were in bed my wife and I had a terrible quarrel about nothing, so that we both got out of bed and were above an hour before we could persuade one another to go to bed again. . . . About 10 o'clock I had a quarrel with my wife. . . ."[105]

All was not grim: Byrd also recorded warm walks in the garden with Lucy and good times in bed: "I gave my wife a flourish in which she had a great deal of pleasure. . . . I rogered my wife. . . . I gave my wife a short flourish. . . . I gave my wife a flourish."[106] Yet, Byrd often seemed driven to seek love or satisfy lust elsewhere, but with little success in a colony where adultery occurred but was not encouraged: He tried to get one young woman to "go with me into my chambers but she would not." Byrd himself saw his extramarital desires as wrong: "I had wicked inclinations to Mistress Sarah

Taylor. . . . Then I returned home and I committed manual uncleanness, for which God forgive me. . . ."[107]

The diary has its share of sadness: Byrd records the death of a son on June 3, 1710.[108] Many diary entries, however, display Byrd's lack of contentment not with the tragedies of life itself but with the tawdriness of life on the frontier. Available pleasures were tainted: "We played at cards and dice till 10 o'clock, and then drank a merry bottle of wine till about 11. When we went to bed it smelled so bad I could hardly endure it. . . ."[109] The way to increase pleasure, Byrd evidently felt, was to advance politically and economically by developing close relationships with the colonial powers. He nervously played host to Governor Spotswood and his courtiers on March 24, 1711: "I gave them several sorts of wine and made them as welcome as I could. . . . The Governor seemed satisfied with his entertainment."[110]

But even Spotswood had limited influence; the road to major advancement lay through London. Byrd held minor governmental positions and tried to use his influence to increase his income: "I wrote another long letter to England, about increasing my salary to £400 a year, in which I hope to succeed because I have some friends in the Treasury."[111] The best investment, however, was to gain more friends in high places, and that would require Byrd to spend several years in England cultivating friendships. Such an option became more appealing as marital difficulties continued; one of the last entries in the 1709-1712 diary, on August 23, 1712, was: "I took a walk about my plantation, and then walked with my wife in the garden, where she quarreled with me. . . ."[112] Byrd's diary for the next several years has not been found, but in 1715 he left Lucy and their two daughters in Virginia and journeyed to London, officially for business purposes and to do what today we would call public-relations and lobbying work for the colony.

Lucy joined her husband in London in 1716 but soon died of smallpox; the two children arrived later and were placed with friends or relatives. That left Byrd, in his forties, free to pursue the high life in London, where the maids seemed far more compliant than those of America. [113] He also relished the masquerades then fashionable in London; at these large parties masked participants could cast aside under cover of anonymity whatever inhibitions they might still have. Byrd recorded the typical result in his diary:

"about ten we went and I was very well diverted and . . . met with a woman that I hugged till I spent. I stayed till 6 o'clock in the morning. . . ."[114]

The imperial capital signified sexual and theological liberation for Byrd. His diary from these years is filled with repeated, graphic descriptions of sexual encounters with women from every station of life: from girls picked up on the street to the aristocratic ladies of London's political elite.[115] Every several months the names changed, but Byrd always seemed delighted to report that he had gone "to Mrs. Smith's to meet a new mistress who was pretty and well humored."[116] London women were not reluctant fornicators like those in America, but were "very sweet and agreeable."[117] There was variety: "I went to see my French whore."[118] There was immediate availability: "After the play I picked up a woman and carried her to the tavern and ate some roast chicken and lay with her."[119] The openness of London for even outdoor sex thrilled Byrd: "I walked in the park and lay with a woman on the grass. . . . About twelve I went home and neglected my prayers."[120]

Byrd typically filled daylight hours with public-relations networking: In 1718 the House of Burgesses officially appointed him agent for the colony, with the goal of laying before the Board of Trade complaints against Governor Spotswood and trying to get some of the governor's laws repealed. Byrd's diary for February 26, 1719, for example, records: "About eleven I went to the Committee of Council. . . . After dinner I went to Garraway's and spoke to my Lord G-l-v-r-s about the government."[121] The diary recounts day-to-day activities like these: "Went to the Virginia Coffehouse where I learned that twenty of the Virginia ships were arrived. . . . Read several letters from Virginia. . . . Received a bill and ate some fish for dinner . . . gave my Lord Orrery a book concerning Virginia . . . "[122]

Byrd's prayer life in London was not much to speak of. He dutifully recorded his sexual emissions and prayer omissions, and when he was content in sin seemed to pray less; he may have prayed more when his lust was unsatisfied.[123] Byrd went to church regularly, but weak preaching gave him a lot of running room. For example, on February 8, 1719, he heard "an indifferent sermon" and headed immediately to a brothel.[124] On March 8, one month later, history repeated itself: "About eleven I went to Somerset Chapel and heard an indifferent sermon . . . picked up a pretty woman and went to the tavern and had a broiled fowl. I found the woman entrancing and gave her a crown and committed uncleanness with her and returned home after 12 o'clock and neglected my prayers."[125]

Early in 1720, due to the press of business, Byrd had to be back in Virginia, where life was different. In London he had often stayed up until the dawn's early light; in Virginia he usually went to bed at about nine. In London he could find available women in drawing rooms, brothels, streets, or parks; in Williamsburg during November and December, 1720, Byrd "endeavored to pick up a whore but could not find one."[126] In London Byrd whirled around to masquerade balls and the theater; at home he "walked about and saw my people working about several things . . . talk[ed] about the repair of my mill and dam at Falling Creek . . . took a walk about the plantation and at night talked with my people and said my prayers."[127]

Byrd, realizing what he would be in for, had brought back with him London maids in the same way that a traveler today might take along a particular stock of pharmaceuticals. "Annie" at first was particularly compliant, and Byrd recorded that, "about 9 o'clock went to bed and kissed Annie until I spent, for which God forgive me."[128] Byrd had prayed in London to a doting God, but back in Virginia he recalled that God has standards that those created in His image are to follow, and a new diary passage began to appear in Byrd's diary: " . . . said my prayers and then I tempted Annie to let me feel her, but she would not let me, for which she is to be commended and for which God be praised."[129]

Byrd and Annie backslid into bed together many times after that, although Byrd made resolutions "to forbear Annie by God's grace."[130] But Virginia and London were two different worlds, and Byrd headed back to London in 1721; we do not know what became of Annie. Byrd spent three years in London apparently leading the life he had lived before, but he was beginning to feel old for such cavorting. In 1724, at age fifty, Byrd married a woman who bore him four children and lived with him, apparently peacefully, for the remaining twenty years of his life; from 1726 on they were back in Virginia. From his plantation home Byrd dispatched to a London friend the plaintive note, "We that are banish't from these polite pleasures [of London] are forced to take up with rural entertainments."[131]

HELL-FIRE PUNCH AND HOLY GHOST PYE

London excited William Byrd II and others from the hinterlands who were turned on by England's low culture—but touring American colonials typically wrote home about visiting the British Museum and cruising the grand shops. Some were impressed by the literary, political, and social clubs that grew up during the first two decades of the century, with names such as the Saturday Club, White's, and the Golden Fleece. Special-interest clubs included the Lying Club and the Mollies Clubs, where young men dressed up as women, sipped gin, and presented to each other lines such as, "Tell me, gentle hobdehoy, Art thou girl, or art thou boy?"[132] The *London Weekly Journal* in 1720 described how members of one club, the Bold Bucks, "attempt all Females of their own Species promiscuously . . . Blind and Bold Love is their motto."[133] As the century wore on, visitors also observed the building boom among the affluent that was changing the face of the English countryside. In 1726, one-fourth of the active peerage held lucrative government jobs; one secretary of state for six years made a clear profit of £50,000 (the equivalent of perhaps $4 million) on the office. Bribe-taking placeholders sunk their gains into ornate decoration and costly artwork that filled the Palladian palaces. Political corruption gave England the architectural heritage that today impresses tourists interested in either elegance or size: one mansion under construction in 1734 had a front that was 260 feet long and a hall that was 64 feet by 53 feet deep and 48 feet high.[134]

The contrast between lordly British lifestyles and those of even the rich and famous of America was overwhelming. For example, the Duke of Chandos maintained on his English estate a collection of exotic birds taken from all the imperial lands: "whistling owls and flamingos from Antigua . . . Virginia fowls and songbirds; a Gold Coast redbird of peculiar prettiness; Barbados 'Powises' and parakeets." Foodstuffs came too, from wherever the British flag reached: rice, kidney beans, and pickles from the Carolinas; hams (sometimes full of maggots, alas) from Pennsylvania; pineapples, cinnamon, coffee trees and berries from Barbados; sugar, raisins, currants, lemons, oranges, musk, and watermelon seeds from other ports. Wealth on its own could be pleasant, but wealth within an empire brought variety that was exceedingly rare in those days of staple diet and local produce.[135]

Americans, impressed by the opportunities of empire, could see that affluence was not only for the aristocracy: Fortunes (sometimes made in the slave trade) bought favor. One foreign visitor, Cesar de Saussure, was impressed to find British merchants who were "far wealthier than many sovereign princes of Germany and Italy. They live in great state; their houses are richly furnished, their tables spread with delicacies."[136] Poverty also was present, and cruelty flourished: Just as some teenage boys bash homeless alcoholics today, so young London aristocrats tossed beggars in blankets and even stole dogs from blind men.[137]

Major colonial cities did have a few brothels, but Byrd's inability to find a Williamsburg prostitute showed that the undercover activities he relished openly in London were less common throughout America.[138] In London also, there was no need to keep secret diaries about sexual activities; one lord who functioned as prime minister early in the century, Henry St. John, Viscount Bolingbroke, was known for having as his mistresses the most expensive women in London, and for occasionally dashing naked through the park. Once, when he received a governmental appointment and his salary was published, a town madam exulted, "Five thousand a year, my girls, and all for us!"[139]

As Byrd and other impressed colonists found out, members of "gentlemen's clubs" in London could openly exchange mistresses and circulate lists of approved harlots, with notes on their talents and peculiarities.[140] Newspapers contained ads such as: "Wanted. A Woman [with] bosom full and plump, firm and white, lively conversation and one looking as if she could feel delight where she wishes to give it."[141] One club printed a *Guide to a Whoremonger's London*. Sacrilege also was fashionable in the metropolis; through 1721 gentlemen could frequent several clubs called "Hell-Fire" that conformed to "a more transcendant Malignity; deriding the Forms of Religion as a Trifle."[142] One club even had on its menu "Hell Fire Punch," "Holy Ghost Pye," "Devil's Loins," and "Breast of Venus."[143]

The most profane groups did have to be somewhat careful after

1721, when King George I issued a royal proclamation against "Blasphemous Clubs," but some continued surreptitiously—there are accounts of a Hell-Fire Club in 1725—and lascivious conduct remained in season.[144] By the 1740s and 1750s rambunctious Saturday-night clubs operated with open infamy once again, and in England, unlike in America, it increasingly came to be believed that, "If a gentleman were a man of Taste, and behaved in public with decorum, his private amusements were his own concern."[145]

These club men were no boy scouts, and their amusements often became public. Young "rakes" in groups often would tour the brothels in the vicinity of Covent Garden both for whoring and to break windows, furniture, and sometimes the bodies of the women who were their freelance employees and victims. William Hogarth's *The Rake's Progress* was only one of the popular series of prints that depicted such nocturnal pursuits; another print showed a scene described in verses beneath the picture: *The Leader of the Rake Pack*, "tho he Risks his life/Will from the Husband force the Wife,/As rudely his companions treat All that in Petticoats they meet./The Women Struggle, Scream and Scratch Loud Swear the men. . . ."[146] Activities of rakes bear some similarity to those of gang members today, except that their social class then was higher and their level of armament lower.[147]

Accompanying the advance of clubs were masquerades—parties where lordly participants could leave restraint behind by putting on a mask that gave them anonymity. Critics at midcentury and thereafter argued that "Masquerades are a market for maidenheads and adultery," but this "dangerous luxury opposite to virtue and liberty" continued to be popular.[148] On the eve of the American Revolution the masquerades were perhaps at their height, and the *Whitehall Evening Post* reported shock at the grossness of "the behavior of the women of the town, and of the bucks of dissipation [at the] nightly orgies."[149]

British gentlemanly dissipation was institutionalized. According to an account from 1708, training to be "crude and unpolished infidels" started in college, where gentlemen thought it was "wit and spirit, to laugh at religion and virtue."[150] Although tyranny and the freedom to practice vice are today often considered to be opposites, political thinkers then commented on their affinity in academic circles: "In the universities, instead of being formed to love their country and its constitution, laws, and liberties, they are rather disposed to love arbitrary government. . . ."[151] During the 1740s Gibbon, later to be famous for writing *The Decline and Fall of the Roman Empire*, observed the decline of a new empire while studying at Oxford. He was struck by the vast array of carousing students, lenient tutors, and jolly good fellows who were supposed to be scholars but spent their time in preferment-seeking politics rather than "the toil of reading, or thinking, or writing. . . . Hedged in from life, fellows and dons meddled in one another's business, talked one another's (and nobody else's) language. . . ."[152]

As Macaulay noted, "the modern country gentleman generally receive[d] a liberal education," then went on a grand tour that included time spent in Italy, where graduates would gain an advanced education in the worship of women and wine; in Venice and Verona they might also pick up some aquaintance with occultism, which flourished in those cities between 1720 and 1760.[153] Upon his return to England, a gentleman had a post-graduate education in extremes. By midcentury, wagering—on horse races at Newmarket; on bear, cock, and bull fights; on boxing matches; on the ability of six elderly women from Lambeth to drink a gallon of scalding tea more quickly than six old women from Rotherhithe—became a mania.[154]

One anecdote and one factual account from the 1750s suggest the tendencies. The story is that when a man apparently dropped dead at the door of one club building and was being carried inside, members were laying bets on whether he truly was dead or not. That may have been made up, but the betting books do show that in 1754 Lord Montforth wagered Sir John Bland one hundred guineas (about $8,000) that one elderly gentleman they knew would outlive another. Bland took himself out of the running to collect shortly thereafter, however: while playing dice he lost his entire fortune of £32,000, or somewhat over $2 million, and then shot himself. Montfort did not win either: he played whist until 1 a.m. on December 31, 1754, and on that last day of the year also committed suicide.[155]

American colonists were not immune to adultery, gambling, and other troubles, but such activities were not accepted on the western shore of the Atlantic as they were in London. For example, most Americans drank alcoholic beverages, but in England at midcentury a one-bottle man was considered temperate; Prime Minister Pitt was a three-bottle man.[156] As one London observer noted, "That a wealthy man should lead a decent life and be a faithful husband was considered to be almost an anomaly."[157] America was far from Eden, but contemporary accounts suggest that the anomaly was common in the colonies.

ENCOURAGE THE TRADE IN THE UTMOST LATITUDE

For many residents of America, economic advantages of the imperial connection were what mattered. Although patriotic journalists during the years immediately before the Revolution pointed out the economic disadvantages, imperial regulation of trade did receive American support throughout most of the century, for at least three reasons.

First, given transportation and communication patterns of the time, Americans had to choose between empire and isolation. Goods and information generally flowed by water; each colony almost might have been an island. (Young Benjamin Franklin's escape from Boston to Philadelphia, for example, was by sea, and he could just as well—although at greater expense—have hopped a ship to Liverpool.) Virginians were far more likely to visit England than New England; all roads, it seemed, led to London.

Second, the complicated regulatory system established by the British trade regulations known as Navigation Acts created winners as well as losers and often the opportunity for special deals to be cut; the system in operation was far different from the pure system espoused in mercantile theory.[158] Established shipmakers found ways to benefit from laws regulating the vessels in which goods could be shipped. Massive tariff regulations could be twisted to promote particular industries. Rebates and export bounties went to those who either made their cases the best or overcame poor logic with good political connections.

Colonial shipowners who wanted to enter into direct England-America trade were pushed out, since that trade was dominated by government-protected shipowners from the British Isles. Protected Americans came to dominate trade between New England and the West Indies, however, as well as trade from one American port to another. They also did well with shipments from the colonies to

Mediterranean, south European, and African ports. The overall goal was to avoid competition, so new facilities that could compete with established industries were prohibited or discouraged. The already affluent liked that.

Third, colonial shippers clearly benefited from the prestige of the British navy. Such was its power that many pirates preferred to prey on ships of other nationalities; the Barbary states even stopped their molesting of British vessels trading in Mediterranean countries. When most countries went to war, insurance costs on their shipping, now threatened by hostile seizure, skyrocketed—but the British navy protected the commerce of its flag, and so powerful was such support that insurance costs for British ships stayed steady during wartime, regardless of the general threat. Essentially, investors in British shipping could look forward to a better return on their investment, and less risk of losing it all, than those involved in any other country's shipping industry.

By 1775, nearly one-third of all ships registered in Britain as English were colonial built. Many New England businessmen throughout most of the century remained content with British regulations that spared their fishing, trading, and shipbuilding enterprises from foreign competition. Nor did typical citizens complain about freight rates very often: Since many Americans entered the shipping business, prices fell despite the lack of foreign competition, and tonnage grew throughout the colonial era.[159]

Similarly, American tobacco planters benefited by high tariffs laid on Spanish and other foreign tobacco. British regulations essentially gave them a monopoly of the market in Great Britain, since tobacco production in England and Ireland was prohibited, and foreign tobacco had to pay a prohibitive import duty. Then as now, tobacco was important to its users and thus important to the British government, for taxes could be piled on tobacco without drastically lowering its use. London's favors helped the tobacco industry boom, and the marketing genius of the great merchants of Glasgow and other British cities also was crucial: They not only supplied capital but also graded and processed tobacco to suit the varying tastes of tobacco users.

Military expenditures and subsidies also produced profits for clever colonists. Producers of tar, pitch, and hemp, vital for the British navy and commercial carriers, could do well: These commodities received not only a virtual monopoly of the British market but liberal bounties as well. Colonial products at first faced competition from producers in the Baltics, but import duties on Baltic products essentially shut them out. Wood products of all kinds, including planks, boards, and barrel staves, also received preferential treatment throughout much of the eighteenth century, culminating in direct import bounties during the 1760s and early 1770s. Not only shippers but planters as well benefited from such preferences. For example, back-country planters and farmers could clear their land and at the same time derive immediate profit from the activity by preparing staves for export to Britain.[160]

British subsidies also encouraged the rice and indigo growers of South Carolina and Georgia. They could have a reliable market for their produce, a dependable supply of products not made locally, and an assurance (through British naval strength) that the shipping flow would not be interrupted in times of war. British control of the seas provided the stability of conditions under which large investments of capital could most securely be made.

Colonists had to pay a price for these marks of royal favor: Increasingly as the century wore on, colonists were told they could not engage in some natural economic acts. For example, domestic production of wool products for family or local use was accepted, but a prohibition on the transport of raw wool and manufactures from one colony to another by water transportation eliminated the possible growth of an American wool-producing and manufacturing industry that could compete with that of the British Isles.[161]

Similarly, the growth of colonial hatmaking in the 1720s made British hatters mad: They complained that New Englanders, New Yorkers, and Carolinians were using beaver and wool to make hats for shipment throughout the colonies and even to the West Indies. The hatters petitioned that colonists be prevented from wearing or selling any hats except those made in Great Britain. The prohibition against wearing hats could not be enforced very readily, but in 1732 London prohibited intercolonial trade in hats and felts, and restricted colonial hatmaking to those who had served a seven-year apprenticeship. The act also stipulated that blacks could not be trained to be hatmakers.[162]

The bark of these laws was worse than their bite, since enforcement of laws drawn too broadly was deliberately lax. For example, laws for the conservation of white pine trees (passed by Parliament in 1711, 1722, and 1729) recognized that the white pine trees of New England made the best naval masts in the world, and mandated the trees' preservation for that purpose. New Englanders, however, knew that white pines that forked within about fifty feet of the ground or were defective could not be used for masts, and they often cut down such trees for lumber and fuel. Although the law allowed no exceptions, there was only one serious attempt to enforce the White Pines Act in Connecticut, and it ended with a British official's being thrown into a millpond and nearly drowned. No one was prosecuted.

Neither the law of 1699 to suppress colonial woolen manufacturing, nor the no-hat act of 1732, set up special enforcement mechanisms, and the colonial records do not show prosecutions. The latter law did irritate some hat merchants who saw the large supply of cheap beaver fur and wanted to set up large-scale manufacturing, but hatmakers worked around it by taking their skills individually to communities and selling directly to customers. The hat industry as a whole prospered, jobs were plentiful, and prices, although not as low as they otherwise would have been, apparently were not a source of complaint. Regulations concerning woolen goods were also more irritating than killing.[163]

The lack of macroeconomic causes for rebellion was still evident at midcentury, even after passage of a controversial Iron Bill in 1750. The iron bill encouraged the nascent steel industry of England by forbidding establishment of new steel mills in the British American colonies and placing some restrictions on American iron making, yet at the same time, it encouraged certain aspects of the colonial iron industry by giving American pig and bar iron favored treatment at English customshouses. The bill worked out well for Americans who followed regulatory patterns because steel mills did not become a major force anywhere until the nineteenth century, and in the meantime the protected colonial iron industry prospered. (In 1774 more iron furnaces operated in America than in England.)[164]

London paid attention to the care and feeding of the colonists along the Atlantic Ocean because they were means to a very important end: the continued functioning of the empire's profit centers in the West Indies. As the discerning trader Samuel Vetch noted in 1708,

> no island the British possess in the West Indies [can] subsist without the assistance of the Continent, for to them we transport their bread, drink and all the necessaryes of human life, their cattle and horses for cultivating their plantations, lumber and staves of all sorts to make casks of for their rum, sugar and molasses, without which they could have none, ships to transport their goods to the European markets, nay, in short, the very houses they inhabitt are carryed over in frames, together with the shingles that cover them, in so much that their being, much more their well being, depends almost entirely upon the Continent.[165]

Furthermore, the London perspective prized the colonies as a market for English manufactured goods. Joshua Gee in 1729 stated the goal baldly: clothing "of ordinary Sort sells with them, and when they are grown out of Fashion with us, they are new fashioned enough there." Gee made the case for keeping the colonists dependent:

> our own Interest is not [to be] mistaken for that of the Planters; for every Restraint and Difficulty put upon our Trade with them makes them have Recourse to their own Products which they manufacture, a thing of great Consequence to us and ought to be guarded against. For if they are supplied with their own Manufactures, one great Part of the Advantage we should otherwise receive is cut off; . . . Care [must be] taken to find them Employment and turne their Industry another Way. . . .[166]

"I'm easy," British trade officials seemingly went out of their way to say all the way up through 1760. Officials generally looked the other way when they had the option of enforcing the Sugar Act of 1733, which levied a tariff of six cents per gallon on foreign molasses brought into American ports. Regardless of what the law said, the custom in Boston was for port officials to settle for "about one tenth" of the statutory duty.[167] When David Dunbar, Surveyor-General of the King's Woods in America from 1725 to 1743, issued a proclamation that allowed such cutting, he was reprimanded by Britain's Board of Trade and ordered to revoke it. (He did.) When British officials were hardheaded, colonists regularly found ways to protect themselves. In 1758, when Governor Benning Wentworth of New Hampshire tried to seize 3,500 white-pine logs, obviously cut down illegally, as proof in a court case, some of the logs were retaken by colonial cutters and the rest were "turned into the river on the Ebb-tide, which soon carried them to sea."[168]

Economically, the British tendency until 1760 was to try a little tenderness whenever their profit-aiding American colonials complained. Government economic regulation, then as now, produced winners and losers, and there were enough winners to preserve the system from unpopularity.[169] Some captains did show their disdain for some of the Navigation Act's mandated import duties by smuggling in whatever goods they thought were taxed too high. Despite that, at least in the 1720s and 1730s, thoughtful British leaders were so committed to an entrepreneur-friendly policy that they generally winked at trade-law violations. Prime Minister Robert Walpole decided to "encourage the trade of the American colonies in the utmost latitude"—by which he meant smuggling—for if by such trade "they gain 500,000 pounds a year, I am convinced that, in two years afterwards, full 250,000 pounds of this will be in his Majesty's Exchequer," through colonial purchase of British goods.

It appears, in short, that the Navigation Acts, apex of the British regulatory system, were not much of an economic cause for revolution. They did, however, have a three-way political effect. First, subsidies paid out to favored industries were a drain on the English treasury and became an economic reason to tax the colonies; thus, one government weakness led to additional weaknesses. Second, some Americans did become accustomed to smuggling and resented later efforts to crack down. Third, British officials became used to thinking in terms of deals: Americans, they believed, would accept new taxes if London added or extended subsidies to favored industries. Manipulative tendencies within the government-expanding mindset eventually undid the empire—but the historical record is disappointing to those who believe that irritation with regulations themselves will create a willingness to rebel.

Our American Subjects Are Children of the State

Hopes of personal advancement contributed to British ability to maintain allegiance in the face of criticism from those prefering small rather than big government. Such hope could spring eternal when centralization of power allowed colonists to gain governmental favors that could make fortunes. London connections could be invaluable, and even though legislatures worked hard to hamstring royal governors, crown appointees in America still had power. Occasionally a colonist even became a governor or, as did James DeLancey of New York, a lieutenant governor. Those who occupied such positions usually ran their colonies and took the profits.

With corruption flourishing, having the ear of the powerful was crucial defensively. Connections with London helped merchant Robert Livingston stop Lord Cornbury's attempts to confiscate his estates. Contacts were also useful offensively, since favored land speculators could hope for substantial grants from royal governors. Those lavish congratulatory addresses that a new governor received upon arrival show that aspirants to his support—lawyers, merchants, and justices of the provincial courts—considered the bowing and scraping worthwhile.

William Byrd's diary shows how important the royal governor was to a wealthy man. Once in Virginia, after remarking that gubernatorial power should be fenced in, he panicked about the consequences: "Somebody had told the Governor that I had said that no Governor ought to be trusted with 20,000 [pounds]. . . . The Governor was angry about what I had said concerning the 20,000. . . . I went to the Governor. He made us wait half an hour before he was pleased to come out to us and when he came he looked very stiff and cold on me. . . . The Governor continued stiff to me. . . . I went to the capitol where I found the Governor complaining that the House of Burgesses had passed several resolutions . . . he dissolved them after a short speech. . . ."[170] Byrd won his way back into some favor by advancing £500 to the governor, who then "did me the honor of a visit this morning without any business and stayed about half an hour. . . ."[171]

Artfully applied appointments to local positions such as justice of the peace or captain of the militia also kept some of the best and brightest from rethinking their allegiances. Throughout the colonial period London-trained administrators tried to corrupt recalcitrant colonists: One Maryland governor argued that offensive assemblymen could be silenced only by "throwing out a Sop [jobs and other patronage] in a proper manner to these Noisy Animals" until they become "tame enough to bear Stroking & tractable enough to follow any directions."[172] Prime Minister Walpole was the top practitioner of this type of legislative management; as one pamphleteer declared, "It is true, indeed, that bribery and corruption had taken pretty deep root long before Sir Robert Walpole was made chief minister; yet he is peculiarly entitled to the honour of having been the first who reduced this practice, as it were, into a regular system."[173] Little Walpoles in America did the best they could with their limited resources, and hoped that little Hogarths would not get around to depicting them in prints with vivid titles such as *The Political Vomit for the Ease of Britain* and *The Compleat Vermin-Catcher*.[174]

London governance consistently appealed to those desiring economic, military, cultural, and personal advancement—but the specifics varied from decade to decade. During the first two decades of the century British officials who tried to push too hard ran out of support. Lord Cornbury thought that New Yorkers were not importing enough woolen fabrics from England and were making too many themselves. Some merchants said the planters should be forced to clothe their servants and slaves in coarse woolen cloths made in Britain. The Board of Trade, though, sensibly replied that British goods should be used for their quality in relation to price and not be imposed in a way that would meet general opposition. Robert Hunter, Cornbury's successor as governor, noted that farmers and poor country people wore clothes that they had made themselves, and a law that required the wearing of English-manufactured clothing would be a law requiring nakedness.[175]

British-American relations were best during the 1720s and 1730s, Walpole's period of ascendancy. His policies of "salutary neglect" enriched hard-working individuals on both sides of the Atlantic, with British manufacturers and merchants able to increase rapidly their exports to America. Salutary neglect in the 1720s meant not only ignoring regulatory violations but sometimes gnawing away at the source of the violations. For example, parliamentary legislation in the early 1720s removed export duties from more than a hundred commodities manufactured in England, and also removed many import duties on raw materials needed for the textile industry.

Walpole knew that as the Americans "increase their foreign trade, more of our own produce will be wanted. This is taxing them more agreeably to their own constitutions, and ours."[176] His bureaucrats became masters of the face-saving nuance. When British West Indies grandees wanted to stop New Englanders from trading provisions and timber to the French West Indies in return for the sugar and molasses that were essential ingredients of rum— West Indies shippers wanted the New England market entirely to themselves— the Walpole administration established taxes that gave the British islands crop preference, but then expended little money for enforcement.[177]

Crucially, throughout the first seven decades of the century, the empire offered one prize more to the affluent and ambitious: the opportunity to be part of something greater than themselves. Many colonists did not want to be little people in frontier places. Proud of what they had accomplished economically, they were ready to take on more political responsibility. London leaders, however, had a different view. In much of official London, "the plantations" were viewed not as lands populated by families with dreams of their own, but as potential profit centers, units of agricultural production that also could function as producers of wealth and acceptors of English goods. Dr. Charles Davenant, a leading public-policy expert of the early eighteenth century, wrote that "The Plantations work for us, their treasure centers all here. . . ."[178]

To make a modern business analogy, governments were big corporations, and the goal of the outlying factories was to make money for stockholders. One analyst described how a suggestion "that Old England shall be made to depend upon the New . . . or that the Lesser should be preferred to the prejudice of the Greater, cannot be the desire of any Honest Man."[179] At the same time, however, London officials typically argued that the British empire could not succeed if it were based on economic exploitation, with those at the periphery slavishly pledging allegiance. In 1723, the Board of Trade tabled a proposal to impose on the colonists a stamp tax, an unimproved land tax, and import duties, with funds going to support six thousand British troops. The British emphasis was on keeping colonists satisfied in their dependency, and on forging enough golden chains to make some of them British partisans.[180]

In their kinder moments, imperial writers even liked to think of Mother England and her colonies as a family. American politicians who like to talk about the nation as family now tend to propose higher taxes; British politicans then told constituents that the children existed to add to the wealth of the family, with the fortune administered by London authorities. Davenant wrote: "That our subjects in the American colonies are children of the state and to be treated as such no one denies; but it can't reasonably be admitted that the mother country should impoverish herself to enrich the children."[181]

Writers regularly stressed that the children's work was crucial for the lifestyle of the parents. Bolingbroke noted in 1728 that the British Isles depended on their

> Trade and Plantations, which breeds Seamen and brings in Wealth to maintain them. The Plantations likewise consume vast Quantities of the British Product and Manufactures' [and] furnish us with many useful Commodities, which we formerly bought of other Nations. . . . If we had nothing more than our own Product . . . could we be able to maintain those mighty Fleets, which render the British Name formidable in all Parts of the known World?[182]

Others noted that the colonies "give employment to many thousands of artificers here at home and take off great quantities, especially of our inferior manufactures."[183] Dumping grounds were useful.

The mercantilists of the empire loved to explain how the imperial whole became greater than the sum of its parts. They talked of the exquisite relationships within the imperial family: mother country, provision colonies such as New York and Pennsylvania, tobacco colonies such as Maryland and Virginia, sugar colonies of the West Indies, fisheries (including New England seacoast towns), and slave-producing territories. They talked of how British subjects in many parts of the world had security in their persons, with London offering protection. (Slaves and impressed seamen could not read the fine print.)

Military benefits did accompany what for many were the economic and social benefits of British rule. Military protection was vital during the early years of the eighteenth century because colonies were deep into plans for invading, or repelling invasions from, New France. The treaty of Ryswick in 1697 had given peace a chance, but in 1701, England entered into the War of the Spanish Succession with the goal of blocking France's Louis XIV and strengthening its own partisans. The American side of the contest was a draw: French-backed Indians hit the frontier and British expeditions in 1709 and 1711 failed to take Quebec. French defeat in Europe, however, led to the Peace of Utrecht, by which France turned over to England territories that included Acadia (now Nova Scotia) and placed the Iroquois (who would have something to say about the matter) under English authority.

That war, although it ended in a tie in the American theater, strengthened London's colonial authority in several ways. First, big brother had come through; with little damage to the colonies, the French danger was slightly decreased. Second, the danger was still present, and the military standoff in North America meant that a rematch seemed inevitable. Militarily, all but the most unconventional thinkers understood that Britain had only two logical moves: either keep the colonies dependent and monopolize their trade, or else desert them and watch another country, most likely France, grab them. The idea that small, struggling entities could be self-governing in a world full of empires-on-the-make did not make sense.[184]

Debauching the Morals of a Whole People

For the ambitious, the small-government tendencies examined in chapter one were more than matched by the appeals of large government. Even when particular governors of the Cornbury mold blundered badly, by the 1730s it looked as if the empire would go on and on. (National projects today are hardly slowed by the failure of experimental programs in Iowa or Oregon.) Economic exasperations were scattered, tax burdens were fairly light, military needs were apparent, personal opportunities for advancement beckoned, and cultural highlights and lowlights had their appeals. As long as colonists abided British corruption and immorality while worshipping imperial strength, the lords of London had nothing to fear.

Yet, while many colonists rested in golden chains, an ethical critique of social and governmental practices began to emerge within the pages of influential English publications. The *Craftsman*, an influential anti-Whig weekly, ran contributions by Henry St. John, Viscount Bolingbroke, the rakish prime minister under Queen Anne who matured while in exile under George I. Knowing from personal experience of what he wrote, Bolingbroke charged that "Luxury and Extravagance, with their constant Attendants, Necessity and Prostitution, are too visible in all Parts of the Kingdom; expecially in this great City, where a general Spirit of Prodigality and Excess is seen to prevail."[185] The well-off were the worst, Bolingbroke observed: "The abominable Crimes of Perjury and Forgery were never so frequent amongst us, as They have been of late; especially amongst Men of Family and Fortune."[186]

British subjects on both sides of the Atlantic became aware of the degree of corruption among those who had family and fortune. Widely known ballads portrayed Walpole, with apparent accuracy, as a corrupt politician. One included the verses, "Bob of Lynn was as lusty as tall,/His Head it was large, and his Belly not small;/With huge goggle Eyes, and a soft fawning Grin . . . A Whig out of Place, and a Tory when in:/And a very great Trimmer was Bob of Lynn."[187] Walpole was accused of debauching public morals through bribery and of draining the treasury: "Gold was the wisdom of Bob of Lynn." Critics called for audits, but audits were delayed for months or even years, with records or authorizations of expenditures lost between departments.[188]

Trends set in the court, Bolingbroke complained, were "debauch[ing] the Morals of a whole People. The same Depravity and Corruption, soon find their Way from a Court to a Cottage; and in Proportion to the Distance, is to be traced in a greater or less Degree through every private Family; so that in a very short Time the very Name of Virtue may come to be lost in such a Kingdom."[189] Societal decline would also have economic consequences: "Distress, Bankruptcy, Dependance and other numberless Evils to the Publick." Bolingbroke predicted in 1729 that immorality in the capital would affect the entire kingdom: Since "Extravagance is of such mischievous Consequence in the Center of Trade, which draws all the Riches of the Kingdom to it; what Terrible Effects must it produce in those parts, which are constantly drain'd to support this great, over-grown Leviathan, and which can subsist only by Labour, Industry, and Frugality?"[190]

Over the next twenty years the slide continued. James Burgh, a political writer who understood that liberty could not survive without virtue, described with scorn in 1748 the "scenes of Wantonness, Pleasure and Extravagance" that filled London nights.[191] He wrote that those engaged in buying and selling used to "employ the Morning in examining their accounts, adjusting their Warehouses and Shops, and preparing themselves for the Busy Hours of the Day . . . they spent their Evenings at home in instructing their Children, Apprentices and Servants, in the Principles of Virtue and Religion, and concluded every day with the laudable Exercise of Family-devotion."[192] In the 1740s, however, many spent nights carousing and never read the Bible: "Is it any Wonder, that the rising Generation have no more Sense or Understanding of Christianity than if they had never heard of it . . . ?"[193]

Personal living had economic as well as theological implications, Burgh explained, as he pointed out a lack of discipline: "In place of these decent and regular methods of living, our Citizens now find it hard to rise by Ten."[194] Some even spent "every Sunday, and at least the two following Days of the Week, in Drunkenness and Idleness."[195] Burgh's summary of common vices of the 1740s was impressively depressing: "venality, perjury, faction, opposition to legal authority, idleness, gluttony, drunkenness, lewdness, excessive gaming, robberies, clandestine marriages, breach of matrimonial vows, self-murders. . . ."[196] The House of Commons itself was filled with "profligates, gamblers, bankrupts, beggars, contractors, commissaries, public plunderers . . . and wretches who would sell their country or deny their God for a guinea."

A decade later, the ABCs of decadence—adultery, bribery, cover-up—were still being recited. John Brown, an honest clergyman, summarized the problem: "The ruinous Effects of this insatiable Thirst of Power and Profit, founded in Parliamentary Influence, together with the notorious Incapacity, Effeminacy, Inaction, and Debility, of those who aspire to the highest and most important Trusts, are at length no longer doubted. All Attention is turned on Gain or Pleasure; Duty is forgot, or laughed at: The main Springs of Government are thus relaxed. . . ."[197] Brown wrote that England's leaders reminded him of "the drunken Crew of the Ship, who were squabbling about the Brandy Casks, while the Vessel was splitting on a Rock."[198] He predicted that once-honest ambition "would be perverted. Not useful, but servile Talents would be applauded."[199]

Brown, in such comments, was distinguishing between those who advanced the commonwealth and those with servile talents—but one of the two most famous Americans of the eighteenth century had both. Benjamin Franklin invented much, organized much, wrote much, and did many other useful things. But as a young man, he also enjoyed London; he implies in his *Autobiography*, which was very much a public-relations document and thus far removed from a Byrdlike secret diary, that his sexual experiences were a poor man's equivalent of Byrd's.[200] What Franklin most certainly had was an unquenchable desire to be at the center and not the obscure periphery. He wrote in a letter from Pennsylvania to one English friend, printer William Strahan, "We have seldom any Newes on our Side of the Globe that can be entertaining to you or yours. All our affairs are petit . . . [they] can seem but Trifles to you."[201]

We will come back to Franklin: The viewpoint he expressed in that letter is key to understanding Britain's ability to keep America in golden chains indefinitely. London, Franklin saw, offered colonists economic, military, and cultural incentives to be loyal. Those prospects, along with the sense of being a ruler of the world rather than just one small person in a frontier place, kept many Americans tied to London. Whenever the colonists attempted to establish a parallel governance process, the lures of London represented a counterattack because their existence posed stark alternatives: cultural freedom, symbolized by high life in a world capital, or obscurity along the frontier. The crucial question in the second third of the eighteenth century was whether and how colonists would learn that they were not little people in little places.

CHAPTER THREE

Theological Battles

Few colonists during the first half of the eighteenth century vociferously criticized London's blandishments. Remnants of the Puritans sometimes were critical, but preachers in established, Anglican churches did not warn that the road to London could be the road to Sodom, because they themselves were compromised: Government and church were the two houses of social control. In the Old Testament book of 2 Kings and in New England election sermons, church and government could countervail the tendencies toward abuse that each might have, but in practice it was all too easy for church and state powers to embrace. In eighteenth-century England's equivalent to today's inside-the-beltway mentality, the Church of England upheld the state and the state attempted to harass dissenters from the Church.[202]

Governors such as Cornbury saw the value of papering over corruption by enlisting Anglican leaders. The eighteenth-century fight against denominational tyranny thus began in New York, but battles soon commenced in the Carolinas as well. There, Presbyterians and other dissenters opposed a requirement that legislators either take the Lord's Supper according to the Anglican rite, or take an oath that they conformed to Anglicanism and had not taken communion at any other church during the past year. In 1704, when the government established the Anglican Book of Common Prayer as the official form of worship and refused to recognize the legitimacy of marriages performed by non-Anglican clergymen, Dissenters struck back. They sent a lobbyist to London, hired Daniel Defoe to write on their behalf a pamphlet entitled *Party-Tyranny*, and pointed out that the Carolina charter had promised toleration of all Christian denominations.[203] The House of Lords agreed, 28-12, and Queen Anne issued an order repealing the two acts.[204]

Anglicans were hurt not only by charges of tyranny but by accusations of priestly laxity and incompetence. When a new governor, John Hart, arrived in Maryland in 1714, he encountered Anglican priests, some politically well-connected but illiterate, who were "a scandal to their profession."[205] In other southern colonies as well where the Church of England went unchallenged, local ministers were often distinguished more by the size of their stomachs than the breadth of their learning or the depth of their compassion.

William Byrd II noted his hearing of "indifferent" sermons in London but several provocative ones in Virginia; fellow colonists rarely were blessed in that way. Virginians paid ministers in tobacco, and since the milder, broader-leaved, "sweet-scented" variety fetched a much higher price in the market, ambitious clergymen were said to learn that, "The best way to get sweet-scented Tobacco is to use sweet-scented Words."[206] Many local parsons, according to a complaint by the House of Burgesses, were known largely for their ability to throw dice, deal cards, and "gabble in a pulpit, roar in a tavern, exact [money] from their parishes, [and] give themselves to excess in drinking or riott."[207] Compulsory tithes went to support one minister who preached required quarterly sermons against fornication and drunkeness while regularly indulging in such activities, and another who was president of the local jockey club and raced his large stable of horses for large bets.

American Anglicanism suffered from the general decline of the Church of England. Many services in and around London were great grist for those who saw Christianity as empty tradition: Some parsons wore riding boots under their cassocks so they would waste no time after church; congregations in high-back pews repaid pastoral disinterest in kind by eating during the sermon, to avoid taking time from subsequent pursuits.[208] English political corruption was built on theological corruption; one pious lady, Hannah More, complained that among the upper classes, "There is but little appearance remaining among the great and the powerful of that righteousness, which exalteth a nation." The Bible, she added, was "the most unfashionable of books."[209]

London's prelates, in short, were like Eli in the Old Testament: old, almost blind, with a history of spoiling their children, ready to fall over when given a prophetic word by the child Samuel and a deserved defeat by the Philistines. Artist Joshua Reynolds once pointed out that the eighteenth-century London elite often lacked even knowledge of the Bible, let alone belief in it: when he showed his painting of the infant Samuel "to some of the great," they asked who Samuel was.[210] But perhaps some knew, and did not want to be reminded of the contrast between Samuel's pure faith and ecclesiastical life in London, with its church conferences that featured Byrd-like sexual promiscuity, heavy drinking, and gambling (where "the Spirit of Avarice glides secretly into the Soul").[211]

Despite some Methodist stirrings in the lower classes during the 1730s and thereafter, the bulk of the English secular and sacred aristocracy remained cold to Christ through almost the entire eighteenth century. At midcentury John Brown, the honest clergyman, painfully recorded gender confusion: "The Sexes have now little other apparent Distinction, beyond that of Person and Dress. . . . The one Sex having advanced into Boldness, as the other have sunk into Effeminacy."[212] Abandonment of family time and prayer followed: "Should you propose to him the Renewal of that Family Devotion, which concluded the guiltless Evening Entertainments of his Ancestry; you would become an Object of his Pity, rather than Contempt."[213] And, once a man took the wrong road, it was hard to get back on course: "How can he get Wisdom, whose Talk is of Dress and Wages . . . Horses, Women, and Dice?"[214]

Church of England leaders, Brown complained, could have spoken out against such practice, but many of them also had fallen into the same "Peculiarities, by which their Contemporaries are distinguished. . . . In their Conduct they curb not, but promote and encourage the trifling Manners of the Times: It is grown a fashionable Thing, among these Gentlemen, to despise the Duties of their Parish; to wander about, as the various Seasons invite, to every Scene of false Gaiety. . . ." The sinfulness of those who were supposed to be shepherds led to a general ignoring of Christian faith and practice: "The Sublime Truths, the pure and simple Morals of the Gospel, are despised and trod under Foot."[215]

The personal soon became political, as wrong belief led to a grasping for special privilege and governmental spoils: "if the great Principles of Religion, Honour, and public Spirit, are weak or loose among us, what effectual Check can there be upon . . . the Great, to controul their unbounded and unwarranted Pursuit of lucrative Employments?" Rotten private lifestyles led to public turmoil: "The present Rage of Pleasure" dissipated interest in honest work, so those who demanded "the Gratification of unmanly Passions" turned to "controuling, bribing, or buying" elections. Brown asked, with words relevant to our own time when such corruption is again on the rise, "Whenever this happens, what can we expect as the Consequence, but a general Anarchy and Confusion?"[216]

Other writers also frequently observed church leaders desiring above all else the world's praises and pleasures. Playwright Charles Churchill noted that job-hunting priests placed king above God: "The trim Chaplain, conscious of a See,/Cries out, 'My King, I have no God but thee.'"[217] Hymn-writer William Cowper cried over the lifestyle of the worldly parson: "Loose in morals and in manners vain/In conversation frivolous, in dress/Extreme. At once rapacious and profuse Frequent in part with lady at his side/Ambling and prattling scandal as he goes./But rare at home and never at his books . . . ." A few parsons were sound, Cowper noted, but the more typical churchman was "Ambitious of preferment for its gold/And well prepared by ignorance and sloth By infidelity and love of world/To make God's work a sinecure, a slave/To his own pleasures and his patron's pride."[218]

Corruption began at the top, since politics clearly outweighed piety within the Anglican hierarchy. Throughout most of the eighteenth century the chief prelates, who made up about one-sixth of the House of Lords, paid back the king for their appointments by spending the parliamentary session in London and generally voting as a block for whatever the king and his court wanted. Most of the prelates did not seem to mind doing their political duty because London was the social center and, as John Brown complained, it was "a fashionable thing, among these gentlemen, to despise the duties of their parish; to wander about, as the various seasons invite, to every scene of false gaity; to frequent and shine in all public places, their own pulpits excepted."[219]

Sloth (except in partying) then sank down to the local church; a foreign visitor commented on "how fat and fair these parsons are. They are charged with being somewhat lazy, and their usual plumpness makes it suspected that there's some truth in it."[220] The end result was that most British churchmen, and some of their favored American appointees, were willing to bless the meanderings of a quasi-pagan ruling party. Although some restlessness on the part of church members was evident, England's centralized church had no structures for dealing with bottom-up theological discontent.

Stained with So Many Odious Vices

Massachusetts by 1700 had a law requiring that each town support and maintain by taxes "an able, orthodox and learned minister"; Connecticut and New Hampshire laws were similar.[221] No denomination was singled out by name for preference, but Congregationalist majorities in towns assured that the Congregationalist minister would gain the subsidy. Minorities, realizing that they would be outvoted, tried to gain exemptions from mandatory tithing. Massachusetts and Connecticut Anglicans in 1727 succeeded in having their religious taxes go to support their own ministers; in subsequent years, Quakers and Baptists with certificates showing membership and regular attendance at their own services gained exemption.

Other colonies had different means of governance, but Christians in all of them strove to obtain ministers who would disciple rather than embarrass. Three of the colonies—Rhode Island, Pennsylvania, and Delaware (a split-off from Pennsylvania in 1704)—prided themselves on their foundings as havens for religious diversity; they had no established churches and were largely free of Anglican control. New Jersey, established by proprietors who allowed considerable religious freedom, came under direct crown (and Anglican) control in 1702, but the New Jersey legislature never agreed to an establishment law and never passed a tax to support Anglican churches.

New York had an ambiguous theological settlement from the time England took over what settlers from the Netherlands—with their Dutch Reformed church—had begun. In New York, as in the other colonies, Britain's Toleration Act gave Congregationalist, Presbyterian, and other dissenting ministers the right to preach, and governors no right to withhold licenses, but New York's experience displayed the tendencies to conflict.[222] The Duke of York had promised Puritan settlers that their mandated tax support for ministers would go to "the Minister being elected by the major Part of the Householders and Inhabitants of the Town."[223] Residents of Jamaica township, twelve miles from Manhattan and inhabited by descendants of New Englanders, had used their tax money to erect a Presbyterian church building and to provide a parsonage house for a Presbyterian minister. Anglicans, claiming (despite the Duke's promise) a monopoly on tax-funded churches, seized the church building in 1793; Presbyterians managed to take it back.

Lord Cornbury involved himself in the controversy in 1703 during a month when smallpox raged through New York City—"the Time of the Great Sickness"—and those who could afford to do so headed for the countryside. When Cornbury, escaping to Jamaica township, sweetly asked Mr. Hubbard, the Presbyterian minister, for the loan of his house, Hubbard graciously moved his whole family out. Cornbury, after a brief stay, repaid the hospitality by delivering house and keys to local Anglicans and instructing the sheriff to keep Hubbard out and seize his lands as well. Presbyterians rioted in 1704 in order to regain posession of their property by force, but Cornbury's high-handed tactics temporarily won the day, and the war turned to the courts.[224]

In the undisputed Anglican establishment—the colonies of Virginia and the Carolinas—colonists tried to assert local control over denominational power. To do so, they had to depart from conventional practice in England, where Anglican ministers received appointments from the bishop that carried not only a form of tenure but a farm or two (the "glebe") that provided financial support. Ministers who were well-connected politically could gain plural livings—glebes from many parishes—whether or not they lived in those parishes or ever visited them, and there was nothing the neglected but tax-paying parishioners could do. Those at the top piled up the glebes, sometimes becoming bishops in one diocese, deans in another, and vicars in a third, with the result that the Archbishop of Canterbury took in £25,000 annually (the equivalent of about $2 million today) and the Bishop of London £20,000.[225]

In eighteenth-century America, though, local Anglicans elected vestrymen who in turn selected the minister, rather than awaiting those appointed by hierarchs. An opinion by England's attorney general, Sir Edward Northey, in 1703 had supported this procedure, and in all of the southern royal colonies except Georgia laws passed by the assemblies moved control over church appointments from royal governors to local vestries. Colonists took advantage of a legal technicality to assure vestry choice of minister and retention only on good behavior. By law a minister was tenured, with full possession of his parish and its glebe, only when "presented" by vestrymen to the royal governor and then "inducted" into his living. Churchgoers in Virginia and other colonies, not objecting to tithing but not wishing to support sloth, stopped presenting and inducting ministers; in that way they made sure that the ministers, essentially on year-to-year contracts, had to do their jobs.

Governors, such as Alexander Spotswood, who tried to bring ecclesiastical appointments under a British-style spoils system found they had overreached. Under fire from the assembly for his economic manipulations, Spotswood in 1718 appointed a minister to a vacancy in St. Anne's Parish; the vestry, refusing to go along, hired another minister. The Burgesses sided with the vestry, but Spotswood would not budge and the legislators directed William Byrd, then in London, to present charges against Spotswood before Crown officials. Legal and public-relations machinations became complicated, but London authorities, seeing one more indication that Spotswood knew how to lose friends and inspire opposition, replaced him with an official who quickly dropped the issue and let the vestry win.[226]

There was some danger in such pure congregational control: In 1727 the Rev. Hugh Jones worried about "such Vestry-Men, who erroneously think themselves the Masters of their Parson, and aver, that since they compacted but from Year to Year with him as some have done, they may turne off this their Servant when they will."[227] In practice, though, vestrymen generally proved to be responsible: In 1724 twenty-three of twenty-eight clergymen responding to questions from the Bishop of London wrote that although they had never received induction, they had on the average served the same parish for twenty years.

This local power was never appreciated by England's Anglican hierararchs, who repeatedly complained of their inability to control far-away colonial Anglicans and argued for the placement of one or more bishops on the scene.[228] King George II agreed that the proposal should be put before the ministers, but the Privy Council did not want to excite opposition from dissenting churches, and the proposals were filed away, not to return until the 1760s. By that time the theological and political landscape had changed radically because the Great Awakening had begun in the fertile soil of churches that saw God, not London, as the center of their being.

The Great Awakening began in New England but quickly spread among all those who were dissatisfied with "labour to build up a Shell, to form a meer Carcase of Godliness." Massachusetts minister Samuel Wigglesworth in 1733 was one of many to complain of regnant hypocrisy: "We have a goodly exterior Form of Religion; . . . [yet] we find our selves stained with so many most odious Vices, especially Uncleanness, Drunkenness, Theft, Covetousness, Violence, Malice, Strife, and others."[229] Words and deeds were in conflict: deeds "be look'd upon with dishonour, yet multitudes are found who are not ashamed to commit them."[230] Those who were ashamed about the lack of shame prayed for an awakening that would help churches succeed in their main objective—the saving of souls and the nourishing of regenerated lives.

The prayers were answered initially by a revival throughout the colonies that led tens of thousands of people into a new appreciation of the holiness of God and their own sinfulness. Beginning in towns such as Jonathan Edwards' Northampton during the 1730s, and fanned into a blaze by the preaching tour of George Whitefield in 1740, the Great Awakening first had Americans asking what they must do to be saved. But the awakening was also a reformation: Those who were saved proceeded to ask how they should live. Awakened piety revitalized old Congregational and Presbyterian churches in the northern colonies and Anglican ones in the south; it also led to the creation of new churches, particularly among Baptists.

The major impact of the Great Awakening, however, may not have been on church growth as such. Revivals led for a short time to large increases in the numbers of those making personal professions of faith and joining churches, but the longer-term results were not so winsome. The Awakening apparently did not lead to a permanent increase in the numbers of people attending church or formally becoming members: Membership/attendance may have rolled down a gentle slope from 1700 to the American Revolution. But the Awakening did have some very decided, long-term effects, as many churches were strengthened and many individuals went from profession to practical application.[231]

Emphasis on a higher allegiance led to stronger families and more conscientious work as short-lived satisfactions paled before the deeper joys of loving God, spouses, and children. God-centeredness also led to a greater willingness to criticize London's appointees. Jonathan Edwards was among those who taught New Englanders to compare the good magistrate with those "contemptible" ones who are "of a mean spirit, a disposition that will admit of their doing those things that are sordid and vile."[232] Such appointees "will shamefully defile their hands to gain a few pounds, are not ashamed to grind the faces of the poor, and screw their neighbours; and will take advantage of their authority or commission to line their own pockets with what is fraudulently taken or withheld from others."[233]

Those who took after Edwards opposed political as well as theological evil, and in that process taught that London was far from the center of the world. When Jonathan Edwards published in 1742 *Some Thoughts Concerning the Present Revival of Religion*, he treated as a secondary matter a new war between England and Spain: referring to the Great Awakening, Edwards wrote, "We in New England are now engaged in a more important war."[234] Connection with God, and not men in high places, was central to successful life, and souls of commoners and kings were of equal value.

The idea that there were no little people and no little places clearly contradicted the belief in London that the chief end of man in the hinterlands was to help the center, and to glory in its pomp. Today, bicoastal Americans speak sarcastically of the fly-over zone; the view of America from eighteenth-century London also was demeaning. Colonies were places where young bureaucrats went to gain dictatorial power in small ponds, to fill out their resumés for an eventual return to the center, and to fill their pockets. London's best weapon against potential opposition was the belief that those who did not follow royal whim would lose out; crucially, the Great Awakening grew people who did not care about missing out, because they had an entirely different set of priorities.

The Great Awakening had the potential to lead to separation from England precisely because it did not, in general, propose separation from the world: The Calvinist background of most revivalists helped them to avoid the common revival-spawned sense that the world is so evil that any political and social action within it also is evil. Revival leaders such as Gilbert Tennett were careful to insist that Christians are "born for Society" and must work for "the Good of the Publick, which we were born to promote."[235] Soon, observers were noting that consistent Calvinists emphasized God's sovereignty over all, including kings; they strove for holiness in government as well as in their own lives. Minister Benjamin Lord noted in 1751 that the colonists were "Prone to act in Civil, as they stand Affected in religious Matters."[236] Minister Mark Leavenworth explained that all problems, whether church, civic, or personal, had a common cause: "Sin."[237]

The Great Awakening, along with changing many individuals, thus led to a decreased distinction between religious and political activities. The signing of a certain political petition could become "a Sabbath-Day's Exercise," and churches sometimes voted as blocs.[238] Leading ministers of the Awakening urged their listeners to avoid lukewarm doctrines and to make the hard decision to separate from ungodly churches, when necessary. Each individual touched by God's grace had to make the decision to follow Jesus Christ in all walks of life, come what may, even if such action infuriated those in authority. Once the willingness to honor God (even if that meant disobeying king or distinguished cleric) was present, the rest followed: It was only one small step to move from leaving a corrupt church to separating from a corrupt government and society.[239]

The Great Awakening, therefore, created the potential for a political awakening. Evangelical Calvinism had a radical social and political ideology that led to greater suspicion of the state church and a willingness to see unity as less important than truth. In the middle of the century, those heavily influenced by economics and by thoughts of man's glory retained the vision of themselves and their posterity as perpetual British subjects; liberal Congregationalists such as Thomas Barnard and John Mellen, and northern Anglicans such as East Apthorp and William Smith, continued to see British cosmopolitan civilization as the hope of the future.[240]

THE TABLE GRACED WITH ABOUT SIXTY BLACK FACES

British leaders, for their part, gave the standard bureaucratic response to a theological or ideological challenge: Offer a bribe. The *Pennsylvania Gazette* reported in 1739 that

> the Reverend Mr. Whitefield's Preaching is become so very offensive to the Clergy of this Kingdom, that 'tis said one of my Lords the Bishops a few Days since, went to the King to desire his Majesty to silence him: Upon which his Majesty enquired whether he preach'd Treason, Sedition, &c., but none of these Things being alledg'd against him, his Majesty see'd at a Loss how to satisfy the Bishop; which a Noble Duke present observing, humbly proposed, that in order to prevent Mr. Whitefield's preaching for the future, his Majesty would be graciously pleased to *make him a Bishop*.[241]

The major British step, however, was attempted suppression, particularly in Virginia where immigrants began to challenge the colony's overwhelming Anglicanism. As Scotch-Irish and German settlers in the 1730s streamed into the Shenandoah Valley and found themselves living in an area without organized Reformed churches, they applied to the Presbyterian Synod at Philadelphia for help. The synod sent a request for toleration to Virginia's Lieutenant Governor William Gooch, who replied that Presbyterian ministers who acted peaceably would not be hindered. But in 1745, as dissent inspired by Whitefield's preaching increased and Dissenters began active proselytizing, Gooch charged a grand jury "to make strict inquiry after those seducers."[242]

Gooch's governor's council, in 1747, declared its concern with the Dissenters' spirit of "enthusiasm," claiming that it would produce confusion and lead to practices that in the midseventh century had led to civil war in England. Gooch ordered all magistrates to keep itinerant ministers from preaching or holding meetings in Virginia.

Presbyterian Samuel Davies was one of the ministers Gooch tried to squelch. Davies, however, argued that Gooch's established church was not doing the job: "Religion has been, and in most Parts of the Colony still is, in a very low State." Davies noted that "Family-Religion is a Rarity, and a solemn Solicitude about eternal Things is still a greater. Vices of various Kinds are triumphant, and even a Form of Godliness is not common."[243]

Virginia authorities liked their vices and sought to crack down further on Davies and other Dissenters, but British attorney general Dudley Ryder observed that the productivity of Americans was tied to their free exercise of religion, which was "so valuable a branch of true liberty and so essential to the enriching and improving of a trading nation."[244] Money talked and religious concerns were not to get in the way. Davies was allowed to preach, and to change the lives of some who heard him: Patrick Henry as a youngster took his Presbyterian mother to hear Davies preach, learned from him, and with Samuel Adams, became one of the two key coalition builders of the prerevolutionary era.[245] (As we will see, both Henry and Adams followed the Great Awakening pattern of appealing to emotions as well as intellect.)

Davies also became an instrument for the salvation of many slaves. He frequently looked to the back of his church and remarked that "Never have I been so struck with the appearance of an assembly as when I have glanced my eye to that part of the meetinghouse where they usually sit . . . with so many black countenances eagerly attentive to every word they hear, and frequently bathed in tears."[246] In 1755, eight years after Davies' arrival in Virginia, he wrote that three hundred blacks regularly worshipped at his church. He invited converted Blacks to participate in the Lord's Supper, and noted in 1757 that "what little success I have lately had, has been chiefly among the extremes of Gentlemen and negroes. Indeed, God has remarkably worked among the latter. I have baptized about 150 adults; and at the last sacramental solemnity, I had the pleasure of seeing the table *graced* with about 60 black faces."[247]

Gradually, blacks who had sympathetic masters also began developing their own churches; the first formal fellowship for worship among slaves may have been established in the late 1750s on the Byrd plantation, then owned by William Byrd III. Black conversions led some white Americans to begin rethinking slavery, which was an integral part of the imperial system: Government-favored owners of tobacco and rice plantations needed slaves if their businesses were to become major profit centers. Since Parliament had worked hard to place the African trade "upon a right establishment," and since British and New England trading companies enjoyed enormous profits from slave trading, opposing the institution was economic treason.[248] Followers of Jonathan Edwards, such as Samuel Hopkins of Newport (a town built on slavery), Levi Hart of Connnecticut, Jacob Green of New York, and Edwards' own son Jonathan, Jr., nevertheless pushed the issue, and began by treating black slaves as brothers fully capable of receiving God's grace.

The British, along with those who saw blacks as inferiors best suited to slavery, tried to suppress such endeavors, as well as others that threatened radical upheaval. While blacks faced the greatest hazards, white Baptists in midcentury Virginia faced persecution of their own. Anti-Baptist campaigns began with ridicule: Baptists were portrayed as "an ignorant, illiterate set," and the *Virginia Gazette* labeled them "a pack of ignorant enthusiasts."[249] One Baptist meeting was broken up when a hornet's nest was thrown in, and one minister was momentarily silenced when a whip was run down his throat. The theologically sedentary—those who opened the Bible only to record births, deaths, and marriages—despised the Baptists' evangelical excitement. [250]

The general mood among leaders of all stripes at first was that many Baptists were seized by a "terrible Distemper" and a "Superstitious Delusion." Some merchants even made an economic argument: Baptists had so many church meetings that work time was lost. (Opponents of the Baptists even counted the number of males and meetings and totaled the loss of productivity.)[251] But the Baptists tended to be separatists, so their surge did not have immediate political significance: British authorities found they could coexist with separatists, as they could coexist with latitudinarians committed to a live-and-let-live creed. The real political threat was from Presbyterians who were potential troublemakers because they increasingly saw themselves as soldiers in a culture war that could become political. They were also a swing vote precisely because they saw a vital role for government: Their ministers frequently preached about how God had established "civil government to keep men from destroying each other."[252]

SUCH RULERS HAVE GONE OUT OF THE LINE OF THEIR POWER

The political question arising out of the Great Awakening was whether criticism of a corrupt church would lead to criticism of a corrupt government. By the time of the Great Awakening the young American press already had a calling. Some journalists in early America were merely propagandists for government's official story, but a general meeting of the Massachusetts clergy in 1681 had requested ministers to "diligently enquire into, and Record such Illustrious Providences as have happened, or from time to time shall happen."[253] Such correspondents were to have a higher task than public relations for the royal governor; they were, as Cotton Mather wrote, "To regard the illustrious displays of that Providence wherewith our Lord Christ governs the world."[254]

By the 1730s, the new press doctrine had been taken one step further: Along with proclaiming that the heavens declare the glory of God, printer-editors performed a ministerial function when they showed how the palaces display the sinfulness of man. An early issue of a new publication, the *New-York Weekly Journal*, pointedly asked, "If we reverence men for their power alone, why do we not reverence the Devil, who has so much more power than men?" The article concluded that respect was due "only to virtuous qualities and useful actions," and that it was therefore "as ridiculous and superstitious to adore great mischievous men as it is to worship a false god or Satan in the stead of God."[255]

Thus, another battle began. William Cosby, the royal governor of New York during the 1730s and a fitting successor to Cornbury, did not appreciate such remarks. When a farmer's cart slowed down Cosby's coach, the governor had his coachman beat the farmer with a horsewhip until they nearly killed him. When Cosby desired some land owned by Indians, he stole their deed and burned it. When Cosby granted new lands to those who applied legally, he demanded and received bribes often amounting to one third of the estates.[256] Cosby, in 1735, read issues of the *New-York Weekly Journal* edited by John Peter Zenger, who played the organ each Sabbath in a Dutch Reformed church and took God's law seriously; Zenger described some of Cosby's transactions, and Cosby had him thrown into jail.

At the trial, Zenger's lawyer, Andrew Hamilton, argued that the editor should be freed because he had been "exposing and opposing arbitrary power by speaking and writing Truth," which Hamilton equated with the Bible. He said Zenger was following the lead of God's inspired authors, who attacked corrupt leaders as "blind watchmen" and "greedy dogs that can never have enough." Zenger, Hamilton argued, was one more victim of "the Flame of Prosecutions upon Informations, set on Foot by the Government, to deprive a People of the Right of Remonstrating (and complaining too), of the arbitrary Attempts of Men in Power."[257] Jury members showed their allegiance to a power higher than the Crown and found Zenger not guilty.

In short, by the time of the Great Awakening, colonists already had begun to move the king from the center of power and to substitute a greater King. By the time of the Zenger trial in 1735, many colonies did not have an established church tied to the crown, and those that did, such as Virginia, were growing policies of church governance that were essentially populist or representative—democratic or republican—rather than top-down. Newspapers were developing the theoretical vision to gain an independent voice: They would be truth-tellers ready to glorify God and expose man's corruption, even if it occurred in palaces and governors' mansions.[258] And colonial assemblies, in which Dissenters often had strength, learned to challenge crown-appointed executives who were almost always Anglican.[259]

Before the Awakening, the Board of Trade in London had received a warning, from Attorney General Bradley of New York, that some of the colonies might have "a strong inclination to take the earliest opportunity of setting up for themselves." Bradley argued that the geographic and cultural base for a war of independence already existed: If several colonies should "join in such a conspiracy . . . it would be extremely difficult and expensive, if not impracticable, at the distance, and in such a thicket of wood and trees as these countries are, to reduce them to their duty and obedience."[260] He proposed that London officials contemplate the colonies' "populousness at present, the skilfulness, strength, and activity of the people who are inured to hardships, can defend themselves in woods and behind trees, can live on roots and what the woods aford without bread, beer or spirits, or forage for horses, &c., and can travel in the woods without guides or the help of roads."

But it was one thing to criticize a governor and dream about independence; Americans would turn dreams into plans only if they believed such an effort was right, and that it would receive God's blessing. George Whitefield became a grandfather of the American Revolution when he argued that Christian subjects must obey divine laws and could, if necessary, break laws that pressed them to do wrong. Accused by the bishop of London of breaking church canons, Whitefield replied firmly but respectfully,

> Your Lordship knows full well that Canons and other church laws are good and obligatory when comformable to the laws of Christ and agreeable to the liberties of a free people; but when invented and compiled by men of little hearts and bigotted principles . . . and when made use of only as ends to bind up the hands of a zealous few, they may be very legally broken.[261]

One of Whitefield's followers, Elisha Williams, played out such thought at greater length in a pamphlet published in 1744, *The Essential Rights and Liberties of Protestants*. The pamphlet examined biblical texts about the kind of respect Christians owed to governing authorities and noted that disobedience was sometimes the right course:

> the Powers that be in Great Britain are the Government therein according to its own Constitution:—If then the higher Powers for the Administration rule not according to the Constitution, or if any King thereof shall rule so, as to change the Government from legal to arbitary, the Power from God fails them, it is then a Power not in the text, and so no Subjection due to it from the Text.[262]

Williams went on to argue that British power "is a limited one: and therefore the Obedience due is a limited Obedience." He argued that when Parliament passes overreaching laws, "a free-born People can never become so servile as to regard them, while they have Eyes to see that such Rulers have gone out of the Line of their Power, . . . There is no Reason they should be Fools because their Rulers are so."[263] Theoretical remarks of this sort had been made before the Great Awakening, but they became far more pointed in its aftermath. By the 1750s, one pamphleteer was even asserting that London's initiatives would work only "in a Popish Country, or in Turkey, where the common People are sunk and degraded almost to the State of Brutes, by Poverty, Chains and absolute Tyranny, and have no more Sense of Liberty and Property, than so many Jack-Asses."[264]

Such pamphlets and sermons were numerous after the Great Awakening. Before it, criticism of leading institutions and a desire to separate from them was viewed as not quite legitimate; afterward, dissent began to be seen not as sinful activity but as protection against corruption. Ideologically dueling newspapers, the *New-York Weekly Journal* explained, made sure that "Injuries on either Side are either prevented or redressed." The argument of a *New-York Gazette* writer became common: Criticism "is not only necessary in free Governments, but of great Service to the Public. Parties are a Check upon one another, and by keeping the Ambition of one another within Bounds, serve to maintain the public Liberty." Political debate, "instead of clogging, regulates and keeps in their just and proper Motion the Wheels of Government."[265]

It became theologically legitimate to think and speak of separation. Peter Kalm, a Swedish scientist who traveled through Britain's American colonies at midcentury, noted a frequent refrain: "that the English colonies in North America, in the space of thirty or fifty years, would be able to form a state by themselves entirely independent of old England."[266] James Abercromby, an Englishman who had lived in South Carolina for at least fifteen years, told Parliament in 1752 that American colonists "formed into separate societies" were ready to "feel their own strength" and decide for themselves "whether they are to remain subjects or become confederates."[267]

One big obstacle to consideration of independence, however, was the presence of New France—Canada—to the north and west of the coast-hugging British colonies. In 1750, Kalm argued that movement to independence could be rapid except for one danger "sufficient to prevent the connection of the colonies with their mother country from being quite broken off." The danger was that "the North American colonies are near a country, under the government of the French," and Kalm suggested that the advantage of retaining that threat had not escaped British authorities: "There is reason to believe that the king never was in earnest in his attempts to expel the French from their possessions there; though it might have been done with little difficulty."[268]

If the colonists believed they needed England for defense, they would not declare independence; similarly, if they believed they needed British expertise in handling a variety of social problems, they also would hesitate. But the Awakened colonists by midcentury were putting faith into practice by caring for the needy in a way far more effective than Britain's various Poor Laws did. Without countermanding from London, vestrymen gained authority over not only the appointment of ministers but the provision of welfare: they placed helpless individuals and families in the homes of volunteers, with expenses paid from the public treasury. Vestries took responsibility for children orphaned during Indian attacks; one parish in the Shenandoah Valley found homes for forty-seven orphans between 1748 and 1752.[269] Vestrymen also levied parish taxes, assessed property for their payment, and prosecuted social crimes such as drunkenness and fornication. They formed, in short, another parallel government.

So significant were church duties, and so limited in function were other governments, that parish taxes were generally greater than other taxes; as late as the eve of the Revolution, Truro and Fairfax parishes in Virginia each had larger budgets than the government of the county in which both were located. Authority over expenditures attracted present and future leaders: Of the more than one hundred members of the Virginia constitutional convention of 1776, only three were not vestrymen. Justices of Fairfax County such as George Washington and George Mason were on the Truro Parish vestry.[270]

Further north, churches and church organizations following the Great Awakening also became a parallel government, particularly in relation to questions of education and welfare. At midcentury in Boston, members of the church-organized Society for Encouraging Industry and Employing the Poor were responsible for "the Distribution of Charity; not being allowed to dispense it promiscuously, but obliged to take due Care to find out suitable Objects; distinguishing properly between those needy People who are able, and those who are *unable*, to employ themselves in Labour. . . ."[271]

In Maryland, which had started out as a haven for Catholics but soon gained a Protestant majority, churches founded charity schools designed to teach poor children the "Knowledge and Fear" of God, and "the Way of providing for themselves by honest industry."[272]

Some British prognosticators had predicted that life on the American frontier would become a war of all against all, with settlers who had left civilization behind descending into savagery. Following the Great Awakening, however, America was looking more and more like a Christian commonwealth that combined the best aspects of individualism and community. Had Britain followed the same course at midcentury, there would have been no trans-Atlantic culture war. But many of England's leaders were on a different course.

Fair Venus Calls; Her Voice Obey

During the 1740s, Americans under the influence of the Great Awakening were examining the major theological issues, and Methodism was making some inroads among the lower classes in England. Many of London's leaders, however, preferred to eat, drink, rut, and be merry; as John Brown wrote at midcentury, there was a "general Contempt of Religion among the fashionable World." Brown argued that this contempt in some ways could not even be called infidelity, "for that would imply a certain Attention to these Subjects; a certain Degree of Self-Converse and Thought; and this would clash with the ruling Manners of the Times"[273]—as it does now.

Many of the leading English social clubs of the era displayed that contempt; one of the most prestigious and infamous was that of the famous "monks" of Medmenham. This group was at its height from 1753 to 1762; its membership during that period included a secretary of state, a first lord of the admiralty, a chancellor of the exchequer, and other cabinet ministers, as well as the leader of the radical opposition and other leading politicians and writers. A host of other influential leaders, including a prime minister, apparently were visitors at one time or another.[274]

It is sometimes hard to separate fact from fiction in both the contemporary accounts of the club's activities and those of more recent historians, but the history of its founder and leader is clear. Sir

Francis Dashwood, a well-connected rake who became chancellor of the exchequer in 1762 and 1763, was an admirer of Voltaire and a student of his works.[275] Like others in his circle, he encouraged the arts, dabbled in philanthropy, married and emotionally abandoned a young lady, and, according to a magazine article in the 1760s, "ingratiated himself with all the celebrated [prostitutes]."[276]

Dashwood in 1752 or 1753 purchased (or perhaps took out a long-term lease on) Medmenham, a semiruined Cistercian abbey in Buckinghamshire, set back from the Thames amid hanging woods, meadows, and a grove of elms. He rehabbed the abbey and landscaped the grounds to make them, in Dashwood's words, a "garden of lust" with statues in poses to appeal to the prurient and shrubbery pruned to resemble a woman's private parts. Inside, Dashwood put in stained glass windows that contained indecent pictures of the twelve apostles, a chapel ceiling with a huge pornographic fresco, a library that was said to contain the country's largest collection of pornographic books, and small rooms with couches placed beneath portraits of past kings and famous prostitutes. Over the eastern porch of the building, Dashwood had workmen paint a motto borrowed from Rabelais: "*fay ce que voudras* (Do as you please)."[277]

That sign could have gone on to cite other words of Rabelais: "Here enter not, religious boobies, sots,/Imposters, sniveling hypocrites, bigots. . . . Your filthy trumperies,/Stuff'd with pernicious lies./(Not worth a bubble)/Would only trouble/Our earthly Paradise."[278] It is clear that Dashwood imported prostitutes from London and provided them to his distinguished friends and visitors, but how far he went beyond that to offend those who had their eyes on a different sort of paradise, is not clear.

An account by Charles Johnstone, in his thinly-veiled novel *Chrysal*, described what Dashwood had to offer in his "monastery": "The cellars were stored with the choicest wines, the larders with the delicacies of every climate, and the cells were fitted up for all the purposes of lasciviousness, for which proper objects were also provided." Dashwood then "selected from among his intimates a number equal to that of those who had been at the first chosen to inculcate the religion which he designed to ridicule, whose names they assumed, as he, with equal modesty and piety, did that of the Divine Author of it." The new apostles and their lord then met in a chapel that featured "walls painted with the portraits of those whose names and characters they assumed, represented in attitudes and actions horrible to imagination."[279]

But Johnstone was not always accurate; for example, he had one prominent member initiated six or seven years later than he actually was.[280] There were rumors but no proof that Medmenham members practiced Satanism.[281] What is unmistakable is that at least twice a year for a decade, political dignitaries reveled for a fortnight at what was at least the eighteenth-century equivalent of parties at Hugh Hefner's mansion: Medmenham members dressed as monks were "drinking wine poured by naked girls."[282] The appeal was that offered in a note from one member, Thomas Potter, to John Wilkes, who like most of the other members was married but unwilling to give up promiscuity: "If you prefer young Women and Whores to old Women and Wives . . . if Life and Spirit and Wit and Humour and Gaity but above all if the heavenly inspir'd Passion called LUST have not deserted you and left you a Prey to Dullness and Imbecillity, hasten to Town. . . ."[283]

The only American known to hasten to Medmenham was Benjamin Franklin; there is no full documentation of his visits until 1772, when the club was on its downside and Franklin was a still hearty sixty-six year old, but he may have been an early guest and, some speculate, a member.[284] Franklin had listened to Whitefield's preaching and was almost swayed by it,[285] but ended up sticking with the peculiar combination of polytheism and deism that he had developed: "I CONCEIVE then that the INFINITE has created many Beings or Gods, vastly superior to man."[286] The Infinite was now out of the picture, but each god, Franklin added, "has made for himself one glorious Sun, attended with a beautiful and admirable System of Planets. It is that particular wise and good God, who is the Author and Owner of our System, that I propose for the Object of my Praise and Adoration."[287] Franklin's local deity was the sweet God of which dreams are made: "He is pleas'd when he sees me Happy. And since he has created many Things which seem purely design'd for the Delight of Man, I believe he is not offended when he sees his Children solace themselves in any manner of pleasant Exercises. . . ."[288]

What most people saw as lascivious conduct, Franklin apparently viewed as a pleasant exercise; Franklin wrote in one letter that "I am in [Dashwood's] house as much at my ease as if it were my own; and the gardens are a paradise. . . ."[289] Franklin wrote in 1745, "Fair Venus calls; her voice obey;/In beauty's arms spend night and day./The joys of love all joys excel/And loving's certainly doing well."[290] Later in life, he was Dashwood's guest for sixteen days when the "monks" were meeting and making use of pornography-filled rooms underground; Franklin during that time mentioned in a letter to a Philadelphia friend his interest in the "whimsical" taste of Dashwood that was "as evident below the earth as above it."[291]

Franklin praised Dashwood as a "a humane, liberal reformer in Church affairs" who made "a handsome contribution to the Unitarian Chapels," as did Franklin.[292] He even worked with Dashwood in an attempt to sap theological orthodoxy by preparing *An Abridgement of the Book of Common Prayer*: Dashwood revised the liturgy by dropping Communion and anything else that emphasized man's sinfulness and need for redemption, and Franklin took charge of the catechism by eliminating all references to the divinity of Jesus, to the Nicene and Athanasian Creeds, and to the Ten Commandments as commandments rather than suggestions.[293] (The publication, however, "was never much noticed," Franklin complained. "Some were given away, very few sold, and I suppose the bulk became waste paper."[294])

Franklin and Dashwood could work well together for several reasons. First, despite the emphasis on virtue in his public-relations dominated *Autobiography*, Franklin was always soft on promiscuity: he acknowledged that as a young man he was looking for love in all the wrong places, and even in the *Autobiography* he argued—as William Byrd II would have also—that venery could be used for purposes of health.[295] Second, up until the eve of the Revolution, Englishmen generally impressed Franklin as superior to the people he found in America.[296] (As Franklin later acknowledged, he was "fond to a Folly of our British Connections."[297])

A third reason also was crucial: In the culture war that escalated after the Awakening, Franklin was on the latitudinarian side. He argued that "Reverend Asses" who preached about original sin and the need to believe in and obey God were attempting to frighten "an unthinking Populace out of their Senses and inspire them with Terror, to answer the little selfish Ends of the Inventors and Propagators."[298] Franklin saw Presbyterians as his "bitter

Enemies," particularly when they emphasized biblical revelation; Franklin insisted that he would not "admit of a Sense contrary to Reason. . . ."[299]

That was almost the crux of the midcentury culture war: The biblical sense that the Great Awakening thrust forward was not contrary to reason, but it certainly maintained that God's reason was higher than man's. The Enlightenment of the eighteenth century, with its emphasis on humanity's light breaking up the darkness of revealed religion, ran directly against the Awakening. The Enlightened, such as Voltaire, often looked to London for political leadership and freedom from the Catholic church; the Awakened would increasingly see London as a latter-day Sodom. When in doubt, the Enlightened looked to literature and the arts. According to Awakened thought, the way to be most reasonable, when opinions and lifestyles differed, was to live by God's standards, and not by the "pleasant exercises" that man devised.

CHAPTER FOUR

The War to End Wars

As spiritual battles continued in churches and homes, the flesh-and-blood battles of a hundred-year war along the frontier also roiled on. For London the issue was empire; for the settlers in mortal combat with New France's Indian allies, the issue at first was survival. The Great Awakening brought a new theological edge to the struggles, as those who had been revitalized saw an opportunity to invade Catholic Canada and, in the words of New England deacon John Gray, "destroy the images there set up and [hear] the true Gospel of our Lord and Saviour there preached." By the mid-1740s the Awakening had peaked and the Reverend Thomas Prince announced that the heavenly shower was over: New Englanders, he said, must go from fighting the devil to fighting the French.[300]

Fighting the French, in theory, was a job for professional soldiers dispatched by London, but by the 1740s imperial strategists understood that the existence of Canada helped to keep the colonists in a state of dependency. As British generals did nothing, the first steps toward relieving military gridlock were taken by New Englanders themselves. The French had an immense fortress at Louisbourg on Cape Breton Island north of Nova Scotia; it functioned defensively as protection for Canada and offensively as a haven for the cruisers and privateers that disrupted New England's fishing interests. It was the logical place to attack, but London indicated no interest in an attempt, and it was up to those on the periphery to assume leadership.

The Massachusetts General Assembly did just that in December 1744, when it urged an expedition against Louisbourg, appropriated £50,000 for supplies, and issued bills of credit to fund the transport and provisioning of three thousand volunteers. Some thirty-three hundred Massachusetts citizens soon headed north, and other northern colonies came through as well: Connecticut sent 516 men and New Hampshire 454. New York sent ten eighteen-pounder cannon that proved very useful during the siege of Louisbourg. The Maine section of Massachusetts, smarting from Indian raids, sent a thousand volunteers, more than one-third of its entire male population of military age.[301]

Colonists stepped out confidently in the belief that God was with them. William Douglass, a deistically inclined Boston physician/politician who saw London as the seat of sophistication, thought the expedition "much above our capacity." Douglass also argued that farmers, fisherman, and mechanics would not serve well as soldiers, and contended that William Pepperell, a merchant appointed to lead the effort, would fail as general.[302] Pepperrell himself wondered whether the expedition was a godly pursuit and whether he was called to head it. He sought counsel from George Whitefield, who assured him but also pointed out that victory would not be easy and that Pepperrell must be prepared for criticism if he failed—and envy if he succeeded.

The expedition did succeed, and scoffers said that Pepperrell was lucky. Colonists who were pious but poorly informed said that God had eased both the travel of New England soldiers to Canada and their travels after arrival, but the pursuit in reality was very hard: The expedition would have been difficult enough under good conditions, but "the weather continues thick and dirty," Pepperell freqently wrote in his journal. The landing of artillery and military stores on the southern shore of Cape Breton, west of Louisbourg, had to be made from an open sea onto a beach with surf so high that even on the best of days flat boats could not reach the shore; men had to wade in the frigid water to haul in supplies. Once landed, cannon had to be dragged through swampy land at night, since the route was exposed to enemy firepower. Men sunk in mud up to their knees.

Nevertheless, morale of the attackers remained high, even when they suffered two hundred casualties while attempting to capture a crucial battery by a surprise nighttime assault. As the Canadian defenders wasted much of their ammunition in foolish shooting, the Americans dug in and waited. While the issue was in doubt, William Pepperrell asked for prayer, and Franklin responded with satire: He wrote that Presbyterian ministers, soldiers, and supporters had been praying for about five months, and during that time had sent an estimated forty-five million prayers to heaven. Their military effort had better succeed, Franklin wrote, or "I fear I shall have but an indifferent opinion of Presbyterian prayers in such cases, as long as I live."[303] Franklin's opinion did not change, but the prayers were efficacious; even those who did not understand the workings of God's Providence could see that, as the battle became a war of nerves, the colonists, who saw themselves as doing God's will, were hard to beat. Three months after the arrival of the first colonial troops, Louisbourg surrendered.

News of the capitulation was greeted with bonfires and rhetorical bombast not only throughout New England, but in New York, Philadelphia, Charlestown, and London as well.[304] Disillusionment followed victory, however. The defeated French soldiers at Louisbourg were allowed to leave for their home country, but the American victors had to stay in a place that proved to be a breeding ground for disease. London officials agreed to send regiments from Gibraltar to take on garrison duty, but the replacements did not arrive until the spring of 1746, and in the meantime dysentery and pestilence raged through the American garrison. By spring almost nine hundred New Englanders had died at Louisbourg.

Even so, New England ministers spoke of those lives as noble sacrifices to make New England, and perhaps Canada as well, safe for Awakened Protestantism. In October, 1748, however, Great Britain signed the treaty of Aix la Chapelle, by which Louisbourg was returned to the French in return for "considerations" on the continent of Europe! Cries of anguish rose up and not only from the families of the soldiers who had truly given their lives in vain. The message was clear: English interests trumped colonial concerns.

Makemie, Zenger, and others had begun a revolution by battling royal governors. The Louisbourg giveaway caused further thought about the London relationship. After all, colonists had put up with

British corruption because of the advantages of imperial status, particularly in terms of economic advantage and military necessity. The economic argument was weakened when those touched by the Great Awakening recalled that they did not live by bread alone. The military argument was weakened when Britain did not come through militarily—colonists' blood won Louisbourg. It even seemed as if London would sabotage future efforts, since the return of Louisbourg was thought by some to be an intentional device to keep the British colonies in need of British soldiery. Should New England battle further for British interests, to the neglect of its own? Never again, was the cry!

The Hairy Scalps Clotted with Gore

Again came soon. Thomas Hutchinson, the Massachusetts governor of the 1770s who became a Tory and wrote a history criticizing Calvinist political fervor, saw the roots of fanaticism in American desire to evict the French from Canada: "This was an object above all others wished for by the people of New England."[305] When a new conflict commenced in 1754, just six years after the Louisbourg giveaway, over one-fourth of all Massachusetts males of military age joined up.[306]

Many in the southern colonies also were ready for battle. Their people had been victims of French-instigated Indian raids that Samuel Davies, preaching a sermon, described in vivid terms: "See yonder! The hairy scalps clotted with gore! The mangled limbs! Women ripped up! The heart and bowels still palpitating with life, and smoking on the ground!" Southerners did not feel the urgency of conquering Canada, but Davies summarized well the self-defense objective of their war: "We fight for our people . . . our tender children, the wives of our bosom, our friends, the sharers of our souls, our posterity to the lastest ages! And who would not use his sword with an exerted aim when these lie at stake?"[307]

The war thus described—as a war to stop hostile Indians by removing their French backers from North America—received support from both north and south, despite the New Englanders' sense of betrayal over the Louisbourg giveaway of 1748, and the southerners' knowledge of that precedent. But leaders from both north and south also decided that this time they would work hard to control the terms of war and peace. This, they asserted, would not be a war in which colonists were subservient, but a war in which they would be full partners with the soldiers that London dispatched.[308] And, this would not be just another imperial war for marginal gains in Europe, but a war for final deliverance from the threat of French Canada, a war to end wars.

Colonial leaders also called for a new contract with London. Major General Edward Braddock in February 1755, denounced the "pusillanimous and improper Behavior" of Pennsylvanians, who astonished him by their "absolute Refusal to supply either Men, Money, or Provisions for their own Defence."[309] But defense was not the issue: The issue was whether colonists would sacrifice lives and lucre merely to pile up imperial bargaining chips. Braddock virtually acknowledged the real debate two weeks after his initial outburst when he attacked not parsimony, but the Pennsylvania Assembly's "endeavouring to take advantage of the common Danger in order to encroach upon his Majesty's Prerogative in the Administration of His Government."[310] Colonists were willing to raise money; they were not willing to give up all control over what they raised.

Colonists remembered Braddock's diatribes against American soldiers—their "Slothfull and Languide Disposition renders them very unfit for Military Service"—when France's Indian allies annihilated Braddock's force. The conventional history tells of an ambush in western Pennsylvania, but that it was not. The French and Indian victory was the result of desperate improvisation following the failure of conventional European tactics that most French commanders embraced as enthusiastically as did their British counterparts. On July 9, 1755, the French force of seventy-two regular soldiers, 146 Canadian militiamen, and 637 Indians, all under the command of Lienard de Beaujeu, frontally charged Braddock's main force of about thirteen hundred men. Volleys from the British stopped the assault and killed Beaujeu. Second-in-command Jean-Daniel Dumas then sent the Indians into the trees on both sides of Braddock's forces. From there the Indians' shots devastated soldiers trained to volley on the open plain.[311]

Even then, the day could have been saved if Braddock had taken the advice of some of his officers, including a young colonel from

Virginia, George Washington: They had called on Braddock to adapt to America, and now those near him wanted the men to take cover and fight back frontier style. Braddock said no, perhaps realizing that if allowed to disperse, many of his men would run away. They did not get the chance to run away; when some tried, Braddock charged into them and used the flat of his saber to force them back into line. The soldiers stood in rank and died: two-thirds of the enlisted men, and nearly three-quarters of the officers, were killed or wounded. Braddock was killed by a bullet—some said it came from his own men—and Colonel Thomas Dunbar, taking command, ordered a retreat to the coast so rapid that cannon had to be abandoned along the way.

The speed of the retreat indicated panic rather than prudence, because even after the rout, British troops—including a reserve of one thousand men who had not taken part in battle—still outnumbered the enemy. British reputation for bravery was not increased when Dunbar asked Philadelphia residents to provide winter quarters for his army—in July.[312] The blow to reputation is important because the battle itself, though fatal for many of its poorly led British participants, turned out to be only a temporary setback in a war that Britain eventually won with ease. Its psychological importance for the colonists was great, however: Benjamin Franklin later wrote in his autobiography that the Braddock defeat and its aftermath "gave us Americans the first Suspicion that our exalted Ideas of the Prowess of British Regulars had not been well founded."[313]

The Braddock debacle had two other effects. First, ministers and journalists began sounding a theme of self-reliance. Pennsylvanian Thomas Barton, in 1755, proclaimed in a sermon, "Dark and dismal is the Cloud that hangs over us! The Troops sent for our Protection sadly defeated, and . . . we who inhabit the Frontiers left an unarmed Prey to a Savage Multitude." Barton spoke of the possibility of being forced, first, "to exchange our holy Protestant Religion for Popish Error and Delusion," and, second, to see "the Fat of the Earth go to feed the Drones of it." Religious and economic freedom seemed most dear when they were in jeopardy, and Barton concluded that God was most likely to protect those who protected themselves.[314]

Second, the need for divine help received renewed emphasis. "Is our Country under no Influence or Power, but what is visible?" Samuel Davies asked. "Are all our Affairs under the Management of Chance or Fortune? . . . Are we to trace the Origin of the Defeat of our Army, no farther than the Power or Stratagems of the French or Indians? If this be the Case, what a miserable World is this? what a State of Anarchy and Confusion?" But Davies noted that this is not the case: "The treacherous French and Savage Indians have routed our Army; but it was all ordered by the Providence of God, and all the Causes and Occasions of it were disposed by him."

Why, then, the defeat? In part, Braddock's pride and subsequent fall was a reminder: "You who can eat, and forget God: you who enjoy the Blessing of the Sun and Rain, and the Fruits of the Earth; and yet go on thoughtless of your divine Benefactor, as the Cattle of your Stall, or who look upon these as Things of Course, or the Fruits of your own Industry . . . you are practical Atheists." God required action, not merely assent: "Whatever you profess in Words, you do in Heart and Life renounce and abjure Jehovah from being the Governor of the World." Davies said the colonies were "over-run with this Kind of Atheism"—and that it had to be fought.[315]

Davies' sermons showed an understanding of the two-level enemy. Davies hated the corruption evident in England and saw that both England and Virginia deserved punishment, but he still pointed to the Catholics of France and Canada as an enemy worse than the squalid squirarchy.[316] He asked Virginians to fight under the British flag while still noting that Britain was a nation heading downward unless a new reformation took root there. And he pointed to Virginian leaders emerging from fields littered with bones; the outstanding example was "that heroic youth, Col. Washington, whom I cannot but hope Providence has hitherto preserved in so signal a manner, for some important service to his country."[317]

The British, however, did not learn their lessons from Braddock's fall and the colonists' unwillingness to put their lives in London's hands. The next major British appointee after Braddock was John Campbell, fourth earl of Loudoun. Lord Loudon had distinguished himself in 1745, during British efforts to put down a rebellion in the Scottish highlands, by losing most of his regiment at one battle and by being bluffed into panic at another. Loudon came to

America in 1756 with seventeen servants, two women (one of them, Jean Masson, his mistress), a selection of fine vintages of wine, and an appointment declaring him "General and Commander in Chief of all and singular our Forces employed or to be employed in North America."[318]

He also came bearing gift horses of financial aid, and colonial legislatures were careful to look inside the mouths of the beasts. When Loudon told Massachusetts legislators that he would be in charge of provisioning troops, the council and House of Representatives debated the offer at length and accepted it only with the assurance that his supplying food would not give Loudoun direct control of the provincial soldiers. Loudoun was upset that his offer was treated so suspiciously; he soon was complaining in letters to London that America was a lawless country in which people respected no authority but their own.

Loudoun had similarly unnerving encounters with other legislatures, and with individuals who did not unthinkingly obey him. Loudoun, in 1756, demanded to be supplied with wagons and horses, did not want to negotiate much about price, and was angry when gridlock resulted: "We can come to no Resolution on this Point, for the evil lies in the Disposition of the People, who will have no Consideration for the Necessity of the Times." Seeing necessity, Loudoun sent his forces throughout the area around Albany to seize the wagons and horses, as well as any people who would not bow and scrape.[319]

Encounters with the actual enemy were even more unsatisfying. In June 1757, Loudoun took his main force to Louisbourg to try to do professionally to the French what the amateurish colonials had done in 1745. Two months later he gave up the effort. In the meantime, the general he had left in command at Albany, Daniel Webb, proved to be not only incompetent but cowardly; sitting at Fort Edward with at least sixteen hundred trained and fit men, he refused to reinforce Colonel George Monro at Fort William Henry only sixteen miles away, and told him to surrender to General Montcalm. Munro did, and the result was the massacre made famous in Fenimore Cooper's *The Last of the Mohicans*.[320]

Infidelity and Gratification of the Appetites

The failures of Braddock, Loudoun, and Webb were examples of what John Brown, three thousand miles away, was writing at the time in his *Principles and Manners of the Times*. Brown complained that Britain's generals and admirals were more "distinguished by their Taste in Dress, their Skill at Play, their Attendance on every Amusement, provided it be but fashionable," than their knowledge or competence.[321] British generals would be more perturbed about losing a wager at cards than surrendering an army after military defeat, Brown suggested: "The Roman killed himself, because he had been unfortunate in War; the Englishman, because he hath been unfortunate at Whist. . . . The first was encouraged by a *mistaken* principle of religion; the latter, by his being void of all Religion. . . ."[322]

Brown suggested that Britain's moral problem in the military, as in the country at large, was more among leaders than among those in the ranks. "Land-Officers in the Capital, are occupied in Dress, Cards, and Tea; and in Country Towns divide their Time between Milleners Shops and Taverns."[323] In the navy the danger also

> ariseth from the Commanders: [young officers are] brave, hardy, and intrepid. But no sooner do they rise to the Rank of Captains, but the Example of the Times infects them: False Elegance and effeminate Parade take Place: French Cooks and Valets are sought after: The Commander of the Ship becomes a Sultan, who lives in idle State, and hath his Duty done by his Vizier, his First Lieutenant.[324]

As Brown's work was being circulated, news of the failure to take Louisbourg and the failure to hold Fort William Henry reached London almost simultaneously, and parliamentary leader William Pitt responded with what was said to be "the finest Oration that ever was made in an English Senate." Pitt attacked the military leadership's "Want of Application to Geography . . . their Insolence to their inferior Officers, and Tyranny over the common Men . . . [their] Extravagance, Idleness and Luxury." Pitt spoke of cowardice and covetousness: "Scarce a Man could be found with whom the Execution of any one Plan in which there was the least Appearance of Danger, could with Confidence be trusted . . . few seem to be affected with any other Zeal than that of aspiring to the highest

Posts, and grasping the largest Salaries." He confirmed, in short, the suspicions of London corruption that colonists committed to either small government or holy government had long entertained.[325]

Pitt spoke of the need to work with the colonists, and not lord it over them; when he became prime minister he won the cooperation of colonial assemblies by promising to reimburse military expenditures.[326] On the battlefield, however, ineptitude seemed inevitable as long as generals who had been promoted because of connections rather than commpetence remained in command. Loudoun's successor, Abercromby, passed up opportunities to attack Fort Ticonderoga in July 1758, before the French could call in reinforcements; then, when French reinforcements had arrived but before much of his artillery was in place at a commanding height, Mount Defiance, Abercromby ordered a frontal assault by bayonet.

The result was told by one soldier, David Perry: "Our orders were to 'run to the breastwork and get in if we could.' But their lines were full, and they killed our men so fast, that we could not gain it. We got behind trees, logs and stumps, and covered ourselves as we could from the enemy's fire. The ground was strewed with the dead and dying. . . . I could hear the men screaming, and see them dying all around me. I lay there some time. A man could not stand erect without being hit, any more than he could stand out in a shower, without having drops of rain fall upon him; for the balls came by handsfull." Again, Britain's professionals had betrayed America's volunteers: Overall, over 550 soldiers died, and fourteen hundred were wounded.[327]

As Americans suffered under Loudon's mismanagement, they also gained a sense of London's scorn for them. General James Wolfe wrote of the colonists, "There never was people collected together so unfit for the business they were set upon—dilatory, ignorant, irresolute." He wrote in another letter that "The Americans are in general the dirtiest, the most contemptible, cowardly dogs you can conceive. There is no depending on 'em in action. They fall down dead in their own dirt."[328] British General John Forbes similarly complained about "the horrible roguery and Rascality in the Country people" of Pennsylvania.[329] Opinions influenced action: A Maryland man wrote that the British treated the colonists "as slaves," and Benjamin Franklin wrote that British regulars "plundered and stripped the inhabitants, totally ruining some poor families, besides insulting, abusing, and confining the people if they remonstrated."[330]

Disputes over the quartering of British troops raged repeatedly. Lord Loudoun, in 1756, faced the problem of finding winter quarters for his regulars, at a time when barracks were few and the custom in England was to lodge soldiers in "Publick Houses . . . here, there are few Publick Houses, and the most of them . . . possess only one room." Loudoun's solution was to promulgate "a new Regulation" that required quartering of soldiers in private homes." Loudoun thought the solution not only sensible but fair, for homeowners would receive compensation. The homeowners, though, knew the reputation of British soldiers for lewdness and profanity; no amount of shillings would make them happy about exposing wives and daughters to the soldiers they had seen in inaction. When the British insisted—Loudoun, for example, placed thirteen hundred men in private homes in Albany in 1757—the British army came to be seen as oppressor, not protector.[331]

American leaders also disliked the bossing they received from British officers who despised them. British general Forbes called the American officers "an extreme bad collection of broken innkeepers, horse jockeys and Indian traders."[332] William Williams, a young Massachusetts officer, wrote that Americans were treated like "Orderly Serjeants. . . . We must do what we are biden and if not, Threatened."[333] Governor Hutchinson acknowledged that, concerning mistreatment of provincials by British officers, "There are a thousand stories all over the Country."[334]

Americans were not fatally wounded in self-esteem by the contempt of the British because they had contempt for the contemners. Americans were depressed by the harshness of British military life: Officers were exempt from corporal punishment, but enlisted men were sentenced to two thousand lashes on the bare back from a cat-o'-nine-tails for stealing supplies, one thousand lashes for stealing a pound of butter, and three hundred lashes for minor infractions of discipline. A physician was on hand to resuscitate the soldier when he fainted, but care was taken not to kill the culprit victim; the physician could order postponement of the punishment when too much blood flowed. Punishments like that could make soldiers fear their officers more than they feared the enemy, and thus keep them moving forward toward death when ordered to do so. The system worked in its way, but colonists who watched saw the British lords of culture as barbaric.[335]

The great difference between British and American enlisted men also was apparent. Provincial armies held two religious services in camp each Sunday and banned bawdy songs, profanity, and card-playing all through the week. The immorality that American visitors to London had noted and sometimes indulged in was now visible in close-at-hand military camps. Private Joseph Nichols walked through the British camp near Ticonderoga and "observ'd but little profanity among our Provantials: But among the Regulars much profaneness." Colonial newspapers played up stories of stealing, drunkenness, and murder among British regulars. Ezra Stiles, a future president of Yale, complained that "infidelity and gratification of the appetites" dominated British appetites; he worried that "American morals and religion" were endangered by contact "with the Europeans in the present war."[336]

So unpopular was the British army and navy among Americans that, even in a popular war, the imperial forces had to resort to a draft of the most vicious kind. Army recruiters adopted ruses to sign up future soldiers. According to British law, taking a coin from a recruiter was equivalent to signing a contract, so recruiters bought men drinks and gave those who got drunk coins to buy more: When they woke up the next day, they had a hangover that would last for years. Colonial leaders who wished to protect their young men taught them to just say no to offers of liquor. Sheriffs sometimes locked up on false charges of indebtedness men who were irresolute, just to keep them out of the way when recruiters roamed.[337]

The naval situation was even worse from the British military standpoint, until Lord Loudoun, in 1757, hit on an imaginative way of breaking this gridlock: He sent three battalions into New York in the middle of the night to conduct a house-to-house search for able-bodied men; by the dawn's early light eight hunded men were in captivity. English law had long established impressment as a royal prerogative, and other impressments had occurred in the 1740s, but not on so massive a scale. Soon, the royal navy was feared as much as the French, for "to be in the navy was in some sense to be a slave."[338]

Eventually, the British army under Pitt's supervision righted itself enough to defeat the French, whose naval inferiority intensified problems of supply and troop transport. (The French, during the 1760s and 1770s, embarked on a major ship-building effort.) Troops under General Jeffrey Amherst seized Louisbourg in 1758, and this time New Englanders pledged grimly that London would hold onto it, or else. The frontier became safer as French resources fell short and, one by one, forts were relinquished; many of France's Indian allies abandoned the losing side and sat out the remainder of the war.

Britain's final push involved warfare aimed at civilians. In the summer of 1759, Major General James Wolfe, like Union generals in 1864 and 1865, was desperate to end the war, so his forces destroyed the farms and villages near Quebec, and his cannon destroyed the civilian houses of the city to the point where the inhabitants wanted to surrender. They refused only because General Montcalm said he would turn loose the remaining Indians on any civilians who gave up.[339]

The climax came on September 13, 1759—a day of triumph in British children's history books, a "day of errors" in the eyes of military historians. General Wolfe, despondent over his inability to win Quebec, led a small force up a tall bluff. An officer fluent in French was able to bluff his way past sentries. Wolfe's men, established on "the Plains of Abraham" outside the city, needed reinforcements, but Wolfe ordered that no other troops be sent. (Psychohistorians conclude that Wolfe was suicidal.) His second in command, Adjutant General Isaac Barre, disregarded Wolfe's order and sent more soldiers. General Montcalm rushed out to face Wolfe but then did exactly what British general Abercromby had done at Ticonderoga. First, he delayed attacking, thus allowing time for British troops to not only take up a stronger defensive position but also for more to arrive. Then, rather than waiting for the imminent arrival of reinforcements from Montreal, he charged Wolfe's line. The British fired off an enormous volley at close range, and Wolfe, dressed in a bright new uniform, led a bayonet attack on the French. In a few minutes Wolfe and Montcalm were both fatally wounded and the battle was decided. Quebec surrendered.

Victory led to misery. Just as the occupation of Louisbourg by New England forces in 1745 resulted in far more casualties than the battle itself, so the posttriumph occupation of Quebec resulted in a thousand deaths from scurvy, compared to 240 who had died during the seige and assault. The British garrison was so weakened that the French came close to retaking the city, but a British fleet came to the rescue just in time.[340]

Geld All the Males

The taking and holding of Quebec proved to be the key to British victory, and the French soon gave up the fight in Canada, hoping to do well enough in the European theater of the Seven Years' War to force the British to sue for peace and give up their conquest. Colonists who had voluntarily joined British forces had done so to protect their homes. They often had been treated scornfully by British colonels such as James Robertson, who wanted the Americans merely to "work our Boats, drive our Waggons, and fell our Trees, and do the Works that in inhabited Countrys are performed by Peasants."[341] Since their duty in the British army was seen as slavery, colonists were quick to seek freedom; once Quebec was taken and the threat to the frontier substantially reduced, Americans saw no need to remain within servitude.

Makemie . . . Zenger . . . the Great Awakening . . . Louisbourg . . . the next large leap toward an American revolution may have begun with small steps by Luke Knowlton and others who became part of the troop mutinees of late 1759. Private Knowlton, a twenty-one-year-old from Shrewsbury, Massachusetts, had enlisted with others from his area to serve until November 1, 1759. They meant to fulfill their contract but were angered on October 28 when their regiment was read orders from General Amherst keeping them in service past the agreed upon date. Knowlton's journal reads as follows:

> November the 1st, 1759 . . . this morning there was a petition drawed up by the men and signed by near two hundred of our men, and sent to our colonel for a dismission. And he immediately sent it to the general [Amherst].
>
> November 2. This morning fair weather. We was drawed up by about six o'clock and our colonel read to us the letter which the general sent as a return to our petition; which is not to have us presume to go home before we have a regular discharge, though he confesses our time is expired. But the men went off from the parade in great haste, and in less than an hour there

> was two hundred of us on the parade with our packs swung in order to march . . . before we had got half a mile our officers came after us with orders to fire upon us if we would not return, but did not, though we refused to obey them and still kept on our march.[342]

They did keep on their march, sometimes evading British patrols, and reached home after about two weeks. The mutineers were not deserters who tried to slip away, but resisters who met publicly as at a town meeting, arrived at a consensus, gave notice, and then openly walked away. The mutineers did not try to kill their commanders: the troops simply decided to leave and then left, as a group. This contractural emphasis and consensual decision-making struck regular British officers as both curious and cowardly.

Along with military mutinees, legislative insurrections spread during the last act of war. The Seven Years' War was the first American war for independence, because legislatures used their leverage over governors and other royal officials to lessen crown authority. Colonial assemblies during that period frequently gained rights to oversee expenditures, and colonial councils gained veto power on judicial appointments.[343] Legislators cut into the administrative authority of London appointees by granting money only when they also could detail the specific purposes for which the money would be used. London generally gave in to wartime demands by colonial legislators for more authority, so as not to hinder the war effort. For example, governors for decades had been instructed to hold out for fixed salaries, but during the war, the Board of Trade instructed the governor of New York to forgo the demand for a fixed salary if he thought that by doing so things would go more smoothly.

England, during treaty negotiations with France, avoided an immediate uproar in America by holding firm in its demands for Canada and relinquishing a cash cow, the sugar island of Guadeloupe.[344] The treaty provisions, finalized and announced in 1763, dismayed British mercantilists who pointed out that even if the colonies stayed under British control, colonists who went across the Appalachians would be too far removed from British merchants to be useful consumers of British goods. But Britain accepted its northern prize in part because, with the Louisbourg return of 1748 not forgotten in New England minds, a second giveaway would have inspired red-hot colonial resentment. British leaders were aware that newspapers such as the *Boston Gazette* and leaders such as Israel Williams of Massachusetts were breathing fire with the prediction that the British would give Canada back "with a political view to keep us Dependent."[345]

A competing view also was at hand: Yes, the French presence in Canada had forced the British colonists into military dependence on London, but it also had made London politically dependent on the colonists. Hard-line plans to harass those power-seeking colonial legislatures often had to be put on hold lest they prompt a nightmare of colonial resistance and consequent French advantage. Evicting the French untied American hands but it also freed those of Britain. During the Stamp Act crisis of 1765, for example, Americans observed that if the French were still in Canada, "the British parlem't would as soon be D[amne]d as to offer to do what they do now."[346]

In this sense British policy immediately after the war was not a departure from past pursuits, but a passage into action of that which for years had been theoretically desirable but practically impossible. Even before the war, some officials had concluded that an army needed to be kept in the colony, with taxes raised from colonists paying for their own shackles. The French and Indian War experience made it clear that colonists were growing insubordinate, but they could not be knocked down while war continued because their bodies and their material were needed. But, as a British customs official proclaimed in 1760, the end of fighting made it "very speedily" possible for England to work on "securing the dependency" of the American colonies.[347]

Comptroller Weare's frank analysis contained several logical steps. First, he wrote, more Europeans will be coming to America, and will be thrilled to see "all mortifying distinctions of rank lost in common equality," with "ways to wealth and perferment [sic] alike open to all men." Disaster will come if new settlers join with old in rebelling against the British system of distinction among classes, Weare predicted. He proposed that the colonies be kept dependent for their own good, or else they would be drowned in "licentiousness."[348] To prevent that, the open American system had to be transformed to a closed system like that of England. Since the colonists were unlikely to put on chains of their own volition, a standing army was necessary to hold them down and teach them what they needed to learn, for their own good.

What if the colonists did not like their chains? That was not a problem, some British officers said upon their return from America. Seeing the unwillingness of colonists to fight in a cause not wholly their own, London officialdom assumed incorrectly that they would fight poorly in any cause. One British officer, irritated by American claims, boasted that he could take a thousand top soldiers across the Atlantic "and geld all the males, partly by force and partly by a little coaxing."[349]

The opportunity to think about independence was made possible by the elimination of a multidecade threat of French aggression. That colonists were thinking privately in such terms even before public agitation began is evident in the business dealings of a young American who fought well during the war and even won praise from British officers, but was ready to give up participation in imperial glory. Biographer James Flexner has pointed out that as a young man "Washington had admired English leadership and dreamed of visiting England. However, that admiration and that dream had been eroded by his tribulations during the French and Indian War with royal governors and officers of the British regular army. . . ."[350]

Washington's education would continue during peacetime as London factors "supplied him with inferior goods in exchange for tobacco they undervalued." But Washington had the discernment and the will to find an alternative: "Well before the Revolution, Washington had reorganized his patterns of planting and distribution so that he no longer had to sell and—by extension—buy in England."[351] More Americans began doing the same, with the goal of liberating themselves and, eventually, a nation. What began with religious fervor as a war to end frontier wars—contain Indian warriors by eliminating their French suppliers—ended with the colonists' beginning to realize that they might have to confront another evil empire.

Discerning British leaders would have used the acquisition of Canada as an opportunity to begin the amicable restructuring of relations with the thirteen colonies. But, given London's arrogance, successful prosecution of the war—whch involved the borrowing of money and consequent postwar indebtedness—made improved relations less likely rather than more. Massachusetts, for example, spent so much early in the war that it almost defaulted on its debt in 1758; the colony's financial structure survived when reimbursements from London arrived, yet those reimbursements took care of only 40 percent of the Massachusetts military costs. The colony had to borrow so much money that provincial taxes stayed at their wartime heights for a decade, and colonists clearly were reluctant to add anything more to that tax burden. London officials were reluctant to raise taxes on the residents of England, however, so they saw no choice but to pressure America for more.[352]

As Mischievous as a Monkey, as Lecherous as a Goat

Why did British officials show so little flexibility? The willingness to pay higher taxes is related not only to the absolute level of taxation but the degree of confidence among taxpayers that their funds will be used rightly. British subjects became more reluctant to pay higher taxes as they lost confidence in the ability of a corrupt government to spend funds wisely. A loss in the Seven Years' War might have been good for England; had that happened, the court in London might have been forced to examine itself critically. But when victory came, the British government, instead of reforming, became even worse. The increased influence of the Earl of Sandwich and John Wilkes, two of Sir Francis Dashwood's Medmenham "monks," shows the problem.

John Montagu, the Earl of Sandwich, was a leader among both those who stressed empire and those who emphasized sexual pleasure. Born in 1718, he followed the usual rakish routes through college. In 1738-39 he sailed to Turkey and into the arms of Turkish prostitutes. Upon his return he had his portrait painted in a turban and, at age twenty-two, married Dorothy Fane, who became the Countess of Sandwich.[353] In subsequent years, Sandwich slept with the Duchess of Bedford, who was the wife of his best friend, as well as noted courtesans Fanny Murray, Kitty Fisher, and many more.[354] On Sandwich's holidays from rutting he was a marathon gambler; once, not wishing to leave the gaming table, he called for two slices of bread and a hunk of meat to stick between them, and thus bequeathed his lower-cased name to the English language.[355]

The fast pace exhausted others. Sandwich's wife slowly went mad, and in 1755 the couple parted formally; the Countess was declared legally insane in 1767 and was made a ward of the court, but she lived on until 1797.[356] During the Seven Years' War, Sandwich dodged duels while carrying on a "uniform, unblushing course of debauchery and dissipation" and further building his reputation as "a tempestuous, rampaging roisterer [who was] as mischievous as a monkey and as lecherous as a Goat."[357] Such were the morals of British high society and government, however, that Sandwich's reputation—"no man ever carried the art of seduction to so enormous a height"—did not keep him from becoming secretary of state for the northern department in 1763.[358] In the cabinet, Sandwich joined Lord Halifax, who had made a mistress his official hostess, and the Duke of Grafton, who neglected his duties while cruelly treating his wife and carrying on very public activities with prostitute Nancy Parsons.[359]

Colonists who had been aghast at perversity among British troops stationed in America could learn about dissipation in London by reading John Wilkes' publications. A skilled cut-and-slash journalist who had rejected the Calvinism of his forebears, Wilkes, by 1760, had married and separated from an heiress and gambled and spent his way through a large fortune.[360] Since Wilkes was a devotee of promiscuity and an up-and-coming political leader, Sandwich and the other so-called monks had added him to their club for the best and the brightest; "I feast my mind with the joys of Medmenham," he wrote to Francis Dashwood.[361]

A practical joke Wilkes played at the abbey in 1759 or 1760, however, had far-reaching consequences. Dashwood and Sandwich apparently kept a baboon as the Friars' mascot, and there is an unsubstantiated tale of Dashwood's putting on a mock Mass and giving the baboon the sacrament.[362] Fuller reports indicated that before a revel of some kind Wilkes unchained the baboon, dressed it in a black robe with horns on its head, and shut it in a box with a string attached to the lid, so that he could open it at the most opportune time. When Sandwich invoked Lucifer—seriously if the tales are believed, "jokingly" if the idea was to just have "fun"—the time was right: Wilkes lifted the lid and the baboon leaped on to Sandwich, who fell to the ground shrieking "The Devil! The Devil!" and pleading for mercy.[363]

Sandwich received almost endless kidding over the incident from his fellow libertines, and tensions between him and Wilkes grew. Whether the personal changed the political or the political the personal is not clear, but Wilkes' increasingly radical politics during the last years of the Seven Years' War changed the nature of a club that had largely been politically homogeneous; the monks learned that it was hard to attack each other by day and drink together all night. Wilkes stopped attending the group's functions and put out a newspaper, the *North Briton*, that became known for its vigorous criticism of King George III and his government. Wilkes also revealed some of the obscene secrets of Medmenham in his pamphlet *The New Foundling Hospital for Wits*, and was behind the publication of prints in which, for example, Sandwich and Dashwood were shown examining a naked women stretched before them on a kitchen table; Sandwich is saying, "My Lord, is not that a Good Motion?"[364+>]

Sandwich's task as secretary of state was to defend king and administration, but he and the other ministers soon found that attempts to suppress Wilkes' publication were so politically unpopular as to endanger their control.[365] Sandwich, still embittered, searched for another route of attack, and found it in Wilkes' publication—probably for very limited circulation to his fellow Medmenham monks—of a bawdy parody of Alexander Pope's *An Essay on Man*.[366] The poem, entitled *An Essay on Woman*, was accompanied by blasphemous "commentaries" Wilkes had penned, and it was those that particularly injured his reputation: British upper-class morality was shot, but it was still not considered proper to equate the Virgin Mary with a prostitute.

Since the publication crudely attacked Anglican bishop William Warburton, Sandwich, late in 1763, used that opening to bring charges against Wilkes for libeling a member of the House of Lords.[367] Sandwich, in Parliament, with tones of righteous indignation, denounced Wilkes for writing pornographic work, and even Dashwood was amazed at the hypocrisy: "I never thought to live and hear Sandwich express such sentiments. . . . Never before have I heard the Devil himself preaching."[368] The House of Lords called Wilkes' work "a gross profanation of many parts of the Holy Scriptures; and a most wicked and blasphemous attempt to ridicule and vilify the person of our blessed Saviour."[369] The House of

Commons expelled Wilkes, who avoided jail time for criminal libel by escaping to France.

Sandwich thus won the debate, but at a cost: less confidence in government, and very little room for the government to maneuver. British leaders who would be faced with American demands could not readily acquiesce, or residents of the British Isles would demand the same solicitude. Similarly, leaders committed to the maintenance of current spending levels and payment of government debt needed tax revenues to pay the bills, and they could not raise taxes in England proper or else domestic problems would intensify.

By 1770, key British leaders were the subject of scornful jests. *The Candidate*, a popular London play by Charles Churchill, depicted a thinly veiled Sandwich as one who "Wrought sin with greediness, and sought for shame/With greater zeal than good men seek for fame."[370] It was hard to ask taxpayers to sacrifice when a jingle circulating among them, following the defeat and exile of Wilkes, went like this: "The King was in his counting house, adding up his wealth;/The Queen was in her boudoir, amusing of herself;/Poor Wilkes he was in Paris, solaced by [the prostitute] Corradini, /While Despencer [Sir Francis Dashwood] down at Mednam languished *in limine*."[371]

The only way out for the British government, if it wished to have its way in America, was to exploit divisions among the colonists, particularly theological ones. Here, Benjamin Franklin was key: The one constant in his career was vituperative attack (different in tone from his quick-witted satires or the mellow tone in his autobiography) on Reformed theology.[372] In the 1760s, Franklin was openly attacking "the Presbyterian Clergy of Philadelphia" and the "mobs" further west that were allied to them and formed "the whole Posse of that Sect." Furthermore, he was so attracted to the pleasures of English life that during the 1750s he had moved to London, leaving his wife behind. He returned briefly to Pennsylvania and fought an unsuccessful anti-Presbyterian political campaign in 1764, but then recrossed the Atlantic and seemed ready to fulfill what he had written to a friend: "Behold me a Londoner for the rest of my Days."[373]

Franklin did become virtually a permanent resident of England, spending the next decade there, with his wife in Philadelphia. Franklin, at both London and Medmenham, became for English leaders the voice of America. In that capacity he may have encouraged British officials in some of their tax-raising efforts by indicating his desire to have the "steady protection" and "security" of a British standing army in the colonies, and making it known to British leaders in 1763 that "I am not much alarm'd about your Schemes of raising Money on us. You will take care for your own sakes not to lay greater Burthens on us that we can bear." He even suggested that a tea tax might be a good way to raise revenue.[374]

Some of his contemporaries speculated that Franklin fawned over London officials in order to protect his own absentee position of deputy postmaster general in North America, which brought him influence and £300 a year. He probably had larger game in his sights, but for someone who preached so frequently a message of "united we stand, divided we fall," Franklin was surprisingly willing up to the brink of revolution to divide himself from most of his countrymen to get in good with the London powers. He even pushed for establishment of the Anglican church throughout America, as a way of diminishing the political power of the dissenters he despised.

The upshot was that just as some Americans were mounting a political offensive against England, Franklin was boasting to British friends that he had consistently "advanced the measures of the Crown, ever since I had any influence in the province." From 1764 through 1769 he even lobbied in London for an increase in royal power over Pennsylvania, with the goal, Franklin wrote, of keeping "Pennsylvania [from] falling totally under the domination of Presbyterians."[375] John Adams wrote that Franklin's "practical cunning united with his theoretick ignorance render him one of the most curious Characters in History."[376] Others gave him the nickname "Old Treachery" and called him "peevish, envious and a slanderer; injuring those with whom he lived, while professing benevolence to all the world."[377] But Franklin in the 1760s was the most famous living American, and as long as the British could count on his support, they rested content in the belief that a serious move toward colonial independence was unlikely.

CHAPTER FIVE

Coalition Building

The disappointments of the midcentury's war to end wars dovetailed with its one major British achievement—the conquest of Canada—to create a new American mood. As colonists thought about the British arrogance and brutality they had witnessed, they realized that England was divided by caste, disjointed by deism, and aggressive. "These Englishmen are going to play the devil with us," Jonathan Sewall told his friend John Adams in 1760. "They will overturn everything. We must resist them and that by force."[378]

But how? Adams knew even then that achievement of independence would require a united effort. The problem, though, was that potential American leaders, divided not only geographically but spiritually, frequently attacked each other more ardently than they criticized the lords of London. In Pennsylvania, for example, as the number of German pietist and Scotch-Irish Presbyterian settlers increased, Quakers and Anglicans feared a takeover: the "torrent of Presbyterianism . . . if not timely prevented will, with more than vandalic Barbarity, bury us."[379] Feelings were so intense that one anti-Calvinist wrote, "Had I any number of children, I would sooner bring them up to the implicit belief of the Alcoran [the Koran], than to make them Pennsylvania Presbyterians."[380]

Other antagonisms also festered. Some factions within colonies had their own agents in London; like business lobbyists today, they often spent most of their effort trying to reverse a rival's success. (Virginia and North Carolina, for example, wanted different tobacco standards; New Hampshire and New York each wanted royal backing to take over what would become known as Vermont.) Even among Christians there were, in Gilbert Tennent's words, such "numerous and scandalous Divisions" that the church was a "Torment to herself, a Grief to her Friends, and the Scorn of her Enemies."[381]

The British kept track of the disputes and were advised by appointees such as Thomas Pownall that they need not fear the prospect of colonial unity; the Americans would remain divided because of "the religious interests by which they are actuated, the rivalship and jealousies which arise from hence, and the impracticability, if not impossibility, of reconciling and accommodating these incomparable ideas and claims. . . ."[382]

The British kept their eyes on the many matters that kept Americans separated, but did not see how concerns about taxes and cultural takeovers could lead to a bridging of the gap between colonists principally concerned with financial wholeness and those whose chief end was holiness.

Tax questions gained the most attention during much of the 1760s. During the first half of the century, Prime Minister Walpole, when he resisted bureaucratic demands to raise taxes on the colonists, said that he would leave that matter to future ministers who might be "less friends of commerce than I am."[383] That day came in the 1760s when English leaders, enjoying their victory over the French, became determined to pay off the debt accumulated in that war, and believed they could do so without much opposition if they played up the theme of common sacrifice.

The bureaucratically brilliant scheme that evolved had two parts. First, since English taxpayers were already burdened, the goal was to force the Americans themselves to supply the funds that would support tax agents and soldiers who would then be in place to command payment of more taxes. Second, since dissenting churches as well as Anglican churches that were essentially under local control were likely to become sources of political as well as theological discontent, London had to impose ecclesiastical as well as political control: as Anglican prelate William Smith declared, "the statesman has always found it necessary for the purposes of government, to raise some one denomination of religion above the rest [and make it] the creature of the government, which is thus enabled to . . . keep all in subjection."[384]

The plan made sense in London, but officials there were showing little understanding of colonists' experiences and ideas. Prime Minister George Grenville, in 1763, sent a British fleet to America to enable rigid enforcement of previously unused restrictions on colonial trade, and, in 1764, presented resolutions to the House of Commons for revenue-producing duties on many colonial imports and exports. Even though the taxation of colonies for revenue was outside existing practice and bound to raise opposition, the bill passed with little discussion.

Americans were not amused by British speeches about common sacrifices and requests for contributions to pay off French and Indian War debt. The colonists, with their understanding of London's profligacy, suspected that any money given would be money wasted. A subsequent argument—that the money was for protection of the colonists against Indian attacks—was seen as specious when it became known that the British regiments left in America were inexperienced in forests and untrained for Indian fighting. Tax collections for more Braddocks and more soldiers taught only to volley were seen as subsidies of future folly.

Taxation to defray costs of a standing British army in the colonies particularly grated because the continued deployment of the army represented a broken promise. Many colonial soldiers had fought to help England gain a complete victory over France in Canada, some to free Canada from Catholicism and others to increase security and save taxes. Benjamin Franklin gave the economic argument: "If we keep Possession of Canada, the Nation will save two or three Millions a Year, now spent in defending the American Colonies . . . ."[385] But when the war was over and victory gained, British forces in North America were not reduced; instead, the number of officers and men was doubled, and costs rose accordingly.

At the same time the British wanted to tax more, they also imposed restrictions on growth by—in the Proclamation of 1763—attempting to keep Americans from settling beyond the Appalachians. Although British public rhetoric emphasized concern for Indians as the reason for the restriction, papers in the archives of the Board of Trade suggest that the real reason for discouraging settlement in the West was to preserve the colonial market for British exports. For example, the secretary to the head of the Board of Trade wrote that colonies are "to be regarded in no other Light, but as subservient to the Commerce of their Mother Country . . . merely Factors for the Purposes of Trade . . . [Colonists] must be kept as near as possible to the Ocean," because those who settled away from the Atlantic would begin manufacturing articles themselves, instead of importing goods from England.[386]

All of this was obnoxious but insufficient fuel for revolution. Colonies during the 1760s were burdened with their own wartime debt and had to maintain higher-than-usual levels of taxation throughout the decade.[387] And yet, the general tax burden the colonists faced in the 1760s was light compared to that faced by inhabitants of England proper.[388] The *London Chronicle*, in 1766 argued, "The taxes paid at present by Americans bear no proportion to the burdens of the English. In less than five years, most of their burdens will cease, as their debts will be discharged; there is no hope of relief here, as the total revenue pays only interest and ordinary expenses of government."[389] American taxpayers then were as reassured by such comparisons as taxpayers on April 15 are today when told that Sweden has higher rates: The pain of others does not eliminate our own. But, for the most part, the tax pain of the 1760s and 1770s was a slight ache, not torture.[390]

Had British officials not been so arrogant, compromises could have been reached, because many merchants tied to London's mercantilism were willing to cut a deal. Thomas Cushing, a Massachusetts merchant and legislator, argued with supply-side logic that a reduction of the foreign molasses tariff to a penny per gallon at most would be greeted favorably and would yield more revenue than was currently obtained through a higher rate.[391] When Parliament levied a duty of threepence per gallon, Americans sensed that they were scorned. When Parliament passed the Stamp Act, by which all colonial legal, commercial, and informational documents had to carry an official treasury stamp, Americans saw their freedoms, not just their wallets, under siege.[392]

It was exceptionally unwise of the British to alienate American editors: The Stamp Act hit newspapers hardest of all, assessing a tax that averaged perhaps 14 percent on newspapers and 40 percent on newspaper advertising. It soon became clear that this was a miscalculation. As a contemporary writer noted, independent newspaper editors "have generally arranged themselves on the side of liberty, nor are they less remarkable for attention to the profits of their profession. A stamp duty, which openly invaded the first, and threatened a great dimunition of the last, provoked their united zealous opposition."[393]

The British were foolish and the colonists mulish, but London, under pressure, did withdraw the Stamp Act, and left the bark of other regulations passed in the 1760s worse than their bite. Occasional incidents of arrogant error made for astonishing stories, but they did not lead people to take up arms, without further cause.

Pomp, Grandeur, Luxury, and Regalia

The level of taxation was not the only colonial concern, however. When the British, in 1759, finally overcame their military debacles, Awakened colonists hoped that London leaders chastened by war would adopt a different moral stance and attempt to live by it. Those hopes were crushed when British leaders in the 1760s not only tried to establish economic control but also embarked on a parallel cultural offensive: They encouraged attempts by the Anglican hierarchy to establish within the colonies a latitudinarian state church, with a theology accepting God as creator of the world but gone on vacation. For those who had been revived by the Great Awakening, such a doctrine was anathema; Joseph Bellamy in Connecticut, Joseph Hawley (a cousin of Jonathan Edwards) in western Massachusetts, and others influenced by the Awakening saw the culture war as more important than the taxation battle.

The pace of cultural imperialism increased during the 1760s. For example, British authorities, in 1761, announced that any schoolteacher emigrating from England to teach in New Hampshire had to be an Anglican, certified by the Bishop of London.[394] Throughout the 1760s, London-based Anglicans attempted to gain control over key cultural institutions, including the College of New Jersey—now Princeton—and the Redwood Library in Newport. (Anglicans accused Princeton of insinuating republican principles among its students.) Massachusetts ministers were furious when they incorporated a missionary society to help in the conversion of Indians to Christianity, only to see London officials disallow the organization because it was not under Anglican control. Minister Andrew Eliot wrote, "It is strange that Gentlemen who profess Christianity will not send the Gospel to the Heathen themselves nor permit it to be sent by others."[395]

Anglican leaders argued that the new forms of governance emerging in the colony were incompatible with their own church order. As a New Jersey Anglican, Thomas Bradbury Chandler wrote in 1767, "Episcopacy and Monarchy are, in their Frame and Constitution, best suited to each other. Episcopacy can never thrive in a Republican Government."[396] Presbyterian William Livingston of New York replied that he was not "prejudiced against any episcopalian for this religion," but was concerned about "the politics of the church . . . its thirst of domination."[397] Pennyslvania Presbyterian Francis Alison declared that the Anglicans should be free to worship as they saw fit, but "what we dread is their political power, and their courts."[398]

Critics of a transcolony Anglican establishment also displayed their social concerns: New England ministers attacked "imperious bishops who love to Lord it over God's heritage," and spoke often of the "pomp, grandeur, luxury and regalia" of Anglican worship and lives. Virginia citizens saw Anglican clergymen who favored establishment of a bishop in America as self-interested money-grabers who loved God less than they did a "pair of lawn sleeves."[399] Southern Anglican laymen who over the decades had developed through their vestries a congregational form of church governance did not want to give up their accomplishments.[400]

The success of this attack on theological pomp was evident not only in Anglican-dominated areas but also in colonies such as Connecticut, where the general assembly appointed Joseph Bellamy to preach an election-day sermon. Bellamy responded by emphasizing the colony's departure from holy living: "pride, luxuriousness, contentiousness, malice, envy, idleness, dishonesty" typified Connecticut life. He argued that "rulers" of the province needed to be not only hearers of God's Word but doers: It was easy to issue a proclamation favoring virtue, but it was more difficult "to act up to the true purpose and spirit of it."[401] The ferocity of concern about corrupt denominational establishment has been largely ignored by twentieth-century historians used to seeing the economy as the central campaign issue, with religious matters relegated to the closet of private concerns.[402] Yet, the centrality of theological concerns to the development of a revolutionary coalition was evident to John Adams and other contemporaries: Adams said that the attempt to impose London's official religion, "as much as any other cause, arouse[d] the attention, not only of the inquiring mind, but of the common people, and urge[d] them to close thinking on the constitutional authority of Parliament over the colonies. . . . This was a fact as certain as any in the history of North America."[403]

Press accounts of the time certainly support Adams' contention. For over a year, during 1768 and 1769, the *New York Gazette* ran articles attacking "ecclesiastical bondage" and calling the anticipated Anglican dominance worse than Britain-imposed taxes because those "affect not the right of conscience."[404] The *Pennsylvania Journal* in 1768 ran twenty-one straight articles on the plan for an American episcopate "totally subversive of our Rights and Liberties," under the pen name "Centinel."[405] Samuel Adams probably hit the hardest of all in three *Boston Gazette* articles that depicted Anglicanism as merely a variety of "Popery"; Adams noted that "revenue raised in America, for ought we can tell, may be constitutionally applied towards the support of prelacy. . . ."[406]

In many American eyes of the 1760s, London Anglicanism was not only imperialistic but abhorrent. The Londoners essentially were Deists who used god-words as covering for attempts to place man—in particular, some important men—above the principles God had handed down. The result of such concern was that in 1767, eight years before Lexington, theistic colonists came to believe that "the Bishops are coming," and they spread the alarm and looked around desperately for allies. They saw that those who emphasized tax issues were ready by the mid-1760s to challenge the British attempt to impose tyranny, but that their emphasis was on personal liberty, material gain, and small government. There needed to be points of contact.

Constructing a garment out of these threads was a task for master tailors. The leaders who were best able to perform the arduous task often were those influenced by both the Great Awakening and the war to end wars. The best coalition builders often were those who understood both camps because they themselves shared the love of God that animated one side and the dislike for bureaucrats and taxes that propelled the other. Patrick Henry was the great southern coalition builder; Samuel Adams was his counterpart in the north. They needed support from writers and politicians such as John Adams who did not necessarily share their faith, but who were able to discern the signs of the times.

YOU TURN ME TO THE PROPHET ISAIAH

Patrick Henry was the first great speaker to tie together the biblical and antitax reasons for opposition to England. Henry, born in 1736, grew up with biblical teaching: His father was a Hanover county vestryman, his mother a supporter of Samuel Davies. In his teens, Henry escorted his mother and sisters to hear Davies preach; he later called Davies the greatest orator he had ever heard. Virginian Edmund Randolph later observed that Henry's "figures of speech, when borrowed, were often borrowed from the Scriptures"; to Pennsylvanian Charles Thomson, Henry resembled "a Presbyterian clergyman, used to harranguing the people."[407] Antagonists of Henry, such as Virginia merchant James Parker, complained that Henry "is so infatuated that he goes about . . . praying and preaching amongst the common people."[408]

Henry came of political age in 1763, the year Britain and France ended their war and the year he argued his first major lawsuit. The case arose after several years of bad tobacco crops and consequently rising prices. Since taxes and compulsory tithes were assessed in pounds of tobacco but generally paid in cash, the bad harvest signalled more income for government and church officials. For example, a Virginian's assessment might be a thousand pounds of tobacco, which in good times was worth two pennies per pound but in poor crop years six cents.

It was irritating enough that Anglican prelates should profit from bad weather, but compulsory tithes were especially resented because many clergymen were viewed as incompetent or corrupt. Shortly after midcentury, for example, the Reverend John Brunskill of King William County was accused of "monstrous immoralities"; testimony uncovered "so many indencies" that modesty kept the governor from reporting details of the case.[409] To relieve farmers of great indebtedness in bad years and to restrict the income of fornicating parsons who were hardly likely to receive any voluntary offerings, the House of Burgesses during the 1750s passed two Two Penny Acts that fixed the price of tobacco for purposes of tithe collection at two cents, though the market price was three times higher. These laws applied largely to compulsory payments, not open-market dealings where tobacco could be bought and sold for whatever price market conditions produced.

The laws allowed tithe payers to pay up either in tobacco or at the fixed price, "as best suited"—which meant, whichever was cheaper. They hit bureaucrats and parsons hard; each Anglican parson, for example, was assigned a fixed sum of slightly over sixteen thousand pounds of tobacco per year, so when he received that tobacco and sold it at six cents per pound his stipend was a pleasant $960 (the equivalent of perhaps $33,000 today). When he was paid only two cents per pound, however, his mandated income dipped to $320, the rough equivalent of a poverty-level $11,000. Ministers beloved by their flocks, of course, could receive voluntary offerings—but the bad parsons suffered and fumed.

Leading Anglican clergymen of Virginia, unwilling to share the pain caused by the terrible drought of 1758 that lowered Virginia's tobacco production by almost ninety percent, fought back. The Reverend James Rowe declared that he would deny the sacraments to supporters of the Two Penny Act. (When critics vociferously pointed out that Rowe was placing mammon above the means of grace, he was compelled to apologize.)[410] Other ministers sent lobbyists to London asking the king to nullify the acts and to require Virginians to pay large retroactive salaries to the established prelates. Bishop Thomas Sherlock of London argued, in 1759, that the Virginia legislature had committed an act of "treason," with theological change pointing to political upheaval: "Within a few years past, Virginia was a very orderly and well regulated colony, and lived in submision to the power set over them. They were all members of the Church of England and no Dissenters among them . . . [now] they seem to have nothing more at Heart than to lessen the influence of the Crown and the maintenance of the Clergy. . . ."[411]

London officials disallowed the two Two Penny Acts and forbade such laws in the future unless the King should approve of them, but they did not mandate the retroactive payment of larger amounts; parsons who desired back tithes would have to bring suit to get them. That is where Patrick Henry came in. In Henry's county, as in others, judges found for the parsons, but it was up to a jury to decide on the amount of money that the complaining clergy would receive—and Henry provided a moral defense for those who did not want to subsidize corruption. He won astonished glances and grateful applause by straightforwardly speaking out against priests who were "rapacious harpies snatch[ing] from the hearth of their honest parishioner his last hoe-cake, from the widow and her orphan children their last milch cow. . . ."[412]

Henry also won the jury to his side. His genius lay in discussing the law not as an economic matter but as a moral concern: Although Anglican leaders wore the garb of humility and preached the beauty of charity, in practice they were greedy. The case itself was proof: The parsons were demanding damages from the people they were ordained by God (and licensed by law) to shepherd and protect. Henry's dramatic expressiveness pushed along his oratory, but even the words he used before the jury were revolutionary: Henry proclaimed that an oppressive king "from being the father of his people, degenerated into a tyrant, and forfeits all rights to his subjects' obedience."[413] The jury, which included both Anglicans and Presbyterians, agreed on a verdict for the local Anglican minister, as required—but established damages of one penny.

When news of the verdict spread through Virginia, Henry was acclaimed not only for winning a case but for uniting theological and tax concerns. Furthermore, as Henry's legal renown and income grew, he personally paid the fines that some Baptist ministers received, and thus helped to begin building a new coalition. Henry showed antibishop forces that they could bring antitaxers to their side by showing how a general tax to support an enlarged Anglican establishment would hit pocketbooks hard. Colonists began predicting that if Anglican bishops were appointed to America, they soon would demand the lavish incomes common among English bishops.[414]

Presbyterians and other Dissenters also argued that American bishops would gain the political power their counterparts had in England; this meant that the question of Anglican establishment was politically as well as spiritually important. Even the Virginia House of Burgesses went on record as opposing "the pernicious Project of a few mistaken Clergymen, for introducing an *American*

Bishop."[415] Those fighting the culture war, in short, were successful when they defined their issues in not only theological terms but in what we would call today a public-policy framework that emphasizes material as well as spiritual results.

Samuel Adams was the writer who did this best. The Great Awakening had made a permanent theological impression on him. That impression is evident in Adams' writings and actions, in his prayers each morning and in his family Bible-reading each evening. He frequently emphasized the importance of "Endeavors to Promote the spiritual kingdom of Jesus Christ," and in good or bad times wrote of the need "to submit to the Dispensations of Heaven, Whose Ways are ever gracious, ever just."[416] During the struggles of the 1760s and 1770s, Adams regularly set aside days of fasting and prayer to "seek the Lord." Once, when Adams wrote to a friend about the high points of a celebration, he stressed the sermon delivered that day. The friend wrote back, "An epicure would have said something about the clams, but you turn me to the prophet Isaiah."[417]

And yet, as Adams led patriotic agitation during the 1760s, he emphasized not Isaiah but his understanding that "the security of right and property, is the great end of government." He wrote of the dangers of dictatorship, whether popular or monarchical, noting that

> the Utopian schemes of levelling, and a community of goods, are as visionary and impracticable, as those which vest all property in the Crown, are arbitrary, despotic, and in our government unconstitutional. Now what property can the colonists be conceived to have, if their money may be granted away by others, without their consent?[418]

Adams always tried to develop positions that the Enlightened as well as the Awakened could embrace. That emphasis on coalition building has led some historians to minimize the importance of his biblical commitments, but Adams always emphasized the connection between attacks on political rights and attempts to restrict "those religious Rights, the enjoyment of which our good forefathers had more especially in their intention, when they explored and settled this new world." He repeatedly explained that "the religion and public liberty of a people are so intimately connected, their interests are interwoven, and cannot exist separately."[419] He saw acquiescence in political slavery as preparation for submission to religious slavery: "I coud not help fancying that the Stamp-Act itself was contrived with a design only to inure the people to the habit of contemplating themselves as the slaves of men; and the transition from thence to a subjection to Satan, is mighty easy."[420]

The battle over the Stamp Act displays how emphasis on common denominators pushed the patriotic movement not lower but higher. When Parliament passed the act in 1765, antitaxers were able to show the theologically concerned that both groups were fighting the same battle. The tax protesters skillfully emphasized one aspect of the Stamp Act that historians today often overlook: Since the act imposed taxes on documents in ecclesiastical courts, and since the act allowed London to require that all transactions be conducted on officially stamped paper to be sold only by government-selected distributors, Anglicans with influence could choke off dealings by dissenting churches by refusing to supply them with stamped paper, and could then jail dissenting ministers if they broke the law.[421]

The concern was this: If the Stamp Act were sustained, how long might it be before officials were required to hold Anglican views and before all had to pay tithes to support luxury-loving bishops? The Stamp Act throughout the colonies led the Awakened into involvement with tax questions, just as the Two Penny Act had done in Virginia. Understanding also flowed the other way: Those with a well-defined Christian worldview helped the broader public see that the Stamp Act was not merely a tax issue but an ideological onslaught. The scenario of Anglican dictatorship seemed farfetched to some, but John Adams argued that "there seems to be a direct and formal design on foot, to enslave America."[422] Even the *St. James's Chronicle* of London acknowledged that "stamping and episcopizing our colonies were understood to be only different branches of the same plan of power."[423]

John Adams, thirty years old in 1765, brought together the two strains of patriotic thought in four essays printed in the *Boston Gazette* during August 1765. Adams first showed historically that British attempts at twin tyranny were nothing new. Within the medieval church, it was understood that

> the temporal grandees would contribute everything in their power to maintain the ascendency of the priesthood, and that the spiritual grandees in their turn should employ their ascendency over the consciences of the people, in impressing on their minds a blind, implicit obedience to civil magistracy. Thus, as long as this confederacy lasted and the people were held in ignorance, liberty, and with her, knowledge and virtue too, seem to have deserted the earth, and one age of darkness succeeded another, till God in his benign providence raised up the champions who began the Reformation.[424]

The Protestant Reformation, Adams argued, was a triumph for liberty within the bounds of God's "benign providence," and brought with it greater literacy as people learned to read in order to read the Bible themselves so that they would not have to rely on those who twisted Scripture to consolidate "the powers of the monarch and the priest. . . ." Adams showed how the Stamp Act was not just a political act but a device to establish ecclesiastical tyranny as well, since literate citizens and inexpensive publications were essential to liberty. The Stamp Act would "strip us in a great measure of the means of knowledge, by loading the press, the colleges, and even an almanac and a newspaper, with restraints and duties. . . ."[425]

In this way Adams, who had one foot in the Awakened camp and one in the Enlightened, saw how antitax and evangelical complaints fit together: "If Parliament could tax us, they could establish the Church of England, with all its creeds, articles, tests, ceremonies, and tithes, and prohibit all other churches." Adams was astute enough to show that the line extended both ways: "If Parliament can erect dioceses and appoint bishops, they may introduce the whole hierarchy, establish tithes, forbid marriages and funerals, establish religions, forbid dissenters, make schism heresy, impose penalties extending to life and limb as well as to liberty and property."[426]

The following year Boston minister William Emerson further developed these ideas in a Thanksgiving sermon that emphasized "the near connection there is between our civil and religious privileges." Emerson contended that the Stamp Act failed because, when it was announced,

> every true lover of Zion began to tremble for the ark of God. For they saw, while our civil liberties were openly threatened, our religious shook; after taking away the liberty of taxing ourselves, and breaking in upon our charters, they feared the breaking in upon the act of toleration, the taking away of liberty to choose our own ministers, and then imposing whom they pleased upon us for spiritual guides, largely taxing us to support the pride and vanity of diocesan Bishops, and it may be by and by making us tributary to the See of Rome.[427]

By the time Emerson spoke, the short-term Stamp Act furor had died with Parliament's repeal of the act. Over the years, however, as alliance-building by Patrick Henry and Samuel Adams proceeded, discerning observers saw that Americans were melding concerns about taxes and religion. One Englishwoman, sister of a customs official, wrote that colonists "believe that the Commissrs. [of Customs] have an unlimited power to tax even their Lands, and that it's in order to raise a Revenue, for supporting a Number of Bishops that are coming over and they are inspired with an enthusiastic Rage for defending their Religion and liberties." The *London Evening Post* noted, "Divided as they are into a thousand forms of policy and religion, there is one point in which they all agree: They equally detest the pageantry of a K__g, and the supercilious hypocrisy of a Bishop."[428]

Sometimes the analysis became even more pointed: the British saw Presbyterians and other Calvinists as the troublemakers. Massachusetts governor Thomas Hutchinson complained that Calvinist pulpits were "filled with such dark covered expressions and the people are led to think they may lawfully resist the King's troops as any foreign enemy."[429] One British sympathizer complained about the coalition of "Presbyterians and Smugglers"; a Hessian captain during the Revolution would call it "an Irish-Scotch Presbyterian Rebellion."[430] Similarly, Pennsylvania officials observed that Presbyterians were "as averse to Kings, as they were in the Days of Cromwell, and some begin to cry out, No King but King Jesus."[431] North Carolina governor Alexander Martin agreed with such analyses, writing that political differences could best be understood as a reflection of the "distinctions and animosities . . .

between the people of the established Church and the Presbyterians."[432]

Crucially, the man who became the best-known Presbyterian patriot, John Witherspoon, did see the need to build a coalition of Presbyterians and smugglers. In 1768, as Benjamin Franklin continued to enjoy the luxuries of London, Witherspoon, a famous Scottish pastor and writer, journeyed west to become president of the College of New Jersey, which soon would be called Princeton. Witherspoon was Franklin's opposite in many ways: while Franklin planned (and described in his autobiography) thirteen-step ways for individuals to develop their own virtue, Witherspoon ridiculed Franklin-style systems. One of Witherspoon's books, *Ecclesiastical Characteristics*, contained thirteen parody maxims for "a Plain and Easy way to attaining the character of a Moderate Man: one way was "never speak of the Confession of Faith but with a sneer;" another emphasized toleration of the "good humored vices."[433]

But Witherspoon turned the College of New Jersey at Princeton into a coalition builder. Before Witherspoon arrived, the college had given honorary degrees only rarely, and then generally to ministers. In 1769, however, colonial leaders known for their politics, not their theological knowledge, were recipients; the list included John Dickinson and John Hancock, who was an antitaxer mostly known for having his ship, *Liberty*, seized by British customs officials in Boston Harbor. Witherspoon justified his coalition building by explaining that political liberty and evangelism were linked, since people needed the freedom to learn about Christ: "The knowledge of God and his truths has been chiefly confined to those parts of the earth where some degree of liberty and political justice were to be seen."[434]

The coalescing of theology and politics continued at the 1770 commencement, where James Witherspoon, the president's son, defended his thesis that subjects were obligated to resist tyrannical kings.[435] Some new graduates spoke out against Anglican cultural hegemony—one argued that "Every religious Profession which does not by its Principles disturb the public Peace, ought to be tolerated by a wise State"—and others provided justification for antitax agitation; the nonimportation agreement was called "a noble Exertion of Self-denial and public spirit."[436] Witherspoon was so effective as a teacher that a British officer later would label him that "political firebrand, who perhaps had not a less share in the Revolution than Washington himself. He poisons the minds of his young students and through them the Continent."[437]

Grand Corruptors and Debauchers of the People

London tacticians tried to dissuade Enlightened antitaxers from an alliance with the Awakened. They raised fears of Cromwell-style hegemony by Puritans and Presbyterians whom they labeled "deformed Pharisees" and "sanctified hypocrites."[438] New York members of the Society of Dissenters, made up of Presbyterians and others who dissented from Anglicanism, took pains to define their organization as Christian but not sectarian: "We are disaffected to no man of any Christian persuasion on account of his religious sentiments. Nor are we prejudiced against any episcopalian for his religion." The Society's enemy, rather, was a state-imposed Anglicanism, "its power and its thirst of domination, a thirst not to be satiated but by our absolute destruction."[439] Dissenter candidates for the New York assembly in 1769 backed statutes that would allow non-Anglican churches to own land and would exempt residents from taxes supporting ministers of churches to which they did not belong.

Colonies with non-Anglican establishments also had to reassess their positions. In Massachusetts, minister Samuel West argued that a citizen should be required to pay "the necessary charges of his own meeting," so as to eliminate "some of the most popular objections against being obliged by law to support publick worship, while the law restricts that support only to one denomination."[440] A Reformed pastor in Newburyport, Jonathan Parsons, argued that residents should have to pay compulsory charges for ministers, but only at their own churches, rather than on a mandated parish basis. Such "natural and constitutional privileges," Parsons argued, were "a legacy left us by Christ," and a wise way to help bring peace among diverse Christians: "equal liberty" for denominations will "naturally tend to beget affectionate union."[441]

John Witherspoon also helped to alleviate concerns about substituting one denominational tyranny for another: He argued for Calvinist doctrine and never embraced the pluralistic faith that all ideas are equal. At the same time, he also developed a position of theistic toleration. Witherspoon pointed out the public repercussions of private belief, arguing that people who did not fear God would do whatever they could get away with, until anarchy reigned and a fearsome government arose in reaction. Yet, he acknowledged that public order did not require the establishment of particular denominations.[442]

Tax protesters in the early 1770s also grew to emphasize common foes and the need to defend common principles of life and liberty. Although men like Richard Henry Lee and Thomas Jefferson were uncomfortable with talk of original sin, they cited the experience of ancient Greece and Rome, spoke of the corrupting nature of power and the tendency to abuse it, and ended up politically in the same place. Both sides analyzed contemporary London politics, wrote of endemic decadence, and tried to focus the attention of official London on not only taxes but also on the cultural crisis as well. Pastor William Gordon of Roxbury, Massachusetts, combined the two emphases in December 1774, when he argued that it was immoral to support through taxes "the luxurious entertainment of lazy, proud, worthless pensioners and placemen."[443] Samuel Adams did his best to allay suspicion that he planned a theocratic dictatorship by warmly welcoming into the coalition Episcopalians who broke from the church hierarchy. "I am no bigot," he explained in 1774: "I can hear a prayer from a man of piety and virtue, who is at the same time a friend of his country."[444]

Official London, however, did not pay attention to prayers. When an empire is in trouble, necessity often seems to be the mother of further weakness. At just the time when top officials were needed, America received a run of mediocrities: One royal governor was said to be "fitter for a bedlam, or other hospital, than to be set over a respectable province."[445] Yet, this is what would be expected, based on insights contained in a remarkable book published in London in 1774—James Burgh's *Political Disquisitions.* The book, according to its subtitle, was "calculated to draw the timely attention of Government and People to a due consideration of the Necessity, and the means, of reforming those errors, defects, and abuses [that Burgh would detail]; of restoring the Constitution, and saving the state."[446] But London was not listening.

Burgh argued that the social decay evident in the 1740s had continued to spread: "The debauching of a virtuous wife, the destruction of a family's peace for life . . . these are what we of this elegant eighteenth century call gallantry, taste. . . ."[447] In times of social decay the character of politicians was particularly vital, because their leadership was needed to fight the blight: "No statesman will look with an indifferent eye on the prevalency of lewdness in his country, if he has any regard for his country, and knows that this vice is not less mischievous by debasing the minds, than by enervating and poisoning the bodies of the subjects."[448] British politicians, however, "far from giving any attention to the general manners of the people, have themselves been the grand corruptors and debauchers of the people. . . ."[449] London was definitely not listening.

Burgh argued that "the men in power have pursued one uniform track of taxing and corrupting the people, and increased court-influence in parliament, while the pretended patriots have exclaimed against those measures, at least till themselves got into power, and had an opportunity of carrying on the same plan of government; which they seldom failed to do. . . ."[450] He proposed many of the same techniques of power reduction that the colonists had put into practice, including frequent elections to limit corruption. Burgh's prime plea was for rotation of offices: "Without exclusion by rotation, the mere shortening of parliaments even to annual would not redress this grievance."[451]

Burgh also dealt with arguments against limitation: "It is pretended by the court-party, that it is necessary to keep in the house some of the great offices of the state, and that a whole house of inexperienced members would be at a loss about the forms, &c." But Burgh noted, "If the majority of the house be not changed every other year, the same men may be reelected for twenty years together," and the result would be a legislative body in league with court rather than country. "There is no solution without exclusion by rotation. But with that regulation and the others, bribery might easily be rendered impracticable."[452] Burgh's writing so impressed John Adams that he strove "to make the Disquisitions more known and attended to in several parts of America."[453] Americans listened—George Washington, John Hancock, and Thomas Jefferson all purchased Burgh's book—but London was filled with denunciations of America's most famous tax protest, the Boston Tea Party. Samuel Adams had carefully instructed the "Indians" who boarded the British tea-carrying ships that nothing except tea was to be destroyed; when the patriots accidently broke a padlock, they later replaced it."[454] And yet, this act of nonviolent defense of basic liberties was viewed with horror by Parliamentary leaders who hastened to cast stones at the "sinners" overseas.

The Tea Party was defended in London by John Cartwright, later to be regarded as "the Father of Parliamentary Reform." Cartwright noted that the colonists had a choice: "either to suffer an insidious attempt against their sacred rights and liberties to take effect, or to destroy the hated instrument. Having had no other choice, they must necessarily have either done this, or suffered that."[455] Cartwright called the tea destroyers "a band of virtuous patriots," and their action "an act of absolute moral and political *necessity* . . . and remarkable temper and forbearance, considering their provocations, since it was done in *self-defence*, with the greatest good order and decency, and unaccompanied with incivility to any one, or the smallest damage to any thing in the ships besides the treacherous tea."[456]

London officials again did not listen. Adams' tea party provoked the harsh reaction from London known as the Intolerable Acts of 1774; one act closed the port of Boston and another effectively banned town meetings. Along with such coercion came the Quebec Act that made Roman Catholicism the state religion in what had been French Canada on the grounds that such an establishment was necessary to maintain order. The Quebec Act eliminated the right to trial by jury in civil cases and gave full legislative authority to a royally appointed council. (Even an already-existing assembly elected by the few Englishmen who resided there was abolished.) Parliament took to itself the levying of virtually all taxes, handed over administration to a military governor to be appointed by the Crown, and placed duties on all goods imported into Quebec, with the proceeds going to pay the salaries of the royal bureaucracy.

The Quebec Act provided the final cement for an alliance between the Awakened and the Enlightened. To make Roman Catholicism the official religion of a British-controlled province was a sellout of New England military efforts as grievous as the return of Louisbourg in 1748. New England Calvinists also argued that if the British would place "order" above religious principle in one territory, they could do the same in New England itself, and the Inquisition might not be far behind.

The Suffolk Resolutions that Masssachusetts placed before the Continental Congress on September 17, 1774, showed that there was no going back. "It is an indispensable duty which we owe to God, our Country, ourselves, and posterity, by all lawful ways and means in our power to maintain, defend and preserve those civil and religious rights and liberties, for which many of our fathers fought, bled and died, and to hand them down entire to future generations," Massachusetts declared. Christians there felt that they were being watched not only by God but by a great cloud of witnesses from the past. London officials had pushed the Awakened into a corner. The Suffolk Resolutions declared that the Quebec Act "is dangerous in an extreme degree to the Protestant religion and to the civil rights and liberties of all America: and, therefore, as men and Protestant Christians, we are indispensably obliged to take all proper measures for our security."[457]

The Enlightened were not theologically upset by the destruction of hopes for a Calvinist Quebec, but they were shocked by London's willingness to eliminate long-held liberties of all English subjects, such as trial by jury. Virginia's Richard Henry Lee called the Quebec Act "the worst grievance," and the Continental Congress of 1774 emphasized the Act in its petitions and declarations.[458] Across the Atlantic, libertarian Catherine Macaulay argued that the Quebec Act showed "that none of the fundamental principles of our boasted constitution are held sacred by the government. . . ."[459]

Macaulay went on to note that "the establishment of Popery, which is a very different thing from the toleration of it, is . . . incompatible with the fundamental principles of our constitution."[460] The Quebec Act, she insisted, embraced "despotism in every line . . . in respect both to their civil and religious rights, [the Canadians] are in a more abject state of slavery than when they were under the French government."[461] For Macaulay, the Quebec Act was the work of a bureaucracy gone mad, with foolish bills penned by those living on "pensions taken from the public treasure" and those who were "dazzled with the sunshine of a court." Macaulay pleaded with her countrymen to "rouse from that state of guilty dissipation in which you have too long remained. . . ."[462]

Peace, Peace, but There Is No Peace

By 1775, much of the American coalition was in place. Britain had only two opportunities to avoid war: by changing its policies, or by influencing members of the colonial elite not to trade the charms of London for minor roles in the hinterland of history. London leaders had trouble changing their policy of punishing America because the alternative was to discipline themselves. As Burgh had argued, before raising taxes "the Ministry ought to have reduced exorbitant salaries, abated or abolished excessive perquisites, annihilated useless places [jobs], stopped iniquitous pensions, withheld electioneering expenses and bribes for votes in the house. . . ."[463] But that the Ministry would not do.

The better alternative, from the viewpoint of London, was to corrupt American leaders. Doubts about the effectiveness of that traditional policy had begun to grow in 1768, however, when John Dickinson turned his back on London. Dickinson, when a law student in London from 1753 to 1757, had assured his parents in letters home that he was not falling prey to "the vicious pleasures" of London—but he had found them tantalizing.[464] Dickinson, observing the corruption and irreligion of British electioneering and life, had written to his father, "It is astonishing what impudence and villainy are practised"[465]—but impudence had its attractions for ambitious young men.

In 1768, however, Dickinson made his choice by writing a series of columns that became an influential book, *Letters From a Farmer in Pennsylvania.* "I am a Farmer," he began his contrast of life in America with the lascivious conduct of London. "I received a liberal education, and have been engaged in the busy scenes of life; but am now convinced, that a man may be as happy without bustle, as with it. My farm is small . . . I wish for no more . . . and with a contented grateful mind, undisturbed by worldly hopes or fears, relating to myself, I am completing the number of days alloted to me by divine goodness."[466] Of life in America, he concluded, "'tis rude, but it's innocent. . . . There we enjoy life, here we spend it."

As other Americans joined Dickinson in throwing aside the golden chains, more eyes turned to the best known of them all, Benjamin Franklin. The British were sure that the person they had pegged as a social climber would stay on their team: Franklin rarely missed an opportunity to hobnob with the English elite, and even cut short a trip to the European continent in 1761 so he would not miss the coronation of George III. In 1763, he wrote enthusiastically to a Philadelphia friend about the young king whose "sincere intention [was] to make his People happy"; George's reign would be "happy & truly glorious."[467] American newspaper articles and pamphlets in the 1760s accused Franklin of a readiness to throw overboard the religious liberties of Presbyterians and other Pennsylvania Christians in order to win King George III's favor and an appointment as the colony's Royal Governor.[468]

Franklin also was most comfortable personally in liberal England. For most of nearly two decades in England he had double-dipped as a London lobbyist and as deputy postmaster general for the colonies, even though he could not possibly do that job from three thousand miles away.[469] Franklin also had income from his print shop as well as free lunches and drinks at virtually any English town or country house he chose to visit, for he was known as both a scientist and as an exotic wit from the frontier. He developed friends among the English aristocracy; according to one account, his two best noble friends were William Petty, Lord Shelburne, whom Edmund Burke referred to as a "Catalina and a Borgia," and Sir Francis Dashwood.[470]

As Franklin was thinking through the problems of colony-London connections, he made various jaunts to Dashwood's Medmenham in 1773 and 1774. With his wife in Philadelphia, out of sight and apparently out of mind except for brief letters and presents, he did not even have to make excuses. But even with all those away-from-home comforts, Franklin was increasingly torn in his allegiances. He attacked the "Court Harpies" who would be the beneficiaries of additional taxes on America, and wrote that it would be far better to tax the "Luxury and Vice" that dominated English life.[471] In 1772, after years of criticizing the Massachusetts he had fled as a youth, Franklin praised "the Happiness of New England, where every Man is a Freeholder, has a Vote in public Affairs, lives in a tidy, warm House, has plenty of good Food and Fewel, with whole cloaths from Head to Foot. . . ."[472]

After years of calling for even tighter connections between Britain and America, Franklin, just before the Revolution, reversed himself: "When I consider the extream Coruption prevalent among all Orders of Men in this old rotten State . . . I cannot but apprehend more Mischief than Benefit from a closer Union."[473] Franklin criticized London's "numberless and needless Places, enormous Salaries, Pensions, Perquisities, Bribes," and concluded that Britain's governmental class would "devour all Revenue, and produce continual Necessity in the Midst of natural Plenty. I apprehend, therefore, that to unite us intimately will only be to corrupt and poison us also."[474]

Early in 1775, Franklin decided to leave London; British officials, fearing that his return would further fire a revolution, considered whether to detain him. Franklin, full of disinformation to the end, quietly ordered that his furniture be shipped to Philadelphia, but told one talkative friend that he would return to America, stay there briefly, and be back in London by the end of the year.[475] British officials let Franklin go, and he sailed for home in March, one month before the skirmish in Lexington.

Some skeptics thought Franklin's last-minute change of heart resulted from economic disappointment, and one recent historian has laid out that documentation.[476] Other colonial leaders feared that Franklin was a spy, but those doubts proved false. Most leaders recognized him as a prodigal son and recognized that late conversions, political as well as theological, testify to God's sovereignty. From London's viewpoint, Franklin's defection was a shock: When a man like Franklin who had been a big-government advocate could not be retained, it was all over for the English lords, unless their troops could pulverize the colonists on the battlefield. That seemed likely—but two speeches, given five and six days, respectively, after Franklin left for America, could have given the London lords pause, had they had ears to hear.

On March 22, Edmund Burke rose in the House of Commons to give the first of the great speeches. Burke, advocating British-American reconciliation, considered "force not as an odious but a feeble instrument for preserving a people so numerous, so active, so growing, so spirited as this, in a profitable and subordinate connection with us."[477] Instead, Burke emphasized "the absolute necessity of keeping up the concord of this empire by a unity of spirit, though in a diversity of operations. . . ." Colonists needed to be treated not as objects but as full participants in freedom: "The more they multiply, the more friends you will have. The more ardently they love liberty, the more perfect will be their obedience."[478]

Samuel Johnson once wrote of Edmund Burke, "You could not stand five minutes with that man beneath a shed while it rained, but you must be convinced you had been standing with the greatest man you had ever seen."[479] But Johnson took a very different position on the Americas than did Burke. In a pamphlet published in 1775, *Taxation No Tyranny*, Johnson attacked the colonists' view that imposition of new taxes was breaking the covenant: "Very well, the longer they have been spared, the better they can pay." Johnson sneered at "delirious dreams of Republican fanaticism," and called the colonists' arguments "abortions of folly . . . too foolish for buffoonery, too wild for madness."

Johnson did strike hard at the soft underbelly of colonial arguments for liberty: the continued existence of slavery. Why, Johnson asked, was he hearing "the loudest yelps for liberty among the drivers of negroes?" But Johnson vitiated his moral appeals by a heavy-handed faith in the importance of continued dominance by London: If colonists were showing "the fecundity of their own rattle-snakes, so that every quarter of a century doubles their numbers," British armed forces should "attack a nation thus prolific, while we may yet hope to prevail."[480] A stronger society would have found better ways to prevail, but England in 1775 could not.[481]

The second of the great speeches came one day after Burke's speech, and three thousand miles to the west. Patrick Henry rose in the Virginia House of Burgesses and topped off the prewar building of the Great Awakening-Enlightenment coalition by explaining that the "great and arduous struggle for liberty" could bring about "temporal salvation."[482] In Henry's words, the struggle for independence would be a "holy cause" under the care of "a just God who presides over the destinies of nations."[483]

Henry's oration in a packed church building was so powerfully appealing that one Virginian, Colonel Edward Carrington, who was listening at an open window, reportedly said, "Right here I wish to be buried"; his widow later fulfilled that request. Henry spoke within the tradition of the colonial jeremiad—a strong speech that emphasized the dire outcome of current trends, should the listeners not change their habits. Speaking before some who were ardent and others who still were lukewarm, Henry used biblical language to decry gentlemen who cried "'peace, peace'—but there is no peace." He noted that words had consequences: "they say, sword and famine shall not be in this land; by sword and famine shall those prophets be consumed." Since no revival came to Jerusalem, "the Chaldeans burned the king's house, and the houses of the people, with fire, and brake down the walls of Jerusalem."[484]

What Henry called for in his famous speech was a political equivalent to the Great Awakening. With Virginia facing a British Nebuchadnezzar to the north, Virginia would go the way of Judah unless its people were bold and courageous. But there was no need to drift any further: Within God's providence, "three millions of people armed in the holy cause of liberty" could separate themselves from Britain's cultural and economic oppression. "Why stand we here idle?" Henry asked. "Is life so dear, or peace so sweet, as to be purchased at the price of chains and slavery?" That was the final question to those who enjoyed the profits and pleasures of big government, and Henry's answer was clear: "Forbid it, Almighty God! I know not what course others may take; but as for me, give me liberty, or give me death!"[485]

Samuel Adams also used biblical language and references to put the finishing touches on the coalition he had helped construct. Just before the Revolution broke out, Adams wrote *The First Book of the American Chronicles of the Times*, a satirical pamphlet that used the language of the King James Bible (by the 1770s already considered antiquated) to equate Britain with Babylon. The pamphlet, published in 1775, began,

1. And behold! when the tidings came to the great city that is afar off, the city that is in the land of Britain, how the men of Boston, even the Bostonites, had arose a great multitude, and destroyed the TEA, the abominable merchandise of the east, and cast it into the midst of the sea 2. That the Lord the King waxed exceedingly wroth, insomuch that the form of his visage was changed, and His knees smote one against the other.[486]

In Adams' account, the king's advisors complained that the "Americanites" did not fear him, and that he should "therefore make a decree to block up their harbor."[487] The economic punishment almost worked, and the British "Babylonians" were ready to proclaim, "She that was great amongst the nations, and princess among the provinces, is about to be made tributary, and bow down to the TEA CHEST, the God of the Heathen."[488] But then New Yorkites, Virginites, Carolinites, and others united in a refusal to worship the "Tea Chest Idol." Realizing that they were east of Eden but west of Sodom, they became Americanites, "and the ears of all the people hearkened unto the book of the law." The Americanites "entered into a solemn league and covenant, that they would obey the book of the law, and none other."[489]

CHAPTER SIX

Vice, Virtue, and the Battlefield

British leaders were militarily confident in 1774 and early in 1775. In the House of Commons, Colonel James Grant said that he "knew the *Americans*" and was "certain they would not fight. They would never dare to face an *English* army. . . ."[490] Colonel Lord Percy wrote that the colonists were "made up of rashness & timidity. Quick & violent in their determinations, they are fearful in the execution of them . . . whenever we appear, they are frightened out of their wits."[491] The Earl of Sandwich in the House of Lords orated, "Supposing the Colonies do abound in men, what does that signify? They were undisciplined, cowardly men. I wish instead of forty or fifty thousand of these *brave* fellows, they would produce in the field at least two hundred thousands, the more the better, the easier would be the conquest. . . ."[492]

That was boasting; battle was different. From Bunker Hill on, the British found combat much tougher than their leaders expected; British soldiers needed skilled and united leaders. Since Lord North, the leading minister, believed in a collegial cabinet and hoped that departments would largely run themselves, and since the war department at that time in London had no strategic role but was designed to be an administrative aid to others, the vision and discipline of two key cabinet members was critical. John Montagu, the tough-talking Earl of Sandwich, was first lord of the admiralty during the prerevolutionary period and the Revolution itself: He was in charge of the war at sea. George Sackville, who by a curious twist of history went for a time by the name of Lord George Germain, was secretary of state for the American colonies from 1775 through 1782: He ran the land war.

Given the corruption of eighteenth-century British high society, it should be no surprise that these two key individuals were notorious for reasons other than their statecraft—but the extent of their decadence was unusual even for those times. Sandwich had been one of Francis Dashwood's "apostles," as noted in chapter 4, and was the leading practitioner of heterosexual promiscuity in the cabinet. Sackville had been court-martialed under accusations of cowardice during the Seven Years' War and was a known homosexual or bisexual. Both men's personal habits led them into erratic professional activities and created a reservoir of distrust among subordinates.

Whether Sandwich himself was responsible for decrepitude in the British navy during the Revolution is still a question for debate among British historians, but the inadequacies of the once-proud (and future-proud) navy during that particular period are not. At the beginning of the war, when Vice Admiral Samuel Graves was asked to blockade the major American ports, he did not have enough ships to do the job; at the end of the war, when a French fleet sailed to the Chesapeake Bay, Rear Admiral Thomas Graves (Samuel's cousin) had to attack with an inferior force. Part of the problem was the assignment of ships, but a large part of it was the nonexistence of ships that should have been there for assignment; the shortage of frigates and other smaller warships was particularly severe. And questions arose: Why did the naval building program falter? England's *Dictionary of National Biography* in 1882 proposed that Sandwich's conduct as first lord of the admiralty "was as great a scandal to public as it had all along been to private morality. Throughout his long administration he rendered the business of the admiralty subservient to the interests of his party. . . ."[493]

Sandwich also has had his defenders who said that he "might serve as a model for a man of business," since "he rose early, and till a late dinner, dedicated his whole time to business."[494] Sandwich was known for quick responses to correspondence most of the time, and for staying at his desk for long periods of time when he was already in his office and a crisis broke out. But he was also unreliable: He sometimes so frustrated his able administrative head, Controller Charles Middleton, that Middleton complained to him,

> If I, my lord, who am a professional man, find myself unequal to the duties of the office I am in, with an application of twelve hours six days in the week, how is it possible that your lordship can manage yours, which is equally extensive, in three or four? Indeed, my lord, it cannot be. The two offices are so nearly connected, that I must be wilfully blind not to see the sad management that prevails at present, and the ruin that accompanies it. . . .[495]

Middleton was a rarity within British officialdom—an evangelical Christian who became involved with the Clapham Sect's movement to reform English life and abolish the slave trade.[496] He was also a person described by one navy office clerk, Robert Gregson, as "the most indefatigable & able of any [official] in my time." So it is no wonder that Middleton was exasperated with what he saw in Sandwich's department, and communicated that frustration in his memo to Sandwich:

> One error has produced another, and the whole has become such a mass of confusion, that I see no prospect of reducing it to order. . . . I know the king's fleet to be equal to any service, if it is properly employed; but is it possible, my lord, that gentlemen who are at an office one day, and following their amusements or private concerns another, can carry on a line of business that requires not only great practical knowledge, but the closest application and attention?[497]

Others made similar observations. In May 1776, as the colonists were moving toward independence and the war was about to enter a new phase with the impending British takeover of New York City, the philosopher David Hume was surprised to encounter at an inn, Sandwich, three companions, and "two or three Ladies of Pleasure" who were all embarked on a three-week fishing and philandering trip. Hume recorded that "Lord Sandwich in particular had caught trouts near twenty Inches long, which gave him incredible Satisfaction." Hume for his part thought it incredible that "the First Lord of the Admiralty, who is absolute and uncontrouled Master in his Department, shou'd, at a time when the Fate of the British Empire is in dependance, and in dependance on him, find so much Leizure, Tranquillity, Presence of Mind and Magnanimity, as to have Amusement in trouting during three Weeks near sixty Miles from the scene of Business, and during the most critical season of the year."[498]

The other member of the cabinet whose competence was crucial for successful prosecution of the war was Secretary of State Lord George Sackville, the comeback kid of his century. Born in 1716 into an illustrious family, he became a member of Parliament in 1741 and a major general in 1755, the year Burgoyne's force was routed. Sackville, however, was posted to the European continent rather than to America, and by the end of 1758 was commander in chief of British forces in Germany, under the authority of German Prince Ferdinand of Brunswick. In 1759, Sackville was court-martialed for refusing to obey Ferdinand's command to advance at a crucial moment in the battle of Minden. Public opinion declared him a coward and the court sentenced him to political disgrace and military exile: "It is the further opinion of this Court, that the said Lord George Sackville is, and he is hereby adjudged, unfit to serve his Majesty in any military capacity whatever."

Sackville retained his seat in Parliament and began a comeback in 1761 by criticizing the defrauding of the British government by military suppliers. He studied the ins and outs of corruption, attacked corruption rhetorically, and yearned for the opportunity to apply what he had learned. In 1769, Sackville was able to change his marred name and gain a fortune in the process: One of his admirers, the widowed Lady Betty Germain, willed her estate to him on the condition he take her last name, and Lord George Germain he became for a time. Rich and cunning, in relation to the American colonies, Sackville allied himself with high-tax Anglicans, and shortly after war broke out, King George III appointed him secretary of state for the American colonies.[499]

The choice was unpopular among army officers: One of Lord George's many military critics, Colonel Henry Lawes Luttrell, predicted that the Americans would fight hard and the British soldiers would have Lord George to lead them—if they ran away.[500] But King George III liked the second-rate George because he displayed a ruthlessness that ranged far beyond that of many of the king's advisors, and thus attracted the favor of a monarch who was affronted when all did not bow to him. While other British leaders favored the usual strategy of bribery, with titles of nobility given to Americans who would convince their fellows to buckle under, Sackville's plan was to use the "utmost force of this kingdom" to force rebel surrender.

It was talk of homosexual conduct that, on top of the reputation for cowardice, chilled Lord George's effectiveness with some of the officers he would need in the focusing of "utmost force." Germain had five children with a lady he married, but accusations concerning Lord George's other sexual urges were common in the 1750s at a time when such activities were not considered proper fare for press and public discussion. It was said that he had formed a three-way homosexual relationship in Ireland, had promoted the "beautiful warrior" who was his domestic partner, and had then been dismissed from the service for both "cowardice and sodomy."[501] Horace Walpole in his letters referred to "gross remarks [made] at the expense of poor Lord George," and made some himself about the three-way "seraglio" involving Lord George, Colonel Robert Cuninghame, and George Stone, head of the Anglican church in Ireland.[502]

Such attacks continued for the next two decades. In 1776, William Jackson's poem "Sodom and Onan"—Jackson wrote it under the pen name Humphrey Nettle—attacked King George III for making Lord George secretary of state. Jackson's critical lines went, "As heaven's Viceregents Kings on Earth are placed,/But George the seal majestic hath disgraced;/Inveigled by Scotch Insinuation/To pardon Sodomites and damn the Nation./Sackville, both Coward and Catamite, commands/Department honourable, and kisses hands/With lips that oft in blandishment obscene Hath been employed. . . ."[503]

Sackville only threw fuel on the fire by appointing to key positions two men also suspected of sodomy. When he made Richard Cumberland secretary of the Board of Trade, diarist Hester Thrale (a friend of Samuel Johnson) noted, "Cumberland is a -. . . . N.B. he is a profess'd favourite of Lord George Sackville, who made his fortune for him. . . . Effeminancy is an odious quality in a He creature, and when joined with low jealousy actually detestable." Later, Mrs. Thrale added that "Cumberland did like the Masculine gender best. . . ."[504] The secretary of state's other curious appointee, New Hampshire tory Benjamin Thompson, became undersecretary in the American department. The crush of business was such that, as loyalist Samuel Curwen recorded, Thompson "always breakfasts, dines and sups with Lord George, so great a favourite is he." Some noble ladies were irate at the individual to whom they were to curtsey; the future Marquess Wellesley would comment about the power of "Sir *Sodom* Thompson, Lord Sackville's *under* Secretary."[505]

In 1777, Sackville's critics in the military sarcastically referred to him as a "buggering hero." In 1779, when the Board of Trade was removed from Sackville's control and given to the Earl of Carlisle, it was said that Carlisle had taken "half of such a buggerer's bed."[506] Since sodomy was a capital crime, it usually was mentioned only in diaries and whispers—but Sackville apparently was so indiscreet that his sexual preferences became the object of London discussion. For example, loyalist and former Massachusetts governor Thomas Hutchinson, describing a conversation in which one British lord had criticized Sackville's homosexuality, wrote, "I was astonished at the freedom with which he spoke of what it's shocking to think of."[507]

Sackville's promotion and protection of young homosexuals also made him unpopular among some of his cabinet colleagues. The Earl of Sandwich believed Thompson was selling naval information to the French and wanted to put him on trial, but Sackville protected him, and Thompson responded by calling him "my dearest."[508] Sackville, faced with "general disrespect for his person" from some of the most able officials, brought in aides who were "adventurers, of doubtful morals, and worse than doubtful integrity"; but what disgraced him most of all was his inveterate habit of corruption. He "might be considered as an object of pity for some of his other failings," but at a time when "it was of the utmost consequence to chose men of the highest eminence and character," Sackville made appointments in return for payoffs: "He had no scruples."[509]

Sackville's corruption in other ways also surprised those accustomed to run-of-the-court avarice. Sackville was very wealthy but always wanted more, and did not care if, in the course of enriching his own family, colonial administration suffered. On March 30, 1776, for example, he informed George III that "by the death of Baron Muir the office of Receiver General of Jamaica becomes vacant. Lord George would be infinitely Obliged to your Majesty if you would be graciously pleased to grant that office to his youngest son. . . ." Sackville's youngest son at that time was seven years old and of course could not do the job, but it paid £600 per year. George III did not follow Sackville's advice in this instance, and instead appointed to the position the son of Prime Minister Lord Frederick North.[510]

When it came to executing the land war in North America, however, Sackville had almost complete say, subject to King George III's approval. He promoted and fired generals, ruled on their promotions and leaves of absence, ordered equipment and provisions, and authorized hospitals.[511]

These Country Clowns Cannot Whip Us

The distinctions between American and British soldiery that had opened the eyes of colonists in the 1750s were even more apparent during the initial battles of the Revolution:

- British infantrymen were trained to point their guns at enemy soldiers a few yards away and then fire on command. They carried the Brown Bess, a smoothbore musket with a walnut stock (thus the name) that in trained hands would miss by only five feet when fired at a target one hundred yards away. (One British major wrote after the war that "a soldier must be very unfortunate indeed who shall be wounded by a common musket at 150 yards, provided his antagonist aims at him.")[512] On the war's first day, the British volleyed at Lexington and demolished a squad of minutemen. Later in the day, with Americans fighting as individuals from behind trees and stone walls, the redcoats in panic scurried back to Boston.
- The typical British infantryman was clothed better for show than for combat: He wore a tight red regimental coat sporting brass buttons and lace, a tight white waistcoat, a stiff collar, tight breeches, a hat with a stiff strap under the chin, and "clubbed" hair (tied up in a queue stiffened with tallow and white powder).

Dressed in heavy wool, he had to carry sixty pounds of musket, bayonet, ammunition, knapsack, and so forth. American soldiers dressed in what they had on hand and traveled lightly.

- The typical British soldier or sailor was fighting because he had no alternative. Many, made drunk by the recruiting sergeant and persuaded to take the 'king's shilling,' woke up to find themselves in the military against their will.[513] Other soldiers had joined by choice, but only because they were criminals pardoned in exchange for enlisting.[514] Their task was to do and die—but Americans who volunteered had to reason why. The reasons for fighting were not self-evident.

Americans were opposing, after all, the empire under whose auspices the colonies had experienced substantial economic growth, and the empire in which some had invested millenial hopes. Could disputes over pennies in taxes trigger the offering of pounds of flesh? Harvard College president Samuel Langdon, preaching a sermon before the Massachusetts legislature in May 1775, explained that fighting had been made necessary by a growing cultural divide: "The general prevalance of vice has changed the whole face of things in the British government." Langdon rhetorically asked, "In what does the British nation now glory"?—and he answered, "in titles of dignity without virtue,—in vast public treasures continually lavished in corruption till every fund is exhausted, notwithstanding the mighty streams perpetually flowing in."[515]

Langdon went on to say that "the pretence for taxing America has been that the nation contracted an immense debt for the defense of the American colonies. . . ." Yet such an appeal was dishonest, since increased taxation could never catch up to immorality: "The demands of corruption are constantly increasing, and will forever exceed all the resources of wealth which the wit of man can invent or tyranny impose." The only solution was for London to eliminate the "vast unnecessary expenses continually incurred by its enormous vices." Taxes would be wasted unless officials "turn[ed] their minds from the pursuit of pleasure and the boundless luxuries of life." But if there were "a general reformation of all those vices which bring misery and ruin upon individuals, families, and kingdoms," Langdon said, "millions might annually be saved . . . and the public debt, great as it is, might in a few years be cancelled by a growing revenue."[516]

Six hundred miles to the south, Patrick Henry, in May 1775, also explained the necessity of fighting in biblical terms that would appeal to those who cared for spiritual liberty, civil liberty, or both. Just as Moses and Joshua presented to the Israelites the need to choose life or death, the Lord or foreign gods, so Patrick Henry told his listeners that the moment was now come in which they were called upon to decide whether to live free or to become the servants of "a corrupt and tyrannical ministry." In William Wirth Henry's summary, Patrick Henry "showed them the land of promise, which was to be won by their valour, under the support and guidance of heaven, and sketched a vision of America enjoying the smiles of liberty and peace."[517]

Henry in his remarks also speculated on why a sovereign God did not eliminate evil by his own command. He spoke of how "God, who in former ages had hardened Pharoah's heart, that he might show forth his power and glory in the redemption of his chosen people, had, for similar purposes, permitted the flagrant outrages which had occurred . . . throughout the continent." He concluded by stressing the importance of responding rightly to God's establishment of a situation in which His glory could shine forth: "They were to remember that the same God whose power divided the Red Sea for the deliverance of Israel, still reigned in all his glory, unchanged and unchangeable—was still the enemy of the oppressor, and the friend of the oppressed—that he would cover them from their enemies by a pillar of cloud by day, and guide their feet through the night by a pillar of fire."[518]

Throughout the colonies in 1775, patriots influenced by the Awakening, the Enlightenment, or both, emphasized the necessity of resisting tyranny whose particular taxes and cultural attacks were manifestations of the deeper evil. In Pennsylvania, the *Evening Post* declared that "resisting the just and lawful power of government" is rebellion, but the colonists' opposition to "unjust and usurped power" was not.[519] In Connecticut, the *Norwich Packet* argued that liberty was like an inheritance, "a sacred deposit which it would be treason against Heaven to betray."[520]

The outbreak of fighting showed that the ideas on which advocates of small government and holy government could agree—

including the necessity of honoring forefathers by upholding contracts—were not merely lowest common denominators: They had the power to move men to the front lines. Joseph Warren, for example, spoke of how "our fathers, having nobly resolved never to wear the yoke of despotism, and seeing the European world, at that time, through indolence and cowardice, falling a prey to tyranny, bravely threw themselves upon the bosom of the ocean, determined to find a place in which they might enjoy their freedom, or perish in the glorious attempt."[521] Warren then perished at the Battle of Bunker Hill.

That battle demonstrated both the strengths and the weaknesses of American and British soldiery. At Breed's Hill and Bunker Hill volunteer American soldiers with a few experienced volunteer commanders waited as a double column of British landing barges ferried from Boston to Charleston twenty-five hundred soldiers with glittering musket barrels and bayonets. They waited as the soldiers in their tight wool, scarlet uniforms—carrying a musket, sixty rounds of cartridges, three days' rations, and a blanket—marched uphill in the afternoon heat. They waited until the whites of eyes were visible, and then shot up the British ranks so badly that fifteen hundred men (45 percent of the invading force) hit the casualty lists.

Later in the day, the battle turned. The British troops, having learned that disobedience on the battlefield brought death at the hands of their commanding officers, returned to the attack despite their enormous casualties. The American troops, without a unified command structure; without a resupply of food, water, and especially ammunition; and with a sense that it was time to get home, were in no condition to resist much more. They had lost few men during the British charges, but their losses during the retreat at the end were so heavy that, of the fifteen hundred Americans who battled the British, 140 were killed and 271 wounded.

Americans concluded from the battle that volunteer militia could win the war, but that they needed a commanding general who could garner contributions of men and supplies from all the colonies and then use what he was given in a disciplined manner. The Continental Congress chose George Washington for four reasons. First, like King Saul, he was tall: Washington looked good in a uniform, was a fine horseman with an upright bearing, and whether walking or riding appeared every inch a general. Second, he was more than a mannequin: Ever since his French and Indian War experience Washington had been viewed as a smart officer, a heroic man's man, and an up-and-coming leader, as Samuel Davies' prediction showed. Third, Washington was from Virginia; John Adams, continuing his role as coalition builder, saw the ascent of Washington as one way to assure Virginian interest in what to that point was a Massachusetts war. Fourth, Adams also saw that Washington had the capability of bringing together small-government and holy-government advocates: Although not identified with either camp, he had ties to both.

Washington early on learned the importance of neither assuming God's blessing nor neglecting his commands. Arrogance was evident late in 1775 as New Englanders under the command of Benedict Arnold assembled for an invasion of Canada. Soldiers gathered at the Newburyport, Massachusetts Presbyterian church that housed the coffin of George Whitefield, who had died in that town five years before. As chaplain Samuel Spring recorded, "They marched in with colors flying, and drums beating, and formed two lines, through which I passed—they presenting arms and the drums rolling, until I was seated in the pulpit." Spring then preached from the text of Exodus 33:15, "Except thy presence go with us, carry us not up hence"; his conclusion was that God wanted them to go hence.[522]

The expedition's way of feeling God's presence, however, was bizarre. After the service, Spring and a group of officers, including the politically ambitious Aaron Burr, "requested a visit to Whitefield's tomb," and the sexton obliged. Then, "the officers induced the sexton to take the lid off the coffin. The body had nearly all returned to dust. Some portions of his grave-clothes remained. His collar and wristbands, in the best preservation, were taken and carefully cut in little pieces and divided among them." Carrying their relics, the American forces journeyed into winter storms and met disaster: They fought hunger by chewing on soap, nibbling on candles, gnawing on cartridge boxes, and eating their mascot dog, but they could not capture Quebec.

Soon, Americans learned to thank God for His providential action after it had occurred, but not to thank Him in advance for that which He had not promised. Unusual happenings, such as rare weather conditions at critical times, signified God's special providence to Pastor William Gordon. Reporting on the American army's successful retreat from Long Island across the river into Manhattan in 1776, Gordon noted that God sent "a thick fog about two o'clock in the morning which hung over Long-Island, while on the New-York side it was clear. Had it not been for the providential shifting of the wind, not more than half the army could possibly have crossed, and the remainder . . . must inevitably have fallen into the enemy's hands."[523] Gordon, after reporting the essential story—*who*, *what*, *when*, and *where*—assessed the *why* and provided evidence for his contention of providential intervention: "It was very unusual also to have a fog at that time of the year. My informer, a citizen of New-York, could not recollect his having known any at that season, within the space of twenty or thirty years."[524]

God was also thanked for befuddling enemy officers and soldiers at crucial times. The *Pennsylvania Journal* commented on a British retreat: "The enemy appear to be panic-struck in the extreme. God prospers our arms in an extraordinary manner."[525] The *Pennsylvania Evening Post* printed an eyewitness account by "a gentleman who was present in the action": the battle, he wrote, "redounds so much to the glory of the Great Lord of the heavens. . . . [it] affords the Americans a lasting monument of the Divine power and goodness, and a most powerful argument of love to and trust in God."[526]

That tendency to thankfulness fought the tendency of some other American leaders to become like many British generals: arrogantly prideful, ignoring God. American general Charles Lee had greater experience than Washington and was considered "a most consummate general" even by one of Washington's key supporters, Nathaniel Greene—but he was also, as Washington correctly surmised, "rather fickle, and violent, I fear, in his temper." When Washington was defeated in and around New York in 1776, Lee campaigned to replace him and was gaining support, but some were reluctant to support him because he lacked both Christian belief and practice.[527] His habit of adultery caught up to him in December 1776, when British cavalry, told that Lee was sleeping with a woman three miles outside the camp, captured him.

The British thought they had seized the only competent general the Americans had, but this was another of their misunderstandings. By removing Lee, they cemented support for the person who could maintain a coalition of liberty and virtue to the satisfaction of those who emphasized either small government or holy government. Washington wanted an army as efficient as that of the British, but with much higher moral standards. At a time when army camps were homes for blasphemy, Washington decried the "foolish, and wicked practice, of profane cursing and swearing," and told his men to "reflect, that we can have little hopes of the blessing of Heaven on our arms, if we insult it by our impiety and folly."[528] Washington demanded the appointment of regimental chaplains and commanded his soldiers to "attend carefully upon religious exercises. The blessing and protection of Heaven are at all times necessary but especially so in times of public distress and danger."[529]

Disunited as the new states often were, they stood together in supporting Washington's endeavors in this direction. For example, the Virginia convention that turned the original colony into an independent state also concluded in 1776 that a commanding officer should "take such steps as to him appear most proper for preventing profane swearing, all manner of gaming, as well as every other vice and immorality among officers and soldiers under his command."[530] Washington's emphasis on high moral standards was pragmatic as well as principled. "With the militia, everybody is a general," General Nathaniel Greene noted: "They must go to war their own way or not at all." The task of British officers was to make their men compliant; the task of American officers was to show volunteers that the patriotic effort was virtually a holy cause. Washington complained about militiamen who "come in, you cannot tell how, go, you cannot tell when . . . and leave you at last in a critical moment."[531] Only the totally committed could be relied on.

Local British commanders, however, mimicked their superiors' commitment to pleasurable pursuits. For example, in December 1776, Johann Rall, who commanded the Hessian forces at Trenton, saw no reason to fortify his garrison or emphasize outposts. (He said, according to testimony at British investigations later, "These country clowns cannot whip us. . . . If the Americans come, we'll give them the bayonet.") Nor did Rall see any reason to pay attention to urgent messages given him; on Christmas Eve, when a Tory farmer delivered to Rall a note saying the entire American army had crossed the river and was marching on Trenton, Rall was intent on his card game and did not read the note, but merely slipped it into his pocket and went on playing.[532]

Washington, however, learned from his mistakes—and it was in defeat that Washington showed best his character. The Americans' famous Christmas victory at Trenton was possible because of Rall's complacency and Washington's realization, after defeats earlier in that year in and around New York City, that Americans could not beat the British in a European-style volleying match. Washington, to win, would have to become an entrepreneurial general, looking for an opening and using surprise. Washington had his men cross the Delaware River on Christmas Eve during a storm that the British thought would stop the best soldiers, let alone those defeated Americans who were supposedly slouching off in dejection. The next morning Rall's men were routed.

When Thomas Paine attempted to profile Washington late in 1776, he noted that "There is a natural firmness in some minds which cannot be unlocked by trifles."[533] British generals, however, were constantly being bogged down by trifles. Eight days after the battle of Trenton, Lord Charles Cornwallis' army at dusk on January 2, 1777, pinned Washington's forces against the Delaware River. Cornwallis, however, liked his relaxation, and is reputed to have said, "We've got the old fox safe now. We'll go over and bag him in the morning."[534] During the night the American army slipped around the British left flank and was able to rout a British regiment at Princeton.

The twin victories made the British withdraw to within a few miles of New York City, where they stayed as commanding general, Sir William Howe, absorbed himself in adultery with his mistress, Elizabeth Loring, wife of a British commissary officer who sought promotion; in the words of Charles Lee, an expert on adultery, "Howe shut his eyes, fought his battles, drank his bottle, had his little whore. . . ."[535] American tories, worried that Howe's mind was unlocked by trifles, circulated a ditty: "Awake, arouse, Sir Billy,/

There's forage on the plain./Ah, leave your little filly,/And open the campaign."[536]

We Have Fled from the Political Sodom

The war was political as well as military. Small-government partisans and holy-government advocates before the war were able to agree that small government was necessary but not sufficient for holy government, and that the British abandonment of holy government was made more likely by their embrace of big government. But it was a long way from coalescing against something to uniting for something else. The task of the Continental Congress that met in Philadelphia was to communicate to the world not only the reasons for separation but the basis for establishing a new union.

The long debates led to a rhetorical compromise. To those theologically enlightened through the Great Awakening, support for personal virtue was of the utmost importance. For those awakened out of allegiance to traditional virtue by the Enlightenment, governmental directives aimed at promoting morality could create new problems. The Continental Congress was not always able to find compromises satisfactory to all, but could adopt language attractive to both sides and subject to varied interpretations. When the deist Thomas Jefferson penned words such as "the laws of nature and of nature's God" and "endowed, by their Creator, with certain unalienable rights," he was expressing his own position while artfully appealing to theists such as Presbyterian minister John Witherspoon. After all, deists also believed that God had created the world; they were happy to have a Prime Mover, as long as he had afterward moved out of the way.

"Laws of nature and of nature's God" was an especially artful Jeffersonian expression. In the sixteenth century, John Calvin had written that "the law of God which we call the moral law, is nothing else than a testimony of natural law and of that conscience which God has engraved upon the minds of men."[537] Early in the seventeenth century, British jurist Sir Edward Coke wrote that "The law of nature is that which God at the time of creation of the nature of man infused into his heart," and law scholar John Selden added, "I cannot fancy to myself what the law of nature means, but the law of God."[538] Many of the signers of the Declaration of

Independence had read the standard law comentary of the time, Sir William Blackstone's *Commentaries on the Laws of England.* Blackstone wrote, "As man depends absolutely upon his maker for every thing, it is necessary that he should in all points conform to his maker's will. This will of his maker is called the law of nature."[539] So when theistic Declaration framers saw Jefferson's expression "laws of nature," their theological warning bells would not go off; they might even be pleased that he added an explicit mention of God to the phrase.

Jefferson and fellow deists, meanwhile, were ready to sign onto a document that emphasized the course of human events without explicit reference to Jesus Christ; the expression "nature's God" even made it seem that nature had created God and now owned Him. Other words also could resonate both ways during the Revolutionary era; the *liberty* of "life, liberty, and the pursuit of happiness," for example, had a theological as well as a political meaning. For Christians such as Connecticut minister Levi Hart, natural man was a captive of sin, and "the whole plan of Redemption is comprised in procuring, preaching and bestowing liberty to the captives."[540] Deists, however, emphasized the political meaning of the word.[541]

Providence was another mellifluous word for a multitude of ears. For deists, *providence* was the general motion of natural forces implanted in a world created by God but left to run on its own: "simply the way the world turned."[542] The Christian understanding, however, was summarized well by John Calvin: *Providence* did not mean that "God idly observes from heaven what takes place on earth, but that . . . as keeper of the keys, he governs all events."[543] American Congregationalists and Presbyterians would have been well aware of the definition of *Providence* in chapter 5 of the Westminster Confession: "God, the great Creator of all things, doth uphold, direct, dispose, and govern all creatures, actions, and things from the greatest even to the least, by his most wise and holy providence."[544] So, for deists, use of the word *providence* downplayed God's current role; for Christians, the word indicated a heightened awareness of God's power and even ruled out the deistic concept. (In Calvin's words, "Unless we pass on to his providence . . . we do not yet properly grasp what it means to say: 'God is creator.'"[545])

Christian leaders like Samuel Adams, who saw the need for

unity, tried to sound the right notes for both segments of the coalition. When Adams analyzed the Declaration of Independence, he noted that the British had tried to make the state a god, but the Americans had seen through the folly: "We have explored the temple of royalty, and found that the idol we have bowed down to has eyes which see not, ears that hear not our prayers, and a heart like the nether millstone."[546]Through the Declaration with its emphasis on Providence and a law above kings, Adams declared that "We have this day restored the Sovereign to whom alone men ought to be obedient."[547]

And what of the future? Adams foresaw attempts once again to set up a political class to which all must bow, but he resolved to fight such attempts: "Were the talents and virtues which Heaven has bestowed on men given merely to make them more obedient drudges, to be sacrificed to the follies and ambition of a few?" The success of America thus far had created a responsibility not to give up: "The hand of heaven appears to have led us on to be, perhaps, humble instruments and means in the great providential dispensation which is completing. We have fled from the political Sodom; let us not look back, lest we perish and become a monument of infamy and derision to the world."[548]

Minister George Duffield spoke similarly to a Philadelphia congregation in 1776: "Our forefathers, who first inhabited yonder eastern shores, fled from the iron rod and heavy hand of tyranny"; the American Revolution, Duffield said, grew out of the "same spirit that inspired our forefathers' breasts when first they left their native shores and embarked for this then howling desert."[549] Freedom was God's gift, as Congress noted in its petition to King George III: "Had our Creator been pleased to give us existence in a land of slavery, the sense of our condition might have been mitigated by ignorance and habit. But, thanks to his adorable goodness, we were born the heirs of freedom."[550]

The new Congress of the United States continued to witness battles on how to preserve the inheritance. John Witherspoon supported the Articles of Confederation plan to give one vote to each state; Benjamin Franklin wanted a stronger national government with voting power to be based on population. Franklin supported the appointment of the radical Thomas Paine as secretary to the Committee on Foreign Affairs; Witherspoon opposed it, contending that a writer who had to "quicken his thought with large draughts of rum" was unreliable. (Paine later had to be fired for betraying confidences.)

I Could Have Borne Anything but This

And the war went on with Americans continuing to exploit British folly to gain occasional victories. The biggest victory of the war, until its close, grew out of the dramatic flair of British lieutenant general "Gentleman Johnny" Burgoyne. Burgoyne, as George Bernard Shaw wrote a century later, was "a man of fashion, gallant enough to have made a distinguished marriage by an elopement, witty enough to write successful comedies, aristocratically-connected."[551] Burgoyne had military experience during the Seven Years' War; he also wrote a successful play, *The Maid of the Oaks*, in 1774, and composed for the play a song that became popular, "The World Turned Upside Down." He combined his military and literary knowledge to produce, in 1776, a report, *Reflections on the War in America*, that gave credit to American fighting skills but argued that "peasants, no matter how intelligent," could not match well-trained British troops.

Burgoyne's proposal was that the British conquer New York City and then send one army north from their new base to link up at Albany with another sent south from Canada. He fought for his idea not by convincing other generals but by visiting King George III and mentioning, in the true spirit of the courtier, that he was distressed as to how the monarch apparently had little time for exercise and was putting on weight. The king agreed to go riding with Burgoyne, and as they cantered for the next two weeks on the bridle paths, "Gentleman Johnny" was able to make George III believe that the campaign would isolate New England and show the rebels who was boss.[552]

Better military strategists than Burgoyne pointed out the folly of his drawing-board dream. Given trade routes between New England and the rest of America, even a successful campaign would have accomplished little. New England land trade with the rest of America had already been restricted by British control of several choke points just north of New York City, and total isolation of New England was not possible unless Britain was prepared to patrol hundreds of miles of coastlines. Burgoyne was marching an army south from Canada for hundreds of hard-to-supply miles when there was no objective at the end but to arrive at a place with no strategic value. Nevertheless, George III gave his charming courtier an army to lose.[553]

Burgoyne, in 1777, thus brought poorly supplied British troops south from Canada into wilderness. His force might still have avoided catastrophe if act two of the drama, a simultaneous movement north from New York City, had gone off as planned. But Sackville messed up here, as was his custom: "Capable of rousing himself to almost frenzied pitches of energy, he habitually lapsed into periods of lethargy little better than a coma."[554] He frequently was lackadaisical about providing for the troops he ordered about; soldiers frequently wrote of sickness "brought on by bad provisions," and wished that the "Government would look after the contractors, or without we are supplied with wholesome necessaries of life, it cannot be expected we will long fight their battles."[555] But Sackville's conduct in 1777 was extraordinary: after sending orders to Burgoyne to march south, he forgot to make sure that orders to march north were sent to his general in New York City, Sir William Howe.

Although the omission could be viewed as a chance occurrence, it was part of the pattern by which minds focused on immorality neglected obligations. As one member of the cabinet, the Earl of Shelburne, recounted in his memoirs, Sackville "had a particular aversion to being put out of his way on any occasion." Heading to vacation pursuits at his country house, Sackville stopped "at his office to sign the dispatches, all of which had been settled, to both these generals [Burgoyne and Howe]. By some mistake those to General Howe were not fair copied, and upon his growing impatient," Sackville signed and sent the one order to Burgoyne, but left before the one to Howe was recopied, and then forgot about it.[556] Burgoyne did as he was told without knowing that Howe was taking his troops to Philadelphia rather than Albany.[557]

The result was British disaster, as American forces swarmed against Burgoyne's unsupported troops, who learned the difference between theater and life: Burgoyne could not twist the plot to save men who marched into hostile territory with inadequate information about terrain. (Similar ignorance, along with communication problems among British commanders who thought as much about embarrassing a London rival as extinguishing a rebellion, would later strand Cornwallis by the waters around Yorktown.) Burgoyne, with failing supplies, no hope of help, and more Americans flocking to Saratoga to surround his forces, surrendered. He and his entire army became prisoners of war.

The American victory was particularly important because it convinced France to enter the war against its old enemy. (The American willingness to enter into an alliance with the nation that had been both a national and religious enemy showed a New World willingness to overcome old antagonisms.) Furthermore, Burgoyne's defeat brought the first uproar in Parliament concerning conduct of the war. Colonel Isaac Barré lambasted Sackville on the floor of the House of Commons—"rather too absurd for an Indian chief," Barre said of Sackville's style of planning.[558] Edmund Burke protested more elegantly "the ignorance of the Minister for the American department"; Sackville, he said, had planned "a conjunction between Howe and Burgoyne," but one to be "produced in the strangest way he ever heard of, [since] Howe was traveling southward and Burgoyne in the same direction."[559]

Sackville continued to receive strong support among Anglican bishops in the House of Lords. Throughout the war they overlooked his lifestyle and that of Sandwich, and received their reward: "Clergymen who in the fast-day sermons distinguished themselves by violent attacks on the Americans . . . were conspicuously selected for promotion."[560] Thus, government-paid ministers continued to disgrace their profession. The only good to come out of the battle for the British was that the incompetent American general, Horatio Gates, who had victory handed to him at Saratoga, was treated as a hero and promoted beyond his capacity, so that three years later he was positioned to lead the American southern command into a rout at Camden, South Carolina. Gates then proceeded to lead his most panicky soldiers out of the battle by abandoning his lines and riding sixty miles on horseback before nightfall, outpacing even his shadow.

There is no indication in any of the battle reports that Washington ever panicked. Nor did Washington ever resign in protest or quit in complete frustration when patriot forces, despite his entreaties to Congress, were poorly supplied. Early in the war, one-fifth of his army had no firearms at all. At Valley Forge during the harsh winter of 1777-78, few soldiers had coats, half were without blankets, more than a third were without shoes, and some lacked other essentials for health amidst winter.[561] One in every four soldiers who wintered at Valley Forge died there. The winter of 1779-80 in Morristown, New Jerscy was even worse. Hungry men, surrounded by snow at one point, had rations only one-eighth of the normal amount.

Finances also were a problem. Rarely during the war were Washington's men paid on time or in full; in January 1781, some Pennsylvania and New Jersey troops mutinied and deserted. And yet, Washington would not give up. When he furloughed militia soldiers to go home to harvest crops, enough came back to hold the British at bay year after year. Washington, it turned out, was the ideal leader for an army of volunteers: He had an awareness of his own limitations, a bulldog strength of perseverance, and an integrity that made him so popular among his soldiers that some who wanted to leave stayed on so as to avoid disappointing him.

Washington, in 1775, had predicted that assumption of military leadership would ruin his reputation and that at times seemed likely; General Friedrich von Steuben said that "Caesar and Hannibal would have lost their reputations" if forced to fight a war under the circumstances Washington faced.[562] Washington's harsh experiences certainly deepened his thinking; in 1778, writing of his army's survival, Washington noted that "the hand of Providence has been so conspicuous in all this that he must be worse than an infidel who lacks faith, and more than wicked that has not gratitude enough to acknowledge his obligations."[563] Characteristically, however, Washington did not specify to Whom he was obligated, but cut off his meditation by writing, "It will be time enough for me to turn preacher when my present appointment ceases, and therefore I shall add no more on the Doctrine of Providence." He did not.[564]

Washington did publicly maintain faith that the Revolution ultimately would succeed.[565] Ultimately often seemed like an eternity as the war wore on. But, as the most critical period of the war approached, the private lives of British leaders continued to affect their public performances and that gave Washington and his American troopers an edge.

Sandwich, from 1760 on, had, along with other liaisons, a live-in lover, Martha Ray. He met her when he was forty-two and she still a teenager, at which time he moved her into his house and trained her as a singer. Sandwich had his Martha perform at musical evenings in his house, but she was not allowed to mix with the guests—and so it went on for years. In 1778, Lord Sandwich invited to his home a young ensign, James Hackman, who listened to Martha Ray sing, fell in love with her, and repeatedly tried to convince her to elope with him. Failing in that effort, he resigned his commission, quickly became an Anglican cleric, and in 1779 went berserk: He shot Martha Ray in the face as she emerged from the theater. When Sandwich was informed of her death, as the British were transporting troops to conquer South Carolina under Cornwallis' command, he flung himself on his bed and cried, "Leave me alone, I could have borne anything but this!"[566]

Sandwich's womanizing also affected his relations with officials who reported to him. For instance, the Portsmouth Dockyard was a crucial venue for shipbuilding and refurbishing, and in 1774 it was administered by Middleton's brother-in-law, Captain James Gambier. Sandwich stayed with Gambier during one visit and later wrote to him about a young lady he had met there and lusted after: "I am capable of receiving very strong impressions from a few hours acquaintance with a very agreeable woman." Sandwich in his fifties had become concerned about rejection—"the fear of her being offended or laughing at me prevented my saying half what I had in my mind. . . . I must own that after 55 a man in love is but a ridiculous being"—so he wanted Gambier to pimp for him. The ambitious captain agreed to do his best.[567]

There is no record as to whether the desired tryst took place, but Gambier received promotion; one historian, apparently unaware of the pimping episode, notes with surprise that in January 1778, Sandwich appointed the "thoroughly lackluster" Gambier a rear admiral.[568] In 1781, as the naval drama along the American coast was coming to a crux, Gambier wanted additional preference, and Sandwich had to spend time convincing the captain that he already had been paid off enough. If Gambier attempted to expose him, Sandwich wrote, "It will probably occasion some ridicule upon me; but I have never pretended to be free from indiscretion, and those who know me have been so long accustomed to forgive my weaknesses. . . ." His bluff called, Gambier bitterly desisted, realizing (as did others) that Sandwich's reputation was so bad that he was virtually blackmail-proof.[569]

Sandwich had other problems with those who knew of his gross unfaithfulness in marriage and had no trust that he would carry out his work faithfully. He antagonized Admiral Augustus Keppel, one of the navy's most admired officers, and lent his support to an attempt in 1779 to court-martial Keppel for largely political reasons. This became known as the battle of the Montagues (playing off Sandwich's family name, John Montague) and the Keppelites. Keppel disclosed that when he had taken command of the fleet against the French in 1778, he had found that Sandwich's claims of thirty-five ships fit for duty were slightly off, since there were only six were ready. Keppel was found not guilty.[570] Some talented officers resigned for reasons such as that given by Captain John Leveson-Gower: Sandwich "never had any decency. . . ."[571] According to the *Dictionary of National Biography*, "Many officers of character and ability . . . refused to accept a command while he remained at the admiralty."[572]

Sackville's reputation for sexual and financial lust also deprived the British war effort of significant support. In 1779, Sackville was accused of pocketing state money. Like Sandwich, he also exaggerated his available forces, so that commanders ended up bitter at promises never fulfilled.[573] One of Sackville's long-time critics, James Luttrell, rose in Parliament to charge that Sackville "considered the post of secretary of state for the colonies at this time as no other than a contractor of emoluments and high honours. . . ." Charles Fox to Sackville's face called him a coward, and others joined in; ordinarily, Sackville might have been expected to fight a duel to vindicate his honor, but he had received so many fact-based insults for so long that he merely continued in his work and habits—and others felt free to continue in theirs, without working for a British victory in America. Both the war effort and the man leading it became increasingly unpopular in England. In the words of a contemporary opponent, "The most odious of tasks was assigned to the most odious of instruments."[574]

In 1780, as the North administration increased taxes to pay war bills, the city of Westminster presented a resolution to the king that criticized "the large addition to the national debt, a heavy accumulation of taxes, a rapid decline of the trades, manufactures and land rates of the Kingdom . . . much public money has been improvidently squandered . . . many individuals enjoy sinecure places . . . with exorbitant emoluments, and pensions unmerited by public services. . . ."[575] Others complained of "treasures squandered . . . by the very men entrusted with the most important and honourable confidence of their Sovereign . . . to make the fortunes of a long train of leeches, who seek the blood of the State. . . ."[576]

Sackville's difficult task was to propel into cohesion diverse armies and civil organizations, but his attachment to some personalities and hatred for others made the work impossible, and British armies in America repeatedly failed to support one another. Sackville was also supposed to work closely with the first lord of the admiralty in coordinating army and navy, but the dislike he and Sandwich had for each other also negated that possibility; they oozed cordiality in public but privately spread the idea that each reverse was the other's fault.[577] According to Horace Walpole, Sandwich was Sackville's "principal enemy," and other correspondents transmitted what was repeatedly the latest news: "a violent quarrel between Lord Sandwich and Lord George. . . ."[578]

Public opinion was increasingly unfavorable to Sandwich. Sarcastic ballads in the streets lambasted him, and he gave up on suing for libel: "Let them sing or say whatever they please about me," Sandwich finally told a servant.[579] Charles Churchill described him best in act three of his play, *The Duellist*: Sandwich was "Too infamous to have a friend,/Too bad for bad men to commend."[580] Sandwich was frequently portrayed as mixing Admiralty business with personal interest. One satirist had Sandwich watching a young lady leave his office and saying, "Enchanting devil! This girl would be the utter ruin of me at seventy years of age, if my fortune was not already dissipated, and my character lost beyond recovery—But I must now to business; and try to raise a sum, by advancing some worthless scoundrel over the head of a hundred men of merit."[581]

In February 1779, disgust of some Londoners for the war and the conduct of it turned to rioting. An angry mob broke the windows of Sackville's London home and, catching Sandwich traveling on the streets, "near massacred" him, according to Horace Walpole.[582] Eyewitness Sir Samuel Romilly described the close call in his memoirs: "I expected . . . to have seen him torn in pieces; but, leaping quickly out of the chariot, he saved himself in a coffee-house, and a very strong party of guards immediately rode up and kept off the mob."[583]

Political opponents almost got him too. Every five years, it seemed, a full-fledged scandal broke around Sandwich, but he kept dodging bullets. In 1773, he was accused of bribery, but there was no irrefutable proof that Sandwich himself had offered the bribes, and the printer of the *Evening Post* was fined for libel. In 1778, Sandwich accused Captain Thomas Baillie of libel after Baillie wrote an expose; Baillie was acquitted, but Sandwich made sure he would never again have a job in the navy as long as Sandwich was in charge. Not until 1783 did an official parliamentary inquiry finally expose corruption in the dockyards, and determined that the problems were the direct outcome of Sandwich's "assigning the charge of departments and of stores to men without a single qualification beyond their votes or their command of votes."[584]

Actors on a Most Conspicuous Theater

By the time of the parliamentary inquiry it was too late for the first British empire. For years Sandwich, Sackville, and others of licentious habits had gained office on the basis of connections rather than competence; not until 1781 did Britain finally reap the full consequences of such appointments. For example, the admiral in command through August 1, 1781, was Sir George Rodney, adulterer, gambler, and debtor. Instead of spending the spring and early summer helping General Charles Cornwallis, Rodney spent weeks improving his own economic condition by seizing and auctioning off goods on St. Eustatius, the tiny Dutch island of the Leeward chain after which he left for London.[585]

Command on land was no better. Cornwallis was Sackville's "special favourite"; Sackville indicated to Cornwallis and to his commanding officer, General Sir Henry Clinton, that he was ready to give Clinton's job to Cornwallis whenever Cornwallis wanted it.[586] Sackville also developed a strategy—"the recovery of the southern provinces and the prosecution of the war by pushing our conquests from south to north is to be considered as the chief and principal object"—that would allow his favorite, Cornwallis, to shine.[587] Clinton, perceiving that political connections were crucial to military office-holding, spent his time wining and dining visiting dignitaries and staging pretend fox hunts through the streets of New York—the general and his friends followed a hound that chased after a Hessian soldier who dragged a bone on a rope.[588] Cornwallis in turn showed his skill by allowing his forces to be pinned in at Yorktown, confident that the British navy could rescue him.

Clinton also followed the tradition of his predecessor, General Howe, in having a pretty mistress, encouraged in that pursuit by a soldier-husband: The wife was complicit and the husband received promotions. Clinton's dislike for Cornwallis made it easier for Clinton to occupy himself not with his duty but with the beauty at hand.[589] Sackville's primping of Cornwallis created animosity between the two generals, who communicated little with each other and were ready to fight a duel. According to Walpole, the two generals "were so ill together that Sir Henry . . . was determined to challenge Lord Cornwallis after the campaign."[590]

Problems of command were also reflected in the ranks. The British navy had regularly recruited crews from prisons and slums or kidnapped drunkards from city streets, but in New York City in the spring of 1781, a press gang went so far as to raid houses and, according to the journal of British lieutenant Bartholomew Jones, literally took "the husband from the arms of his wife in bed."[591] New York neutralists taken against their will did not make fervent fighters. On land toward the end of the war, as at the beginning, British soldiers fought when they could not avoid it, but otherwise dedicated themselves to gambling, drinking, and cavorting with camp prostitutes. In 1781, Cornwallis became so disgusted that he finally sent out a notice: "Lord Cornwallis has lately received the most shocking complaints of the excesses committed by the troops. He calls on the officers to put a stop to this licentiousness."[592]

It was a little late—for George Washington was using the late summer of 1781 to embark on one of history's great flank attacks. His original inclination, like Lee's four-score years later at Gettysburg, was to attack frontally the strong British positions in New York City, with the help of French soldiers under Count Jean-Baptiste de Rochambeau. Rochambeau demurred, so Washington went to a second plan that avoided frontal attack folly but carried with it immediate risks and the possibility of embarrassment and heartache so great that the American war effort might collapse.

American and French forces on the Hudson would have to march about nine hundred miles and link up on Chesapeake Bay with a French fleet that all the while could be scattered by storms, the British navy, or erratic command decisions. Washington would have to hope that Clinton in New York City would remain lethargic—if he were to make a full assault while the American and French forces were moving across his front, they could be shattered—and that Cornwallis would stay put in Yorktown as his army's doom was slowly being sealed. The odds seemed long, but Washington trusted Providence and his understanding of British complacency.[593]

By the beginning of September, thanks to Clinton and Cornwallis, the great flanking maneuver was on the brink of succeeding—but all depended on the French fleet's ability to keep British ships out of Chesapeake Bay, where they could readily pick up Cornwallis' army and transport it to safety. The crucial British-French naval battle came on September 5, with the British hampered in three ways, at least in part because of Sandwich's malfeasance: First, they were outnumbered, twenty-four ships to nineteen, and some of their nineteen were in poor shape. The HMS *Terrible*, whose name mirrored her decayed condition, received enemy fire but sank largely because she had never been properly repaired.[594]

Second, the British fleet lacked a cohesive command. Admiral Thomas Graves, distinguished largely by being Prime Minister North's brother-in-law, was in charge, although he never had commanded a fleet in battle. Graves had met the two junior admirals of this fleet, Sir Samuel Hood and Francis S. Drake (great nephew of the Elizabethan hero), only a week before; neither knew his tactical thinking. At a time when ships communicated with signal flags, Graves used one signal book and Hood another; the flags were the same, but different flags and different sequences signalled the same maneuver. The result was confusion. When the two fleets met in combat on September 5, Hood's squadron never became engaged, and the French ships bashed their British counterparts so badly that Graves decided it was time to limp back to New York.[595]

Third, when Clinton in mid-September heard the news of the fleet's defeat, he decided that Cornwallis's force, which now could not be evacuated, should be reinforced—with Clinton's typical alacrity, he thought the troops should be sent in about a month or so. When the battered British ships themselves arrived in New York on September 19, Clinton almost was moved to action, but sixteen-year-old Prince William Henry, King George III's third son, arrived in New York and had to be entertained with concerts, carriage rides, parades, and parties. Meanwhile, Washington's and Rochambeau's forces were arriving in Yorktown. On September 28 a siege began.

The siege lasted only three weeks. Cornwallis, outnumbered 16,650 to about 7,000 and outgunned, surrendered his troops on October 19 after reporting that his supplies were depleted. American and French soldiers found in the British camp 144 cannon and mortars, thousands of big gun cartridges and 120 barrels of powder, 800 muskets and 266,000 musket cartridges, 73,000 pounds of flour, 60,000 pounds of bread, 75,000 pounds of pork, 30,000 bushels of peas, 1,250 gallons of liquor, and enough other military materials and foodstuffs to hold on for many more weeks. Clearly, the British at Yorktown did not have the will to win, and gave in as soon as they could semihonorably do so.

Americans accepted Cornwallis's surrender without demanding revenge for the way some of his troops had acted as they marched through the Carolinas and Virginia. (One credible account by a contemporary observer describes how "on a beautiful estate a pregnant woman was found murdered in her bed through several bayonet stabs," with words written on the wall above the bed: "Thou shalt never give birth to a rebel.")[596] Washington, not wanting victory to slip away and not knowing how long British commanders in New York would dally before dispatching a relief expedition, formally accepted the surrender. (The expedition did not leave New York until October 19, the day Cornwallis was surrendering; one of Clinton's last acts was to give a copy of his will to his mistress. The British fleet arrived off Yorktown one week later, much too late, and then meekly sailed back to New York, with some time lost from parties and parades, and the colonies lost to London.[597])

Many Americans had the sense that the victory was God's gift. Immediately after the British surrender, George Washington noted the "surprizing and particular interposition of Providence in our favour," and ordered that "divine service shall be performed tomorow in the different brigades and divisions."[598] Yorktown was the culminating development that impressed leaders such as Elbridge

Gerry of Massachusetts, who exulted (in a letter to Samuel Adams) as to how history could "hardly produce such a series of events as has taken place in favor of American opposition. The hand of Heaven seems to have directed every occurrence."[599]

The war was not settled officially for two more years, but Washington's task was essentially completed. His clearest philosophical statement came in his last official communication to the thirteen state governors as commander of the army. In the letter, sent on June 8, 1783, a few months after the conclusion of a preliminary peace treaty, Washington predicted that Americans would be "Actors on a most conspicuous Theatre, which seems to be peculiarly designated by Providence for the display of human greatness and felicity."[600] He wrote of the current era as one aided by products of both the Enlightenment and the Great Awakening: "the free cultivation of letters, the unbounded extension of Commerce, the progressive refinement of Manners, the growing liberality of sentiment, and, above all, the pure and benign light of Revelation. . . ."[601] The sense of playing a role in a drama not his own making, and his tendency to unite the two strands of American eighteenth-century thought, were pure Washington.

The conclusion of the letter, however, was extraordinary. "I now make it my earnest prayer," he wrote, "that God would have you, and the State over which you preside, in his holy protection." Washington added, in a reference to Micah, his hopes that God "would most graciously be pleased to dispose us all, to do Justice, to love mercy, and to demean ourselves with that Charity, humility, and pacific temper of mind, which were the Characteristicks of the Divine Author of our blessed Religion, and without an humble imitation of whose example in these things, we can never hope to be a Happy Nation."[602]

James MacArdell, c. 1728–1765, after Benjamin Wilson, Mezzotint, 1761, National Portrait Gallery, Smithsonian Institution

Benjamin Franklin

Changed sides just before the Revolution

1706–1790

Valentine Green, 1739–1813, after John Trumbull, Mezzotint, 1783, National Portrait Gallery, Smithsonian Institution

George Washington

Symbolized steadfastness

1732–1799

James Barton Longacre, 1794–1869, after Lawrence Sully, Watercolor on artist board, c. 1835, National Portrait Gallery, Smithsonian Institution

Patrick Henry

Built the Virginia coalition

1736–1799

Attributed to George Graham, active c. 1796–1813, after John Johnston, Mezzotint, 1801, National Portrait Gallery, Smithsonian Institution

Samuel Adams

Built the Massachusetts coalition

1722–1803

Charles Willson Peale, 1741–1827, Oil on canvas, replica after 1784 original, c. 1795/1805, National Portrait Gallery, Smithsonian Institution

Richard Henry Lee

Predicted government centralization

1732–1794

John Trumbull, 1756–1843, Oil on canvas, 1793, National Portrait Gallery, Smithsonian Institution

John Adams

Survived turmoil

1735–1826

Michel Sokolnicki, 1760–1816, after Thaddeus Kosciusko, Hand-colored aquatint, 1798–1799, National Portrait Gallery, Smithsonian Institution

Thomas Jefferson

Promoted radical forces

1743–1826

Unidentified artist, probably after Charles Willson Peale, Stipple and line engraving, 1796, National Portrait Gallery, Smithsonian Institution

James Madison

Led the federalist campaign

1751–1836

CHAPTER SEVEN

Agitated Peace

The structure of American government immediately following independence was easy to predict: Identify what the British had done that colonists did not like, and be sure to avoid it. Independent executive power a problem? Get rid of it and congressional committees would perform executive functions. Judicial power a threat? Congress itself took on the very limited judicial tasks that state courts could not find a way to handle. Taxation by the central government? No, Congress would rely on grants of funds by the independent states. Legislative corruption? The Articles of Confederation established a rotation principle by which members of Congress could serve only three years out of every six, with the option of recall at any time.[603] Legislative steamrollers? The Articles leaned toward principled gridlock by requiring two-thirds votes for passing legislation and a unanimous vote of the states to amend the articles. Other stipulations also placed the central government thoroughly under state control.

John Dickinson and other framers of the Articles felt that passing a bad law was worse than failing to pass a good law. They saw particularly strongly the need to restrict taxing power. The *Providence Gazette* argued that federal reliance on state treasuries would preserve liberty, because "taxation is the necessary instrument of tyranny. There is no tyranny without it."[604] The *New York Packet* noted that "no important revolutions have taken place in any government, till the power of raising money from the people has been put into different hands."[605] In 1782, the Virginia Assembly resolved that a granting of tax power to any group other than the assembly "may prove destructive of the rights and liberty of the people."[606]

Americans saw such containment of power seekers as particularly important because representatives in Congress often had little trust in those from other states and backgrounds. Even after it was understood that the patriots would hang together or would otherwise hang separately, John Adams wrote of the secret fears and jealousies that delegates from one colony had of another.[607] Even in the Continental Congress, as one delegate noted, "jealousies, ill-natured observations and recriminations take the place of reason and argument."[608] Libertarians who feared governmental power and Christian conservatives who emphasized sin could agree with those who simply distrusted each other: Authority must be circumscribed.

Limited as the power of the federal government was, some thought it still too great. Halfway through the war, the town of West Springfield, Massachusetts, complained to its representatives about "the growing thirst for power," and argued that under the Articles "the sovereignty and independence of particular states [are] nearly annihilated." Town-meeting participants trusted current leaders but had no confidence in those who might arise: "We entertain no jealousy of the present Congress but who knows but in some future corrupt times there may be a Congress which will form a design upon the liberties of the People. . . ."[609]

The greatest fear, in many ways, was that members of one denomination would take the opportunity to throw out the Anglicans, only to put in equally obnoxious substitutes. Most new state constitutions displayed the libertarian/Christian consensus: no state church, but an honoring of the scriptural God whom virtually all either revered or thought useful. The Maryland constitution of 1776 was typical in its embrace of Christianity but separation of denomination and state: The constitution proclaimed God's worship not to be an option ("it is the duty of every man to worship God. . . .") but noted that the particular style was up for grabs (" . . . in such manner as he thinks most acceptable to him").[610]

Crucially, there would be no established denomination: no one would "be compelled to frequent, or maintain, or contribute, unless on contract, to maintain any particular place of worship, or any particular ministry." The establishment of Christianity, however, might be constitutional: In Maryland, for example, "the Legislature may, in their discretion, lay a general and equal tax, for the support of the Christian religion; leaving to each individual the power of appointing the payment over of the money, collected from him, to the support of any particular place of worship or minister. . . ." This system of denominational choice applied to aid to the poor as well: if the legislature passed a tax for supporting the poor, a taxpayer could have his money go to "the poor of his own denomination, or the poor in general of any particular county."[611]

Two years later, the South Carolina constitution established "the Christian Protestant religion . . . all denominations of Christian Protestants in this State, demeaning themselves peaceably and faithfully, shall enjoy equal religious and civil privileges." The South Carolina framers did not think it an impossible task to define the common beliefs of those who would receive such protection—they had to agree that "there is one eternal God, and a future state of rewards and punishments . . . that the Christian religion is the true religion. That the holy scriptures of the Old and New Testament are of divine inspiration, and are the rule of faith and practice." There was no proscription on taxes going to support churches where such doctrines were taught, as long as no one was "obliged to pay towards the maintenance and support of a religious worship" not his own.[612]

Maryland . . . South Carolina . . . the Massachusetts constitution of 1780 . . . all recognized God in the preamble, "acknowledging with grateful hearts, the goodness of the Great Legislator, of the universe . . . and devoutly imploring His direction. . . ." The Massachusetts framers then proceeded to the practical application in a series of logical steps. First, opportunity and obligation: "It is the right as well as the Duty of all men in society, publicly and at stated seasons to worship the Supreme Being, the great Creator and preserver of the Universe." Second, toleration: "No subject shall be hurt, molested, or restrained, in his person, liberty, or estate, for worshipping God in the manner and season most agreeable to the dictates of his own conscience. . . ."[613] Third, encouragement: "The happiness of a people, and the good order and preservation of civil government, essentially depend upon piety, religion, and morality

. . . these cannot be generally diffused through a Community, but by the institution of the public worship of God, and of public instructions in piety, religion, and morality."

With such an emphasis on worship in the public interest, establishment of particular denominations was unnecessary: "Every denomination of Christians, demeaning themselves peaceably, and as Good subjects of the Commonwealth, shall be equally under the protection of the Law; and no subordination of any one sect or denomination to another shall ever be established by Law." Towns were to make "suitable provision, at their own expense, for the institution of the public worship of God, and for the support and maintenance of public protestant teachers of piety, religion and morality, in all cases where such provision shall be made voluntarily." The local bodies could choose the particular objects of support, depending on local denominational nuances, but support of some kind was essential.[614] The goal was to empower alternatives to state churches, but not to go to the opposite extreme by separating government and God.

The aforementioned state constitutions were written during the Revolution, when God was a frequent subject of newspaper accounts of battle. The *Pennsylvania Journal* reported that in one fight, "Through Divine Providence not one of our men were [sic] hurt."[615] The *Virginia Gazette* commented on one battle in which American lives once again were spared, "Heaven apparently, and most evidently, fights for us, covers our heads in the day of battle, and shields our people from the assaults of our common enemies."[616] The *Gazette* reported similarly about a later battle: "The Almighty was on our side. Not a ball struck or wounded an individual person, although they went through our houses in almost every direction when filled with women and children."[617]

Official pronouncements during the war were similar. The United States Congress, in 1778, proclaimed that the "God of battles, in whom was our trust, hath conducted us thro' the paths of danger and distress to the thresholds of security." In 1779, Congress told the world that "America, without arms, ammunition, discipline, revenue, government or ally, with a 'staff and a sling' only, dared, 'in the name of the Lord of Hosts,' to engage a giant adversary, prepared at all points, boasting of his strength, and of whom even mighty warriors 'were greatly afraid.'"[618] But once fighting ended, remembrance of God dropped off, just as it had for several years following the French and Indian War.

How exact were the historical parallels? In 1766, the Presbyterian Synod observed, "Under the calamities of war, and the wasting ravages of Indian cruelty, we were repeatedly brought to approach the throne of grace, with solemn fasting and prayer; and thereby openly professed our resolution to forsake the ways of sin, and turn unto the Lord. But alas! we rendered not to God according to the multitude of his tender mercies, for no sooner was the rod removed, and the blessings of peace restored, but we became more vain and dissolute than before." The Synod declared that, "The Almighty, thus provoked, permitted counsels of the most pernicious tendency, both to Great Britain and her colonies . . . an almost total stagnation of business threatened us with inevitable ruin."[619] Would poor political decisions and economic collapse come again?

People in General Seem Ready for Anything

Politically, Americans understood that they needed to build a political structure that supported both liberty and virtue. They saw these as connected: no liberty without virtue, and maybe even no virtue without liberty. Unless concerted efforts to support both continued, the tendency would be to fall back into a monarchy. Already, in 1782, Colonel Lewis Nicola sent Washington a letter proposing that Washington be designated George I; Washington responded that the idea filled him with "abhorrence."[620] Others kept the idea alive: Talk of a crown to be forced on Washington was common gossip in some Philadelphia circles, but Washington just said no.[621] Discussion of a stronger government did not die, however, and every time Americans feared economic downturn, the talk resumed.

Economically during the five years after Yorktown, the United States faced simultaneous boom and bust. Those years were the centerpiece of a period of growth evident in the statistics for the years from 1775 to 1790, during which time Virginia's official population increased from 400,000 to almost 750,000, South Carolina's from 150,000 to 250,000, and Georgia's from 50,000 to 82,000. During this time, Southern states became populated far from the seashore, as settlers moved across the mountains. Population in the frontier areas also swelled. Kentucky, in 1775, had a population of 150 male colonists but no women, but by the 1790 census had nearly 75,000, with families rather than lone hunters predominating. Tennessee's settled population during those fifteen years increased from about 7,000 to well over 35,000. Northern states also saw some population growth in their westward parts, but there the big story was cities. Philadelphia's population increased from 30,000 to 42,000, New York's from 22,000 to 33,000, and Baltimore's from 6,000 to 14,000.[622]

In most of the country from 1781 through 1786, farming was on the increase. Tobacco exports grew as tobacco growing spread far into inland areas of South Carolina and Georgia and even into Tennessee and Kentucky.[623] Americans shipped more grain to Europe, as the South particularly stepped up its corn and wheat production. Alexandria, Virginia, became a great grain port.[624] Liberation from the British empire gave enterprising merchants new opportunities. Commerce with France and the French West Indies produced individual profits and a favorable balance of trade. American ships not only went to Holland and Sweden, they also opened up trade with China.

In the cities, jobs were plentiful, especially in the building trades. The *Pennsylvania Packet* reported that Philadelphia workmen built six hundred brick houses during the summer of 1784.[625] When George Washington that year attempted to find carpenters and masons to work on Mount Vernon, he was told that wages would be higher than he expected: Master builders, to gain workers, had to "agree to release a four years' [indentured] servant at the expiration of one year and a half."[626] Immigrants flocked to what they saw as a new world. The *Pennsylvania Gazette*, in July 1784, reported over fourteen hundred people's arriving in Philadelphia within a week, and noted that thousands more wanted to come.[627] Manufacturing increased, and newspapers regularly published reports of successes such as that of the Bridgewater, Connecticut, factory that produced "61,500 good tenpenny nails" before 9 a.m.[628]

But some occupations, particularly those that had been dependent on trade with the British, were depressed. The British colonies on the North American mainland and in the West Indies had enjoyed extensive trading, but London officials in 1783 declared that key American products could be shipped from the United States to the British West Indies only in ships built and owned by

British subjects. London officials, thinking they had taken revenge, soon were to claim that the declaration of 1783 preserved "the navigation and maritime importance of this country and strangled in the birth that of the United States." But because British mercantilist policy had artificially encouraged rice planting, without a subsidy, total rice exports for the five years beginning in 1782 were less than half what they had been in the five-year period before the war. Indigo also had been encouraged by British bounty, but without a prop the industry rapidly declined in the 1780s.[629]

Other postwar behaviors also created hardship. Residents of seaport cities went on a buying spree in 1783, with credit extended by French and Dutch merchants anxious to develop new customers. By the spring of 1784, markets were glutted and credit was overextended. The United States as a nation was also overextended, with loans taken out during the Revolution past due. As James Winthrop of Massachusetts delicately put it, "The embarrassments consequent upon a war, and the usual reduction of prices immediately after a war, neccessarily occasioned a want of punctuality in publick payments."[630] Meanwhile, rural New England also experienced hard times. Worn-out land became less productive, and some of the more enterprising individuals headed west and south. Worn-out farmers who stayed behind opposed the new requirements to pay taxes in money rather than in bartered goods.[631]

The severity of the economic crisis of 1784 and 1785 is still a matter of dispute—but in 1786 a sense of economic unease was evident.[632] Richard Henry Lee of Virginia, who opposed governmental centralization, wrote in that year that the war had "disturbed the course of commerce [and] introduced floods of paper money," and that the United States was "like a man just recovering from a severe fit of sickness."[633] Some, worried that the 1780s was becoming a decade of greed, saw the sickness only continuing: "Money is the only object attended to, and the only acquisition that commands respect," James Warren complained to John Adams.[634]

Amid economic unease, political embarrassments developed. The *Massachusetts Gazette* noted that state governments readily put down small outbreaks of lawlessness: "In Connecticut, the treason was restrained while it existed only in the forms of conspiracy. In Vermont, the conspirators assembled in arms, but were suppressed by the exertions of the militia, under the direction of their sheriffs.

In New Hampshire, the attack was made on the legislature, but the insurrection was in a very few hours suppressed, and has never been renewed."[635] But Shays' Rebellion, which disrupted Massachusetts court proceedings and even set Boston legislators quaking, was more troublesome.

The protest received its name through the actions of Captain Daniel Shays, formerly of the Continental Army, and others who began drilling as a military band: They were concerned primarily with hard-money laws and heavy taxes designed to pay off the state and national debt.[636] Fueled by declining land values and agricultural prices in rural Massachusetts, the protest swelled and may have involved as many as two thousand men (not over twelve thousand as General Henry Knox hysterically wrote to Washington).[637] The rebellion was readily put down once the governor of Massachusetts called out the militia to stifle it. Yet the uprising was I-told-you-so ammunition for British leaders and others who had predicted that a republican government would lead to anarchy. As George Washington worried in an October 1786 letter, Shays' Rebellion was "melancholy proof of what our trans-Atlantic foe has predicted."[638]

This became for Washington a continuing concern. Early in November 1786, he complained to Madison, "How melancholy is the reflection, that in so short a space, we should have made such large strides towards fulfilling the prediction of our trans-Atlantic foe! 'leave them to themselves, and their government will soon dissolve.'"[639] At the end of December he enunciated the same concern in a letter to Knox about "the disorders which have arisen in these States. Good God! who besides a tory could have foreseen, or a Briton predicted them! Were these people wiser than others, or did they judge of us from the corruption, and depravity of their own hearts?"[640] Washington concluded, "The latter I am persuaded was the case, and that notwithstanding the boasted virtue of America, we are far gone in every thing ignoble and bad."[641]

At many times during the Revolution it seemed that the American army had been held together by Washington's confidence. In 1786 and 1787, Washington's loss of confidence signalled the sinking of the Articles of Confederation. To a physician friend he wrote, "It is but the other day, that we were shedding our blood to obtain the Constitutions under which we now live; Constitutions of our own choice and making; and now we are unsheathing the sword to overturn them. The thing is so unaccountable, that I hardly know how to realize it, or to persuade myself that I am not under the illusion of a dream."[642] The accelerating disillusionment was even more evident in a letter to Knox in February, 1787: If three years ago "any person had told me that at this day, I should see such a formidable rebellion against the laws and constitutions of our own making as now appears I should have thought him a bedlamite, a fit subject for a mad house."[643]

James Madison also received firsthand knowledge of the changed mood of the man whose judgement Americans revered. In a March 1787 letter to Madison, Washington wrote, "My opinion of public virtue is so far changed that I have my doubts whether any system without the means of coercion in the Sovereign, will enforce Obedience to the Ordinances of a Genl. Government; without which, every thing else fails."[644] The *New York Journal* would argue later that year that radical political change was unnecessary: "The country is in profound peace, and we are not threatened by invasions from any quarter. The governments of the respective states are in the full exercise of their powers; and the lives, the liberty, and property of individuals are protected." But George Washington felt that something had to be done—and when Washington spoke, people listened.

Some were skeptical. One pamphleteer argued that "all the powers of rhetoric, and arts of description, are employed to paint the condition of this country in the most hideous and frightful colors"—although America, the writer insisted, was not in crisis.[645] But Richard Henry Lee noted that the summer of 1787 was a politically impatient one despite the improving economic situation: "Now the cry is power, give Congress power. Without reflecting that every free nation, that hath ever existed, has lost its liberty by the same rash impatience, and want of necessary caution." Lee argued that "we ought carefully to distinguish those which are merely the consequences of a severe and tedious war, from those which arise from defects in the federal system," but he observed that "people in general seem ready for anything."[646] When Washington joined the chorus for dramatic change, it swelled so fully that change was inevitable.

We Are Paying Off Our State Debt

The demand in 1787 was for change—but would it be incremental or radical? Evident economic improvement in 1787 provided ammunition for incrementalists.[647] "Industry and frugality are taking their station, and banishing from the community, idleness and prodigality," the *New York Journal* noted.[648] "Agriculture has been improved, manufactures multiplied, and trade prodigiously enlarged," James Winthrop wrote in the *Massachusetts Gazette.*[649] Many other writers also told of recovery, and Richard Henry Lee made the key point that governmental structure could not overcome human depravity: "It is more in vicious manners, than mistakes in form, that we must seek for the causes of the present discontent."[650]

The government under the Articles of Confederation was unable to deal with some mistakes in form, because any changes required unanamity. The American government clearly required limited powers to regulate trade; Boston's *Independent Chronicle* noted that "the important object of our commerce could be effected by a uniform navigation act, giving Congress full power to regulate the whole commerce of the States."[651] Although experience with British economic and political regulations had created an unwillingness to hand over significant power to members of a central government who were likely over time to develop a culture of abuse, at least two-thirds of the states supported federal regulation of interstate commerce.

A second correctable mistake in form concerned power to tax: the federal government under the Articles of Confederation had none. Decentralizers such as Luther Martin of Maryland and George Mason of Virginia, well aware of London's tax abuse, "candidly acknowledge[d] the inefficacy of the Confederation" but did not want to make the mistake of giving a central government unlimited powers. Instead, they proposed to "give the general government the power of demanding their quotas of the states, with an alternative of laying direct taxes in case of non-compliance."[652] Such a two-stage method avoided the establishment of a permanent federal tax-gathering bureaucracy that could become oppressive, and gave states a ready means to express disapproval of federal tax grabs. The method might err on the side of slowness, but it made overtaxation unlikely. Richard Henry Lee agreed with the two-step idea and suggested one additional protection: If state legislatures representing a majority of American citizens agreed that a taxing measure was improper, they could nullify it.[653] Lee, joined by James Monroe, also proposed requiring a super majority—two-thirds or even three-fourths—for any tax requisition.[654]

A third question about form also received attention: Did the Articles of Confederation make it impossible to deal with the national debt of $12 per capita? Congress clearly was slow in handling the matter: William Grayson, in 1787, noted that "public credit has suffered, and our public creditors have been ill used . . . owing to a fault at the head-quarters—to Congress themselves—in not selling the western lands at an earlier period."[655] By then, however, the Articles-of-Confederation government was rising to the task of privatizing public lands, with the goal of ending the debt crisis by selling 360 million acres of available, ungranted lands at a little over sixpence per acre.[656]

The state legislatures also deserved some blame for the slow repayment of the national debt, but by 1787 their behavior also had improved, as a report from New Hampshire noted: "We are paying off our state debt, and the interest on the domestic, as fast as Congress call[s] upon us for it."[657] That year Richard Henry Lee on the floor of Congress was pleased that the plan to privatize land to reduce the national debt was moving forward: "We have now something to sell that will pay the debt & discharge the greatest part of the Taxes. . . ."[658] Overall, James Winthrop could note accurately, in 1787, that "the publick debt has been very considerably reduced . . . Congress this year disposed of a large tract of their lands towards paying the principal of their debt . . . applications are continually making for purchases in our eastern and western lands."[659]

In short, radical centralization of power was unnecessary, but the central government clearly needed the power to regulate commerce and to make and enforce treaties. One writer concluded that power to regulate interstate commerce and to make treaties was "all that is wanting to render America as prosperous as it is in the power of any form of government to render her."[660] But how much power did the form of government have? In Boston, the *Independent Chronicle* wondered whether Americans were able to "distinguish between the evils that arise from extraneous causes and our private imprudencies, and those that arise from our government." The paper went on to say that if trade deficits resulted from the desire of Americans to consume more than they produced, "it does not appear that the embarrassments of our trade will be removed by the adoption of [a new] Constitution."[661] Maintenance of liberty and virtue required more than proper organizational form. An improved structure could be useful in the development of holy government, but holy people were essential.

Absolute and Uncontrollable Powers

Traditional historians tend to portray the Constitutional Convention first as a battle between the large states, with their "Virginia plan," and the small states, with their " New Jersey plan." Then, along comes the "great compromise," with the House of Representatives reflecting population and the Senate equality by state, and all go home happily. The New Jersey plan, however, focused on more than representation. For example, New York delegates Lansing and Yates favored the New Jersey plan not because they were enamoured of small states, but because it embodied the Articles of Confederation plus essential changes in form. Congress under that plan gained the right to regulate trade, to lay duties on imports, and to have a two-tier taxing mechanism that allowed Congress to make requisitions and collect directly if states balked. The New Jersey plan expanded other central powers also but strictly limited them. For example, the nation would have a supreme court, but one with a very narrow authority.

The Constitutional Convention quickly rejected changes such as these that would have dealt with the pressing problems of the day without opening up new problems for the future.[662] Historians offer a variety of reasons. Some—most famously Charles Beard—suggested that the Framers were driven by their own economic considerations, yet historians as critical of the Constitution as was Beard, but less conspiratorially inclined in their analysis, have shown that personal economic considerations among the founders tended to cancel out each other.[663] It is more likely that ideology trumped specific economic interests: Those who favored a stronger central government generally had their way, since, as French minister Louis Otto observed, the economic difficulties had "happily arisen" and given the centralizers "a pretext for innovation."[663]

But if the circumstances did not require radical innovation, and if personal economic interests were not key, why was the desire to innovate so great? Here is where examinations of the Constitutional Convention itself, or analyses of conditions in the 1780s, are by themselves inadequate: We need to think back on the history of the entire eighteenth century. The colonists had established dual governments that became duelling governments, but their creations were reactions to British corruption, not stand-alone systems. The framers, self-conscious as they were about constructing "a new order for the ages," wanted not the antithesis that the Articles of Confederation represented but a new synthesis. They saw the Articles as a new testament without the old, and they felt excited but organizationally inadequate.

The Articles of Confederation as they existed during the early 1780s, after all, violated the checks-and-balances wisdom that had grown throughout the century by having neither an independent executive nor an independent judiciary. The framers of the Constitution were successful in arguing that the preservation of liberty required the sharing of power by elements of monarchy (represented in the presidency), aristocracy (represented in a Senate elected by state legislatures), and democracy (represented in the House of Representatives): If one of the three major elements began to assert itself too greatly, the two others would be jealous enough for their own authority to force down the aggressor. In theory, the Supreme Court would also be on hand to adjudicate among the combatants for governance and make sure a potential dictator was stopped.

Other remembrances of things past also contributed to the decision to make the nation's capital a point of importance, a new London. With independence won, Americans had to face the reality of what the British had for years propagandized—"leave us and you're a nobody." Patrick Henry, who had already achieved much and was growing seventeen children, could be happy sitting "under his vine and fig tree." Statements and actions of young leaders such as Hamilton, however, make it evident that, once having played on national fields, they were not content with the provincialism to be found in state capitals.[665] Those who had grasped the Great-Awakening understanding—that there are no little places and no little people—could be happy gaming with the small stakes of local politics. Others, recalling the attractions and repulsions of London life, did not want to be kept down on the farm.

Mixed throughout the federalist calls for a stronger central government was the desire to make the country safe for ambition. The United States would never have a world-class capital if Congress insisted on keeping power in the states. No one publicly favored selling out the liberty obtained on the battlefield just to have a capital like all the other countries had—but those who could speak in the name of "We, the People of the United States," would have far more authority than those who followed state legislatures and could thus speak only in the terms Patrick Henry preferred: "We, the states." Richard Henry Lee accurately noted that big government partisans were excited by the prospects of a new empire: "The dazzling ideas of glory, wealth, and power uncontrolled, unfettered by popular opinions, are powerful to captivate the ambitious and the avaricious."[666]

Americans needed a compromise acceptable to both the Enlightenment and the Awakening sides of the revolutionary coalition. Ticklish problems emerged all along the way. For example, since state constitutions typically had a religious test for office, the Constitutional prohibition of a religious test for federal office worried some Christians. At the North Carolina ratifying convention, delegate Henry Abbot complained, "If here be no religious test required, pagans, deists, and Mahometans might obtain offices among us . . . senators and representatives might all be pagans."[667] But, most Christians from dissenting traditions accepted the prohibition, which freethinkers also obviously relished; Presbyterians, Congregationalists, and Baptists had just finished fighting a culture war against a corrupt Anglican church that required officeholders to swear fealty to it.

The Great Compromise of the Constitution, in other words, was not just between large and small states; it also papered over differences among members of the revolutionary coalition. The intentional elasticity of some of the writing portended problems. Skeptics such as Thomas B. Wait of the Maine district of Massachusetts complained: "There is a certain darkness, duplicity, and studied ambiguity of expression running through the whole Constitution. . . . As it now stands but very few individuals do or ever will understand it, consequently Congress will be its own interpreter."[668]

Studied ambiguity of expression was also a logical outcome of the double-mindedness that existed among the Constitution writers themselves. Madison and several other key framers, while influenced indirectly by the Great Awakening, did not accept all of its teaching. They wanted the hope for rapid societal progress that accompanied the Awakening, but they lacked confidence in the concept that personal holiness would lead to governmental improvement. Those who had absorbed Enlightenment ideas understood faction but may have underestimated sin. Envisioning a steady state of virtue and vice, they set up measures to preserve balance—but what if individuals like Sackville and Sandwich took power in America?[669] The Constitution, with its emphasis on checks and balances within the federal system is a masterpiece of construction—but did it plumb the depths of political depravity and protect liberty as well as a revised Articles of Confederation might have?

Madison was aware of the problem. He wrote in Federalist 57 that the chief guardian against oppression was "the vigilant and manly spirit which actuates the people of America—a spirit which nourishes freedom, and in return is nourished by it. If this spirit shall ever be so far debased as to tolerate a law not obligatory on the legislature, as well as on the people, the people will be prepared to tolerate anything but liberty."[670] Would it not have been wiser to guard against the decline of that spirit through decentralization? Madison did acknowledge in Federalist 44 that all could go wrong if the executive and judicial leaders allied themselves with usurpers of power, but he argued that in the last resort voters would provide the remedy by electing "more faithful representatives."[671] And yet, if virtue did decline, wouldn't a more centralized political system cement into power the vicious?

The incrementalists of 1787 asked Americans to enjoy their current situation. Americans, they argued, had both freedom of worship and freedom of commerce, with the ability to "purchase grain, bread, meat, and other necessities of life at as reasonable a rate as in any country. . . ."[672] But *as good* was not good enough for those who, having left the British empire behind, still wanted to be somebody. When Patrick Henry decided to oppose the Constitution, he said,

"Consider our situation, sir: go to the poor man, and ask him what he does, he will inform you that he enjoys the fruits of his labor, under his own fig-tree, with his wife and children around him, in peace and security."[673] For Henry, the risk/return ratio in investing in a new system of governance was too high. That in many ways was the key difference between Federalists and anti-Federalists who, aware that the postrevolutionary crisis was ending, became averse to risk throughout 1787 and 1788.

Richard Henry Lee was one not willing to take the risk. When he saw the Constitution he immediately was alarmed, and quickly expressed to George Mason his concern that "the greatness of the powers given, and the multitude of places to be created, produce a coalition of monarchy men, military men, aristocrats and drones"—exactly what the Revolution had been fought to avoid.[674] Lee, like John Brown of England a generation earlier, was concerned about licentiousness, but he considered a strong government more likely to "oppress and ruin the people" than to point the way toward virtue.[675] Lee did not oppose radical change, but wanted proof that it was needed: "Unless there be great and awful dangers, the change is dangerous, and the experiment ought not to be made. . . . It is not sufficient to feign mere imaginary dangers; there must be a dreadful reality. The great question between us is; Does that reality exist?"[676]

Lee's alternative to Madisonian checks and balances was a division of power not only within the nation's capital, but a division of states vs. center. He complained that "instead of seeing powers cautiously lodged in the hands of numerous legislators, and many magistrates, we see all important powers collecting in one centre, where a few men will possess them almost at discretion."[677] Lee urged those of the revolutionary generation not to depend on the character of their successors. "Good men will generally govern well with almost any constitution: but why in laying the foundation of the social system, need we unnecessarily leave a door open to improper regulations?"[678] He also argued that "we ought to give power to the union, so far only as experience and present circumstances shall direct, with a reasonable regard to time to come. Should future circumstances, contrary to our expectations, require that further powers be transferred to the union, we can do it far more easily than get back those we may now imprudently give."[679] Backers of the

Constitution were not dormant, of course, as bad reviews continued to emerge. James Madison, Alexander Hamilton, and John Jay used the pseudonym "Publius" to pen the newspaper columns that became known as *The Federalist Papers*. In them they insisted that the Constitution's complex set of mechanisms would allow needed federal action but prevent dictatorship. For example, the president would be selected by electors appointed according to the will of the state legislators, and senators would be elected by state legislators: Both mechanisms were a way of preserving state authority. Madison even predicted (in Federalist 45) that "the State governments will have the advantage of the federal government," because "without the intervention of the State legislatures, the President of the United States cannot be elected at all. They must in all cases have a great share in his appointment, and will, perhaps, in most cases, of themselves determine it. The Senate will be elected absolutely and exclusively by the State legislatures."[680]

Madison contended that "each of the principal branches of the federal government will owe its existence more or less to the favor of the State governments, and must consequently feel a dependence, which is much more likely to beget a disposition too obsequious than too overbearing towards them."[681] That prediction eventually proved inaccurate. In Federalist 57 Madison described with similar enthusiasm a protection against the possibility of oppression by the House of Representatives: "They can make no law which will not have its full operation on themselves and their friends, as well as on the great mass of the society." [682] That and many other Madisonian expectations were destroyed in the 20th century by lust for power.[683]

Anti-Federalists anticipated the drive for more democracy and argued that centralization over time would lead to more centralization. For this, Hamilton ridiculed them, contending in Federalist 31 that his opponents were not those who saw the consequences of certain actions, but were those who were controlled by phobias: "The moment we launch into conjectures about the usurpations of the federal government, we get into an unfathomable abyss and fairly put ourselves out of the reach of all reasoning." Hamilton claimed that anti-Federalist brains were "bewildered amidst the labyrinths of an enchanted castle . . . [they] imagine an endless train of possible dangers [through] an excess of jealousy and timidity."[684]

Yet, it is history, not imagination, that shows how power that is there for the grabbing will be grabbed. Hamilton's most articulate journalistic opponent, "Brutus," went through the logic. First, "This [new] government is to possess absolute and uncontrollable powers, legislative, executive and judicial, with respect to every object to which it extends."[685] Second, federal officials "may so exercise this power as entirely to annihilate all the State governments, and reduce this country to one single government." Third, history suggested extreme wariness: It is the "naturally unerring experience of ages, that every man, and every body of men, invested with power, are ever disposed to increase it, and to acquire a superiority over everything that stands in their way." Fourth, knowledge of humanity and history allows for a firm prediction: "This disposition, which is implanted in human nature, will operate in the Federal legislature to lesson and ultimately to subvert the State authority."[686]

Certain specific applications arose from these general historical understandings. Richard Henry Lee proposed strict limitations on the federal government's power to tax: If stringent limits were not in place, not only would tax rates tend to become oppressive, but "to lay and collect taxes, in this extensive country, must require a great number of congressional ordinances, immediately operating upon the body of the people; these must continually interfere with the state laws, and thereby produce disorder and general dissatisfaction."[687] Federal officials, Lee predicted, would pass laws to increase the number of those dependent on them: "Should the general government think it politic, as some administration (if not all) probably will, to look for a support in a system of influence, the government will take every occasion to multiply laws, and officers to execute them, considering these as so many necessary props for its own support."[688]

Although Lee thought it "not probable that any prudent congress will attempt to lay and collect internal taxes, especially direct taxes, [the power] might be abused by imprudent and designing men." His Virginian colleague George Mason had no doubt that the broad tax power, "being at discretion, unconfined, and without any kind of control, must carry every thing before it."[689] And New York's George Clinton pointed out the repercussions: Although "there are politicians who believe that you should be loaded with taxes, in order to make you industrious . . . what can inspire you with industry, if the greatest measure of your labors are to be swallowed up in taxes?" Clinton even laid out a supply-side theory, with higher taxes leading to reduced governmental revenues: "If heavy duties are laid on merchandise, . . . the price of the commodities . . . must be increased; the consumers will be fewer; the merchants must import less; trade will languish, and this source of revenue in a great measure will be dried up."[690]

Along with predictions of high taxation came a concern with judiciary powers that, in Elbridge Gerry's words, had "no well defined limits" and were "left as a boundless ocean."[691] George Mason argued that federal courts would "absorb and destroy the judiciaries of the several states; thereby rendering laws as tedious, intricate, and expensive, and justice as unattainable by a great part of the community, as in England."[692] An anonymous essayist offered a prescient prediction of federal judges and federal legislators cooperating for the aggrandizement of both: "As the general government acquires power and jurisdiction, by the liberal construction which the judges may give the constitution, those of the states will lose their rights, until they become so trifling and unimportant, as not to be worth having."[693]

Some observers also doubted the adequacy of bicameralism, arguing that the two houses of the legislature would be made up of "men having similar interests and views, feelings and connections. . . . The partitions between the two branches will be merely those of the building in which they sit."[694] But restrictions on taxing power would help, and so would the limitation that colony after colony had adopted: rotation in office. A Massachusetts writer complained that lack of term limits could mean "office in the same hands for life."[695] Elbridge Gerry, who as a last resort later shook up the political system with audacious "gerrymandering," also complained that "there is no provision for a rotation . . . By this neglect we lose the advantages of that check to the overbearing insolence of office. . . ."[696] The omission was glaring: Continental army officer William Findley worried that "Rotation, that noble prerogative of liberty, is entirely excluded from the new system of government."[697]

George Mason was among those who foresaw the development of what today is called a Beltway mentality: "Those gentlemen, who will be elected senators, will fix themselves in the federal town, and become citizens of that town more than of our state."[698] The solution was clear: term limits, in line with the rotation principle that would not permanently exclude talent and experience from office, but would allow "a man who has served four years in congress to return home, mix with the people, and reside some time with them. This will tend to reinstate him in the interests, feelings, and views similar to theirs, and thereby confirm in him the essential qualifications of a legislator."[699] Twelve years was the maximum time in office usually proposed.[700]

The common denominator of these suggestions was Madison plus: checks and balances, yes, but extended out to the states. Antifederalists argued that the best checks and balances came not by strengthening the federal government with the hope that parts of it would fight against each other; instead, "Infuse new strength and spirit into the state governments; for, when the component parts are strong, it will give energy to the government although it be otherwise weak. . . ."[701] In Pennsylvania, Samuel Bryan took on the charge that a strong state system would lead to a "split into separate confederacies or republics, that might become rival powers and consequently liable to mutual wars from the usual motives of contention."[702] Bryan argued that the threat of impending separation was a "hobgoblin . . . sprung from the deranged brain of *Publius*, [who has] with herculean labor accumulated myriads of unmeaning sentences, and mechanically endeavored to force conviction by a torrent of misplaced words. . . ."[703]

Power to Perpetuate the Worst of Mischiefs

The torrents came out in the newspaper debates (the appendix to this volume, "Soundbites from the 1780s for the 1990s," includes many press quotations) and during the state ratifying conventions. At the South Carolina convention, for example, James Lincoln asked, "What is liberty? The power of governing yourselves. If you adopt this Constitution, have you this power? No: you give it into the hands of a set of men who live one thousand miles distant from you. Let the people but once trust their liberties out of their own hands, and what will be the consequence? First, haughty, imperious aristocracy; and ultimately, a tyrannical monarchy." [704]

Dissenters from Pennsylvania's ratification of the Constitution similarly worried that "the powers of Congress under the new constitution are complete and unlimited over the purse and the sword, and are perfectly independent of and supreme over the state governments, whose intervention in these great points is entirely destroyed." Looking down the road, the dissenters predicted that federal power "must necessarily annihilate and absorb the legislative, executive, and judicial powers of the several States, and produce from their ruins one consolidated government." That government, the Pennsylvanians predicted, will "multiply officers in every department; judges, collectors, taxgatherers, excisemen and the whole host of revenue officers, will swarm over the land, devouring the hard earnings of the industrious—like the locusts of old, impoverishing, and desolating all before them." [705]

The decisive battle came in Massachusetts. Many respected leaders—Samuel Adams, Elbridge Gerry, James Warren, and others—opposed the Constitution, and as the state convention opened in January, 1788, anti-Federalists clearly were in the majority.[706] The turning point was the Federalists' offering of a resolution to ratify, but with a strong recommendation that the new government immediately adopt a list of proposed amendments. A Dutch observer, P. J. van Berckel, wrote that the Constitution "would have been absolutely rejected in Massachusetts had not [John Hancock] proposed some changes whereby the rights of the people are more precisely stipulated and insured."[707]

Van Berckel added his observation that the changes were mostly cosmetic—"The Federalists consider these changes as merely pro forma and stand them in the wind"—but they did the job, and Massachusetts ratified the constitution.[708] When Madison wrote to Washington about "the favorable result of the Convention at Boston," he commented that "the Amendments are a blemish, but are in the least offensive form."[709] Federalists then came to the Virginia ratifying convention with momentum and a strategy: ratify now, with the promise of rights-guaranteeing amendments later.

At the convention particular issues, such as control over western lands, were less significant than the overall question: Given the danger of governmental centralization but the advantages as well, what risk/return ratio was acceptable?[710] George Mason was conservative: "Gentlemen may talk of public virtue and confidence; we shall be told that the House of Representatives will consist of the most virtuous men on the continent, and that in their hands we may trust our dearest rights. This, like all other assemblies, will be composed of some bad and some good men; and, considering the natural lust of power so inherent in man, I fear the thirst of power will prevail to oppress the people."[711] James Monroe spoke of "how prone all human institutions have been to decay; how subject the best-formed and most wisely organized governments have been to lose their checks and totally dissolve; how difficult it has been for mankind, in all ages and countries, to preserve their dearest rights and best privileges, impelled as it were by an irresistible fate of despotism."[712]

The ratifying convention was Patrick Henry's last major effort as a great orator, and he gave it all he had. The Constitution will work if leaders "shall be honest," he said, but it also gave them "power to perpetrate the worst of mischiefs, should they be bad men . . . [a president of] ambition and abilities, how easy is it for him to render himself absolute."[713] Like Samuel in the Old Testament, Henry warned against copying other nations: "Shall we imitate the example of those nations who have gone from a simple to a splendid government? . . . If we admit this consolidated government, it will be because we like a great, splendid one. Some way or other we must be a great and mighty empire; we must have an army, and a navy, and a number of things."[714]

The ratifying-convention Federalists, however, muted the effect of Henry's trumpet calls by promising a careful look at amendments once Congress convened. Most of the amendments suggested by the Virginian ratifiers found their way into the Bill of Rights, but other restrictions on federal power did not. For example, Monroe's last short argument in the convention was, "to render the system under consideration safe and proper I would take from it one power only—I mean that of direct taxation."[715] The third of Virginia's proposed amendments to the Constitution read,

> When the Congress shall lay direct taxes or excises, they shall immediately inform the executive powers of each state, of the quota of such state, according to the census herein directed, which is proposed to be thereby raised; and if the legislature of any state shall pass a law which shall be effectual for raising such quota at the time required by Congress, the taxes and excises laid by Congress shall not be collected in such state.[716]

That amendment did not make it past the first Congress.

The process was similar at the New York ratifying convention, where anti-Federalists were discouraged by the news that Virginia had ratified. Delegate Melancton Smith warned that "this is an extensive country, increasing in population and growing in consequence. Very many lucrative offices will be in the grant of the government, which will be objects of avarice and ambition. How easy will it be to gain over a sufficient number, in the bestowment of offices, to promote the views and the purposes of those who grant them!"[717] But the promise of protective amendments down the road again was sufficient to garner enough delegates to ratify. When delegate Gilbert Livingston tried to insert a clause for rotation of office—"no person shall be eligible as a senator for more than six years in any term of twelve years"—the delegates, advised to give straight assent to the document as written, went with what they had.[718]

The votes in the key states were close—Massachusetts ratified 187 to 168, Virginia 89 to 79, and New York 30 to 27. What made the difference at the margin? Clearly, younger delegates accepted more risk than those with greater experience: It has become conventional among historians to note the division between generations, with the leaders from the 1765-75 period opposed to centralized government and those who came of age during the war, when disintegration seemed likely, inclined to just say yes. Also, the immediate risks were less than the long-term ones: Patrick Henry emphasized "latent consequences" and pointed down the road—"who knows the dangers that this new system may produce?"—but many delegates focused on the immediate benefits of a new system.[719] Clearly, the tactic of accepting amendment recommendations for later considerations gained crucial votes. [720]

Crucially, Federalists succeeded in neutralizing objections from dissenters who were suspicious of centralization. Some Presbyterians and Baptists in the Shenandoah Valley, for example, favored the Constitution because they believed that a promised amendment would guarantee religious liberty; one historian calls this "an all-important factor" in Virginia's ratification.[721] Crucially, many Presbyterians who had revolted against the British did not follow the calls of Samuel Adams and Patrick Henry to oppose the

Constitution; at the Pennsylvania state ratifying convention, Presbyterians were evenly divided.[722] Baptists in back-country South Carolina, North Carolina, Pennsylvania, and New York tended to oppose the Constitution, but others who worried about a powerful central government were more concerned about the possibility of majoritarian religious pressure in their states; since the federal government would not apply religious tests, they swung to its support.[723]

And above all, there was the position of the trusted leader whom everyone knew would be the first president. Washington—who had seen his army barely survive under a weak government during the Revolution—was the key to the entire process of Constitution making; as James Monroe later wrote to Jefferson, "Be assured, his influence carried this government."[724] Virginian legislator William Grayson similarly proclaimed that "were it not for one great character in America, so many would not be for this government."[725]

Washington's presence influenced not only adoption of a new document but the document itself: Pierce Butler of Georgia wrote in one letter that the presidency would not have been given powers so extensive "had not many of the members cast their ideas towards General Washington as President; and shaped their Ideas of the Powers to be given to a President, by their opinions of his Virtue."[726] Yet, one Massachusetts convention delegate, Nathaniel Barrell, looked down the road: He thought it likely that "exalted, amiable characters as the great Washington" would be "faithful guardians of our liberties," but asked, "What assurance can we have . . . that their successors will be such?" Americans could not have found a better leader than Washington, but he was mortal.

CHAPTER EIGHT

Tempests to Come

The governing structure was not the only structure that had to be rethought following the Revolution. In the majority of colonies where the Anglican church had been established or propped up by governmental favor, and in New England where Congregationalism dominated, the structure of organized religion, which also meant the structure of organized charity and education, was up for debate. Some states had moved toward a multiple establishment during the Revolution, and others during the early 1780s had agreed that while no particular denomination should be established, religious belief was a public-policy concern. For example, the New Hampshire constitution of 1784 noted that "Morality and piety, rightly grounded on evangelical principles, will give the best and greatest security to government, and will lay in the hearts of men the strongest obligations to due subjection . . . knowledge of these [principles] is most likely to be propagated through a society by the institution of the public worship of the Deity and of public instruction in morality and religion. . . ."[727]

The key debate on church-state cooperation came in Virginia. The jailing of some Baptist ministers in 1774 had infuriated James Madison, then twenty-two years old. He condemned the "diabolic, hell-conceived principle of persecution."[728] Such experience with governmental abuse of powers led to skepticism among Madison and others not only concerning the establishment of a particular denomination, but even the establishment of Christianity generally. Virginia, during the Revolution, disestablished Anglicanism and wavered between a multiple establishment and complete disestablishment.[729] As soon as the land was at peace, Patrick Henry offered a Bill Establishing a Provision for Teachers of the Christian Religion; the bill declared Christianity to be "the established Religion of this Commonwealth" and proposed a property tax for support of Christian ministers and teachers.[730]

The bill proposed that "all Denominations of Christians demeaning themselves peaceably and faithfully shall enjoy equal privileges." Each person who paid the tax could name the religious society to which he dedicated the tax. If the taxpayer did not designate a particular organization, the tax would be applied to the maintenance of a county school.[731] Multiple establishment had broad support from Virginian leaders such as George Washington and John Marshall, who both understood the social usefulness of biblical religion (whether or not its truth claims were acknowledged). George Mason, later known as the moving force behind the First Amendment, also spoke for the bill, noting the public interest in supporting religious teaching, since "justice and virtue are the vital principles of republican government. . . ."[732] Jefferson opposed the bill, but his deism was a known commodity and his opposition expected.

The critical role was played by Madison, who referred frequently to the persecution of Baptists and attacked the bill as bad precedent that could lead once again to denominational monopoly.[733] In one letter to Jefferson, Madison called the bill "chiefly obnoxious on account of its dishonorable principle and dangerous tendency." The dishonorable principle was that religion benefits from state support. Madison argued, as did the Baptists, that "religion flourishes in greater purity, without than with the aid of Government."[734] Madison called multiple establishment at the state level "dangerous," but in *The Federalist Papers* he argued: that security of religious rights depends on a multiplicity of sects, and that a multiplicity at the national level secures religious rights even if states establish denominations (provided that different states establish different denominations). There was thus less to fear in a state level multiple establishment—but Madison, determined to end all establishments, pushed ahead. Through clever legislative strategy, Madison was able to delay voting on the bill until 1785, by which time Patrick Henry was governor once more, with his rhetorical skills removed from the assembly debate.[735]

What proved equally critical was the coalition that formed among pietistic Christians such as Baptists, who wanted separation from society; deists and "freethinkers," who wanted to knock Christianity off its social pedestal; and low-taxers, who suggested that a general assessment would lead some Virginians to leave the state and other potential settlers not to come.[736] Madison ably handled the public agitation through the use of "remonstrances" and petitions, and then with great facility shepherded through the legislature a bill for total disestablishment. That became the Virginia model, and within the next several decades all states would adopt it in preference to multiple establishment, with long-term effects that may be appearing only now.

An immediate effect, however, was a change in many modes of aid to the poor. Charity in Anglican states such as Virginia had largely been in the hands of church vestrymen, who served a semi-official function. Following disestablishment, the idea of handling charitable needs through voluntary organizations—nonchurch, but often parachurch—began to spread, and America was on the way to becoming what Alexis de Tocqueville in the 1830s called a nation of associations.[737] The idea was to attack problems not by governmental paternalism or coercive action but by genuine compassion based on a personal involvement that stressed both spiritual challenge and material help.

The last decade of the century displayed many examples of such neighborliness. In 1791, for example, some residents of New York needed health care and could not afford it, so Christian volunteers there set up the New York Dispensary to care for the sick poor. Some residents of Massachusetts, in 1794, saw their homes burned down, so the Massachusetts Charitable Fire Society launched its work of "relieving such as suffer by fire." In 1797, ministers in several cities preached about children at risk, and volunteers formed the Society for the Relief of Poor Widows with Small Children. Soon, hundreds of similar organizations, a so-called benevolent empire, were successfully presenting the alternative to British imperial welfare.[738]

Late in the century there also was movement on a desperate problem that had plagued thoughtful Americans throughout the century: slavery. John Jay of New York, wrestling with attempts to reconcile Christianity and slavery, proposed during the peace negotiations in 1783 that Great Britain and the United States jointly adopt measures against the "diabolical institution." That idea was stillborn, but when Jay returned to America, he and several others, in 1785, organized the New York Society for Promoting the Manumission of Slaves; Jay, the society's first president, proposed that "all our inhabitants of every color and denomination shall be free and equal partakers of our political liberty."[739]

Many plans for gradual liberation were afoot in America during the last two decades of the century. For example, John Witherspoon chaired a committee on the abolition of slavery in New Jersey and proposed that all slaves be freed when they reached the age of twenty-eight. When Jay was governor in 1799, New York passed a law for the gradual abolition of slavery: All children born of slave parents after July fourth of that year were declared free but were subject to apprenticeship. Exportation of slaves from New York also was forbidden.[740] Many Christians supported gradual abolitionism not because owning a slave was necessarily a sin—the Bible does not ban all modes of slavery—but because the institution of slavery tended to be specially productive of sin and therefore was to be avoided and abolished when possible.[741]

Since such a position did not demonize slaveholders, moderates could join with radicals in moves to contain and eventually end the institution. Laws like that of New York spread through the north, and the Northwest Territory maintained its no-slavery status. Even more crucially, blacks were receiving theological liberation. Richard Allen, one of the early black church leaders, was born as a slave in 1760 and converted to Christianity in 1777 while working on a plantation in Delaware. Allen's master allowed him to do extra work for pay, and Allen saved enough to purchase his freedom. In 1786, he arrived in Philadelphia and "saw a large field open in seeking and instructing my African brethren, who had been a long forgotten people and few of them attended public worship. . . . I frequently preached twice a day, at 5 o'clock in the morning and in the evening, and it was not uncommon for me to preach from four to five times a day."[742] Allen cofounded the Free African Society, a fraternal organization that provided material aid and spiritual help to Philadelphia blacks, and in 1793 established the Bethel Church for Negro Methodists.[743]

In the South, some whites taught slaves to read, opened up the Bible to them, and helped them establish churches. White Georgians helped Andrew Bryan, a slave in Savannah, to be ordained and installed as the organizing minister of a black church there. After other white Georgians imprisoned and whipped Bryan and members of his congregation, Bryan's master helped him reestablish the congregation in a barn on his plantation, and there the church meetings flourished. At the end of the century, the congregation numbered seven hundred, and Bryan reported that they were "worshipping in our families and preaching every Lord's day, baptizing frequently from ten to thirty at a time in the Savannah [River] and administering the sacred supper, not only without molestation, but in the presence, and with the approbation and encouragement of many of the white people."[744] At the same time, however, the absence of a southern legal breakthrough laid the foundation for a century of stagnation and sorrow.

Feeble and Doubtful Words

Even though the Constitution had been adopted, decisions about governance still had to be made. Soon after seeing a draft of the Constitution in 1787, Lee had written that "in its present state, unamended, the adoption of it will put Civil Liberty and the happiness of the people at the mercy of Rulers who may possess the great unguarded powers given. . . ."[745] Many of those who approved the Constitution did so on the basis of pledges that amendments to protect against governmental tyranny would be added, but Lee, in a letter to Samuel Adams, was skeptical: Federal authorities would have "the power of judging what shall be for the general welfare," with the decisions of such judges becoming "the supreme Law of the Land."[746]

Samuel Adams agreed. As the new government was organizing itself in 1789, Adams predicted to Lee that a combination of mistakes ("the weakness of the human Mind often discovered even in the wisest and best of Men") and malice ("the perverseness of the interested, and designing") would lead to "misconstructions" of the

Constitution that "would disappoint the Views and expectations of the honest among those who acceded to it, and hazard the Liberty, Independence and Happiness of the People." Adams was "particularly afraid that unless great care should be taken to prevent it, the Constitution in the Administration of it would gradually, but swiftly and imperceptibly run into a consolidated Government pervading and legislating through all the States."[747]

Adams asked Lee, elected to the first Senate, to persevere in the amendment process as a way of stopping the greatest mischief. Lee did, despite his realization that the Bill of Rights would be at the mercy of the Supreme Court. "So much for the propriety of a Bill of Rights as a necessary bottom to this new system," Lee sniffed. "It is in vain to say that the defects in this new Constitution may be remedied by the Legislature created by it."[748] But he still fought on to provide whatever remedies he could, and was shocked to find amendments written not for clarity but for purposeful ambiguity so that members of the first Congress could satisfy constituents of different minds. "The English language has been carefully culled to find words feeble in their nature or doubtful in their meaning," Lee complained.[749]

The writing of the First Amendment is an example. Madison, early in the process, proposed that, "The civil rights of none shall be abridged on account of religious belief or worship, nor shall any national religion be established, nor shall the full and equal rights of conscience be in any manner, or any pretext, abridged."[750] That wording was challenged by those who feared that "a support of ministers or building of places of worship might be construed [by courts] into a religious establishment," and by those who wanted assurance that state and local aid to religion would not be banned.[751] Madison replied that the crux of the amendment was the prohibition on national establishment: "He thought if the word 'national' was introduced it would point the amendment directly to the object it was intended to prevent."[752]

Madison assured members that the amendment's language would not cut off government from support of religion generally. The amendment was needed, he said, because "the people feared one sect might obtain a preeminence, or two combine together and establish a religion to which they would compel others to conform."[753] His assurances notwithstanding, the legislative battle focused on questions of whether state and federal governments could directly support religion. Senators shot down an attempt to ban state and local action, and instead stated that Congress would "make no law establishing articles of faith or a mode of worship or prohibiting the free exercise of religion."

That wording suggested that the federal government could financially support churches and church schools.[754] The House of Representatives, however, went for a proposal introduced by Representative Samuel Livermore of New Hampshire, wherein residents paid town taxes to support churches. Congress was to make "no laws touching religion, or infringing the rights of conscience." Restrictions on laws touching religion were to apply to Congress only; Livermore wanted to insure that Congress would not interfere with local and state denominational support.[755]

The final draft, prepared by a conference committee that Madison chaired, was neither Livermore's outright ban on any Congressional legislation's touching religion, nor the Senate's specific enumeration. Instead, the compromise wording read, "Congress shall make no law respecting an establishment of religion or prohibiting the free exercise thereof." In the language of the time, *establishment* meant requiring allegiance or giving financial support to one particular denomination's articles of faith or mode of worship; future generations of judges made accidental or deliberate misinterpretations. (Students today make a simpler misinterpretation by thinking that *respecting* means "honoring" rather than "concerning.")

One determination did seem clear at the time: The Senate rejected Madison's last-ditch attempt through the conference committee to insert a prohibition on state-level support of religion.[756] The Revolutionary coalition was still powerful enough to combine subsidy of religion with an unwillingness to establish any particular denomination nationwide. A strong religious presence without a government-supported denomination was an oddball concept in London, but in America the rejection of denominational establishment became an important way of promoting religion and its evident social benefits without threatening freedom. As Supreme Court justice Joseph Story wrote in 1833, the First Amendment allowed "Christianity . . . to receive encouragement from the state, so far as was not incompatible with the private rights of conscience, and the freedom of religious worship."[757]

Some other amendments also would receive 20th century twisting. For example, the Tenth Amendment was a key reiteration of the common understanding: "The powers not delegated to the United States by the Constitution, nor prohibited by it to the States, are reserved to the States respectively, or to the people." The Tenth Amendment was—and is, or should be—a clear restraint on federal power. But, if "we the people" rather than "we the states" were the constituents of a central government whose task was to "promote the general welfare," and if Congress was given many powers and then allowed "to make all laws which shall be necessary and proper" for the task, could not ambitious schemers extend their influence by arguing that the central government had elastic powers, and that "the people" might assign it more, regardless of the wishes of state legislatures?

Lee publicly expressed disappointment with the constitutional amendments: "It is impossible for us not to see the necessary tendency to consolidated empire in the natural operation of the Constitution, if no further amended than now proposed."[758] In a letter to his brother Francis Lightfoot, he predicted that the federal government would come under the control of the north, and that the result would be dire: "It is very clear, I think, that a government very different from a free one will take place e'er many years [have] passed."[759] The First Amendment did not reduce the theological concerns of some Christians. Many, while noting the omission of God from the Preamble, assumed that the Constitution was not an original contract among individuals but a derivative compact among the states, one that assumed the sovereignty of God and was based on previous, explicitly theistic compacts. However, two small Presbyterian groups, the Associated Church and the Reformed Presbyterian Church, opposed the Constitution and asked that it be amended to make the assumed explicit. It was not.[760]

Optimists took heart in the Constitution's emphasis on federal governmental restraint rather than empowerment—the Constitution made twenty grants of authority to Congress but put in place seventy restraints. The optimists argued that the Constitution was the pact that would help the country survive. The alternatives, they argued, were dictatorship or foreign takeover.

They expressed concern over the general-welfare clause but saw it as designed to help all citizens generally. They saw a distinction between general welfare and individual, class, or ethnic-group welfare.[761] Furthermore, while the Constitution established a government to *provide for* the common defense, that same government would only *promote* the general welfare: They trusted that constitutional government would suggest, not command.

For the time being, the safety of the young republic depended on the self-restraint of those in power. When George Washington, early in his first term, was taken ill with pneumonia, and—according to Jefferson's account—"pronounced by two of the three physicians present to be in the act of death," Jefferson was "in total despair." He wrote to a friend, "You cannot conceive of the public alarm on this occasion. It proves how much depends on his life."[762] Providentially, Washington recovered, and he continued to prove his trustworthiness and his desire to retain honor rather than to heap honors on himself.

It was good for the country that Washington was president and that he recovered. Vice President John Adams was trustworthy, but prone to take offense and often tactless. Furthermore, while Washington was every inch a president, Adams' rotundity made him look like a chipmunk rather than a lion: One vituperative journalist described Adams as "that strange compound of ignorance and ferocity, of deceit and weakness, [with] neither the force and firmness of a man, nor the gentleness and sensibility of a woman."[763] Adams also had the disadvantage, in the Jeffersonians' eyes, of being a New Englander. People from that section of the country, according to Jefferson in 1798, had "such a perversity of character" that they are bound to create a "reign of witches."[764]

Secretary of the Treasury Alexander Hamilton, another possible replacement for Washington, was rumored to be a monarchist and an Anglophile. He was certainly a centralist, having called for state governors to be appointed by the federal government, and to be given an absolute veto on all actions of the state legislature. In his one speech to the Constitutional Convention, Hamilton (according to Madison's notes) had called the states "not necessary" and had said that "if they were extinguished, he was persuaded that a great economy might be obtained."[765] The financial proposals that Hamilton made to Congress in three papers during 1790 and 1791 called for heavy governmental regulation of business, higher taxes, and substantial governmental spending. None of this made him acceptable to those who had fought for liberty.

Secretary of State Jefferson, a third possible presidential replacement, attracted supporters through his vivid attacks on Europe. He said he "wished that this country was separated from Europe by an ocean of fire." But Jefferson repelled many of those who understood that a virtuous society could not be founded on man's reason alone; without a fixed compass, Jefferson was brilliant but inconsistent.[766]

Washington, on the other hand, had "bottom," to use an eighteenth-century expression: He was steady. Washington fought against dictatorial London and its Tories in the 1770s, and he opposed dictatorial Paris and its American leftist lobbying groups ("Democratic Societies") in the 1790s. Jefferson largely wrote his own material and Washington at times made use of talented ghostwriters, but while Jefferson's letters over the years wavered in their views, Washington's showed a coherent vision that did not vary as his counselors and assistants changed.[767]

It was also good for the young United States that the American with as much renown as Washington, Benjamin Franklin, was not president. Franklin was consistent in a different way. Franklin's son William was born out of wedlock, as was William's son, William Temple Franklin. The latter, while living with his grandfather Ben in France, committed adultery with a neighbor's wife, so *his* son was illegitimate also. As Franklin received news of the illegitimate son of the illegitimate son of his own illegitimate son, he might have seen that the sins were visited unto the fourth generation—but Franklin never accepted the Christian concept of sin. George Whitefield, the Calvinist revivalist, had seen "mere morality" as damning. Franklin had tried to set up a method by which mortals could work to become moral on their own recognizance. His own family showed what worked and what did not.

For all his proverbial understanding, Franklin never gained theological wisdom. When John Jay and Franklin, in 1783, were meeting with British officials in Paris to negotiate American independence, Mr. and Mrs. Jay lived at Franklin's house in the Parisian suburb of Passy and spent many evenings with him, not always happily. Jay, trying to be a good guest, developed several strategies to avoid verbal blows with his host. For example, when

Franklin began to discuss the Bible in his typically irreverent way, Jay asked him to play the harmonica.[768] (Franklin played poorly but in this realm, as in others, he had high self-esteem.)

Franklin did make a famous call for prayer at the Constitutional Convention that would appear to suggest theistic faith, but Franklin's writings suggest not belief in God but belief in prayer as a social glue capable of relieving tension within troubled meetings; such an attitude was common among deistic instrumentalists. Franklin repeatedly in his writings emphasized the usefulness of religion for influencing "weak and ignorant Men and Women."[769] But Franklin, though he wavered at times, never deviated from his young man's faith in himself and in a god created after his own image.

There was one other consistency in Franklin's life: He always asserted his independence from man or God. While a young man, he demonstrated his determination to succeed as a printer (in a six thousand-inhabitant Philadelphia that already had five printers) by taking a porridge bowl, filling it with sawdust, stirring in a little water, and then eating the mixture.[770] As an old man, he apparently continued to trust in his dry deism even as Christian colleagues proposed to him a much more savory feast.[771] Franklin died in 1792, before he could see what the radical ideas he played with had wrought in the Paris he loved.

From 1792 through 1794, French revolutionaries progressed rapidly: Having dethroned a king they decapitated him, and then did the same to each other.[772] The French reign of terror provoked varied reactions among Americans. Jefferson was apologetic, but some of his Francophile followers glibly accepted guillotining in a supposedly good cause. French customs remained popular among radicals, who considered salutations such as "sir" or "madam" aristocratic, and so substituted "citizen" and "citess."[773] In 1793, the Democratic Society of Pennsylvania, with Benjamin Franklin Bache (another Franklin grandson) the first name on its list of Corresponding Committee members, issued a proclamation that praised "the successive Revolutions of America and France."[774]

In Paris there was terror; in Pennsylvania the Francophiles toasted a new order. On both sides of the Atlantic, revolutionaries hurled invective at anyone who got in their way. When Washington, informed by Lafayette of what was transpiring, became an opponent of the French Revolution, American poet and journalist Philip Freneau compared George Washington to a crocodile and a hyena. Freneau wrote that the President was "lulled by an opiate of sycophancy," and implied that a guillotine might end Washington's "temporary" presidency. Other editors of the Left reprinted Tory-forged letters from the American Revolution that portrayed Washington as the seducer of his own servants.

The attacks got to a man who cared deeply about his reputation for personal honor and civic virtue: Washington hated being written about "in such exaggerated and indecent terms as could scarcely be applied to a Nero or a notorious defaulter or even a common pickpocket. . . . I would rather be in my grave than in this place. I would rather live out my days on the farm than be emperor of the world!"[775] Even as Washington voluntarily left the presidency in 1797, proving to even the most rabid that he did not aspire to dictatorship, the radical beat—and the verbal beating—went on: Pro-French newspaper editors attacked Washington's "farce of disinterestedness" and predicted that "posterity will in vain search for the monuments of wisdom in your administration." Thomas Paine called Washington "the patron of fraud . . . treacherous . . . a hypocrite."[776] Celebrating the day Washington left office, Benjamin Franklin Bache wrote that Washington, "the source of all the misfortunes of our country, is this day reduced to a level with his fellow citizens and is no longer possessed of power to multiply evils . . . the name of Washington from this day ceases to give a currency to political iniquity and to legalize corruption."[777]

Such invective was the tip of an iceberg that seemed to be thickening during the mid-1790s. French ideas were spreading—and to some, the world seemed to be coming to an end. Publications reported rampant deism and atheism in upstate New York, rural Connecticut and Vermont, parts of North Carolina and Kentucky, and urbane Philadelphia and New York.[778] Leaders who rejected biblical revelation included Willie Jones of North Carolina; Governor Edmund Randolph of Virginia; Ethan Allen of Vermont, who in 1784 published *Reason, the Only Oracle of Man*; and Thomas Paine, author of *Common Sense* in 1776 but *The Age of Reason* in 1794.[779] Samuel Adams feared that republicanism would be identified in the public mind with deism, in large part because of Jefferson's identification with irreligion. But this did not happen, in part because many state republican leaders such as William Findley, a Presbyterian elder from western Pennsylvania, tolerated Jefferson but stood firm against local deists. Findley was willing to lose an election rather than accept a gubernatorial candidate who was part of the "Tom Paine crowd."[780]

The colleges also seemed corrupted. At Yale, in 1795, the majority of sophomores were said to be skeptics who chose to address each other by the names of Voltaire and Rousseau.[781] Reports from Harvard, Columbia, and the new University of North Carolina were dire, and at Dartmouth only one member of the class scheduled to graduate in 1799 would publicly profess Christ; Bowdoin College was said to be the same, and at Princeton only three or four "pious" students remained.[782] The Presbyterian Church's General Assembly in 1798 decried the growth of deism and proclaimed a day of humiliation, prayer, and fasting.

As a new century began, there would be a response by man and God to such a trend: It was called the Second Great Awakening. But, in the late 1790s, concern about Francophile atheism and radicalism led to the Alien and Sedition Acts. The Alien Act allowed the federal government to deport suspected French agents, and the Sedition Act allowed Federalists to prosecute four of the five major Jeffersonian newspapers for "fake, scandalous and malicious writing" aimed at President John Adams.[783]

The climate of the time justified such restraints, according to their backers. As the Massachusetts legislature argued, "Congress, having been especially entrusted by the people with the general defense of the nation, had not only the right, but were bound, to protect it against internal as well as external foes."[784] But the legislation was a political blunderbuss, and it blew up in Adams' face.

Encroachments Disguised by Expediency

The Alien and Sedition Acts received vigorous opposition from Thomas Jefferson, who saw them—accurately—as a direct attack on himself and his followers. Jefferson framed opposing resolutions that the legislature of the new state of Kentucky approved. The federal government, Kentucky stated, has limited authority, and any acts reached beyond delegated power are "unauthoritative, void, and of no force." Nor should the federal government be "the exclusive or final judge of the extent of the powers delegated to itself . . . as in all other cases of compact among parties having no common judge, each party has an equal right to judge for itself." Anti-Federalists had predicted that the Supreme Court, if made final judge, would favor an increase in centralized power. Jefferson and the Kentuckians were blunt in proclaiming "that [if] the general government is the exclusive judge of the extent of the powers delegated to it, [courts will] stop not short of despotism. . . ."[785]

The Alien and Sedition Acts also awakened Federalists such as Madison who, in pushing for a stronger central government, had said their goal was to avoid a new London, not create one. Yet in 1798, only ten years after the Virginia ratifying convention in which anti-Federalists were accused of fulminating about fantasies, Madison had to tackle the question of whether Patrick Henry had been right. Madison's belated acknowledgment that the concerns were substantial came in the form of the "Virginia Resolutions" that he drafted and saw approved by the state's legislature in December 1798. Those resolutions charged that the federal government was out to "enlarge its powers by forced constructions of the constitutional charter," including dramatic and distorted use of the elastic clause, with the goal of "consolidat[ing] the states, by degrees, into one sovereignty"; the states, Madison asserted, had the right to nullify such power grabs.[786]

The Virginia legislature sent its resolutions to other states, and accompanied them with an "Address to the People" that included statements similar to those made by anti-Federalists ten years before: State legislators warned citizens of "encroachments, which, though clothed with the pretext of necessity, or disguised by arguments of expediency, may yet establish precedents which may ultimately devote a generous and unsuspicious people to all the consequences of usurped power." The Virginia legislators insisted, "It is evident that the objects for which the Constitution was formed were deemed attainable only by a particular enumeration and specification of each power granted to the federal government; reserving all others to the people, or to the states."[787]

The response from other states to their nullification gambit disappointed the Virginians. Suspicious Rhode Island had been the last state to enter the Union, but its legislators now condemned the "unwarrantable resolutions" from Virginia.[788] Delaware legislators resolved to "consider the resolutions from the state of Virginia as a very unjustifiable interference with the general government and constituted authorities of the United States, and of dangerous tendency. . . ."[789] The legislatures of New York, Connecticut, New Hampshire, and Vermont responded similarly, and those from Massachusetts challenged "the right of the state legislatures to denounce the administration of that government to which the people themselves, by a solemn compact, have exclusively committed their national concerns."[790] (Ten years before, Patrick Henry had objected to the Constitution's emphasis not on state jurisdictions but on "We, the People.") The Massachusetts legislature justified the Alien and Sedition Acts by pointing to Article I, Section 8: "Congress shall have power to make all laws which shall be necessary and proper. . . ." (And all of the objections concerning the "elastic clause" had a new resiliency.)

Madison, forced to address the original intent of that clause, presented a report to the Virginia House of Delegates during its 1799-1800 session. Madison began by noting that "in all the contemporary discussions and comments which the Constitution underwent, it was constantly justified and recommended on the ground that the powers not given to the government were withheld from it."[791] Madison added that any lingering doubt was removed by the "reserved to the states" amendment. He argued that the Supreme Court could not be the final arbiter between federal officials and the states, since it was "a plain principle, founded in common sense, that in a dispute between parties one party could not be the sole judge." The Supreme Court could be the last resort on all disputes within the federal government, but some other mechanism would be needed to arbitrate national-state disputes. Although Madison did not specify the mechanism, he emphasized states' rights: Since the Constitution was accepted by each state "in its sovereign capacity," the states "must themselves decide, in the last resort, such questions as may be of sufficient magnitude to require their interposition."[792]

Madison was thus belatedly coming to grips with the anti-Federalist concern that "the judicial authority is to be regarded as the sole expositor of the Constitution in the last resort"; he was finally acknowledging that "the judicial department, also, may exercise or sanction dangerous powers beyond the grant of the

Constitution."[793] Of course, for a state to have authority in federal-state disputes also made one of the parties the sole judge, but Madison argued the logical necessity of state supremacy over the Supreme Court: "On any other hypothesis, the delegation of judicial power would annul the authority delegating it." In words as loaded as those uttered by any anti-Federalist, Madison noted that the Supreme Court could become dangerous: "The concurrence of this department with the others in usurped powers, might subvert forever, and beyond the possible reach of any rightful remedy, the very Constitution which all were instituted to preserve."[794]

Madison also attempted to diminish the elasticity of the constitutional clauses that anti-Federalists had most lambasted. Madison explained that he had taken some wording straight from the Articles of Confederation, and that "similarity in the use of these phrases" should make the Constitution "less liable to be misconstrued," because no one could reasonably say that the Articles created dictatorial power.[795] Madison insisted that those who wished to expand central authority were making "rather a mockery than an observance" of the Constitution.[796] He also tried to narrow the "general welfare" clause of the Preamble.[797]

Finally, Madison reviewed the history of the ratification process:

> When the Constitution was under the discussions which preceded its ratification, it is well known that great apprehensions were expressed by many [about] the power to make all laws necessary and proper for carrying [Congress'] other powers into execution. In reply to this objection, it was invariably urged to be a fundamental and characteristic principle of the Constitution, that all powers not given by it were reserved; that no powers were given beyond those enumerated in the Constitution. . . .[798]

Because some doubted, the Bill of Rights was enacted: It should have stopped usurpation, but "it is painful to remark how much the arguments now employed in behalf of the Sedition Act, are at variance with the reasoning which then justified the Constitution, and invited its ratification."[799]

Painful to remark, indeed. Throughout the report, Madison showed exasperation with those who wished to twist the clear meaning of constitutional sections such as the empowering paragraph of Article 1, Section 8. "In its fair and consistent meaning, it cannot enlarge the enumerated powers vested in Congress," Madison wrote. "It is not a grant of new powers to Congress, but merely a declaration, or the removal of all uncertainty, that the means of carrying into execution those otherwise granted are included in the grant."[800] He also expressed concern about "an excessive augmentation of the offices, honors, and emoluments, depending on the executive will. . . ."[801] So soon after the Revolution, the world was turning upside-down again, and the still-unbuilt capital threatened to become a new London.

It Is the Lot of Man to Die

Samuel Adams, governor of Massachusetts in 1796 when French revolutionary fervor was at its height, appointed December 15 a "Day of Public Thanksgiving and Praise to our Divine Benefactor." God, Adams noted, had blessed America economically ("He hath regarded our Pastures and Fields with an Eye of the most indulgent Parent"), politically ("Our civil Constitutions of Government, formed by ourselves, and administered by Men of our own *free Election*, are by His Grace continued to us), and theologically ("We still enjoy the inestimable Blessings of the Gospel and right of worshipping God according to His own Institutions and the honest dictates of our Consciences"). Adams included in his proclamation a prayer: "Together with our thanksgiving, earnest Supplication to God is hereby recommended for the forgiveness of our Sins which have rendered us unworthy of the least of his Mercies; and that by the sanctifying influence of his Spirit, our hearts and manners may be corrected, and we become a reformed and happy People."[802]

How reformed and happy could we become? By 1798, New England ministers were perceiving clearly what had only been glimpsed at the beginning of the century: America (even after gaining independence from the British Sodom) was not the new Jerusalem, and American Christians had much to learn from how God's people had conducted themselves in Babylon. The Massachusetts election-day sermon for 1798, given by Nathaniel Emmons (pastor of a small church in Franklin), centered on life in ancient Babylon and the importance of having leaders such as Daniel: "The captive tribes were struck with his pious and exemplary conduct, in the midst of the worshippers of idols."[803] Emmons then enumerated Babylonian aspects of America, where some leaders "have lately spread atheism and infidelity through a great nation; and attempted to diffuse the poison of their irreligious and disorganizing sentiments among the people of America." The Francophile spirit, Emmons said, was not progressive but regressive: "Such champions of infidelity endeavor to shake our faith in natural and revealed religion, by carrying us back into the dark regions of antiquity."[804]

Emmons' citing of both natural and revealed religion meant that he was accusing the Francophiles of not just deism, but atheism. He pleaded with the legislators to stand firm against anti-Christian thought, and proposed a combination of small government (to restrain power) and holy government (to restrain immorality). Emmons also stressed the consequences of disobedience: "If you cast off fear, and restrain prayer before God, despite all his warnings and admonitions, the day is coming, when that invisible hand, which is now recording all your deeds, will write on the table of your hearts, in a language which will need no interpreter, this final and fearful sentence: 'You are weighed in the balances, and are found *wanting*.'"[805]

Another typical sermon in 1798 raised the question of whether morality could be separated from religion. Minister Ashbel Green of the Second Presbyterian Church in Philadelphia argued against the notion "that morality can exist without religion" and called the idea "destitute of proof. . . . No nation has ever yet existed where this phenomenon of morals without religion has made its appearance; and there is no reason to believe that it is even possible from the very nature and structure of the human mind."[806]

Green warned that the desire of some to separate religious and governmental concerns was part of a deeper strategy. "Infidels first endeavor to exclude religion from the state that they may give the name of morality to any set of principles they may choose to adopt." But, he argued, "Be warned that without religion and morality harmoniously united we are an undone people. Without these our civil liberty and social happiness cannot possibly be preserved. Let us esteem these our principal and most essential defense."[807] President John Adams, not a believer himself, understood that linkage when he issued thanksgiving proclamations with expressions such as

"Redeemer of the World," "the grace of His Holy Spirit," and "The Great Mediator and Redeemer." In March of 1798 and then again in 1799, as political hurricanes raged around him, he issued proclamations for days of "solemn humiliation, fasting, and prayer."[808]

Americans would need to be praying for new leaders as well. In 1789, during Washington's first term as chief executive, Samuel Adams had asked in a letter to Richard Henry Lee, "Who will succeed the present President, for it is the Lot of Man to die? Perhaps the next and the next may inherit his Virtues, [but] the Time will come when the worst takes over."[809] Ten years later, with Richard Henry Lee dead and Samuel Adams close to the grave, the questions were raised again as two of the Virginia giants went to their Maker.

George Washington died suddenly in 1799 without leaving behind any remarkable last words, and so the words of his farewell address were replayed in the press. "Of all the dispositions and habits which lead to political prosperity, religion and morality are indispensable supports," he had said in 1797. Washington, dodging the question of his own personal faith but emphasizing social utility, noted that the fear of God is the beginning of civic trust: "Where is the security for property, for reputation, for life, if the sense of religious obligation desert the oaths, which are the instruments of investigation in Courts of Justice?"[810] Francophiles spoke of atheistic morality, but Washington had no faith "that morality can be maintained without religion."[811]

Patrick Henry also died in 1799, after adding to his will these words: "This is all the inheritance I can give to my dear family. The religion of Christ can give them one which will make them rich indeed."[812] To the will he added a copy of the resolutions that he had written in 1765 in opposition to the Stamp Act and attached a new addendum: "Whether this will prove a blessing or a curse, will depend upon the use our people make of the blessings which a gracious God hath bestowed on us. If they are wise, they will be great and happy. If they are of a contrary character, they will be miserable. Righteousness alone can exalt them as a nation."[813]

Among the younger generation, Hamilton and Jefferson continued to vie for power. Hamilton's electoral opportunities suffered a fatal blow, however, when he was accused of illegitimate financial dealings and attempted to escape the charge by claiming that the accuser was angry with him for another reason: "The charge against me," he wrote in a newspaper column, "is a connection with one James Reynolds for purposes of improper pecuniary speculation. My real crime is an amorous connection with his wife. . . . This confession is not made without a blush."[814] Hamilton blushed, but others were angry: Abigail Adams called Hamilton "wicked" and "lascivious," and John Adams labeled him "a proud, spirited, conceited, aspiring Mortal, with as debauched Morals as old Franklin, who is more his Model than anyone I know."[815]

John Dickinson, the Pennsylvanian whose *Letters from a Farmer* had been so influential in 1768, lived on. He never turned back on his resolution to prefer the simple pleasures of America to the thrills of London, and his reputation for decency grew during the 1790s. He opposed the "reign of monsters" that resulted from the "flood of atheism and democracy" that swamped the new Sodom of France, and he continued to praise American attempts to avoid foreign entanglements both in action and thought. Dickinson ended one letter in March, 1800, with words about the future near and far: "I confess I look for nothing but deceitful calms, to be succeeded by the most furious and tempestuous agitation which ambition, avarice, and revenge are capable of exciting."[816]

A Useful Show of Virtue

Leaders like Dickinson could look back over the progress of a century and see how Americans had learned to check ambition, avarice, and revenge. They could see how the American way had become one of legislative minimalism. Not only were British appointees checked in their activity, but colonists had placed restrictions on legislative power as well by discouraging legislators from staying on the job for more than a few years. Colonists had learned to restrict the franchise so that voter independence could be emphasized. In short, they had placed restrictions on bureaucrats, legislators, and voters themselves, so that the slogan "No taxation without representation" was in spirit coupled with a second, "No representation without taxation."

Americans had learned the importance of constricting governmental opportunity to offer bribes. When the colonies were lost, the common British explanation was that

> the King and government of Great Britain held no patronage in the country, which could create attachment and influence suficient to counteract that restless, arrogating spirit which in popular assemblies, when left to itself, will never brook an authority that checks and interferes with its own."[817]

Virginia's governor Dunmore had complained in 1772 that he had not "the disposal of one Single place of Consequence in the Government," and his counterpart in Massachusetts had claimed that "the Root of the American Disorders" was "the Want of a certain and adequate civil List to each Colony." [818] Americans, wishing to remain free from governmental tyranny, would for a time make sure that the government was small enough so that officials had few jobs to offer and few bribes to offer voters.

Americans, by 1800, also had gained an appreciation for messy organization charts. Martin Bladen, a member of London's Board of Trade, had complained in 1739 that the colonies were

> divided into so many different Provinces, spread over so immense a Tract of Land . . . Ruled by so many various Forms of Government; so little concerned for each other's Prosperity, and as devoid of all Care for the Welfare of the whole, as if they were not the Subjects of the same Prince. . . .[819]

Bladen had demanded appointment of a "Captain General" with agents in every colony to report on the "Dispositions of the People" and "dissuade the Planters from the persuit of Manufactures deterimental to their Mother Country, and . . . to engage them to pay more Respect to the orders of the Crown. . . ." Americans had understood proposals such as Bladen's to be logical, efficient, and wrong. One cost of liberty was a certain governmental inefficiency; paying less respect to the orders of those who lacked virtue was far better than a greased track for ambitious rule.

Americans, by 1800, had learned that virtue in high places was not merely preferable, but essential, since its presence or lack affected everything else, including the economy. For example, they discerned that the willingness to pay higher taxes was related not only to the absolute level of taxation, but to the degree of confidence among taxpayers that their funds would be used rightly. British subjects became more reluctant to pay higher taxes as they lost confidence in the ability of an evidently corrupt government to spend funds wisely, and they knew that future governments would face the same scrutiny.

For that reason, Americans realized the importance of electing leaders who continued to think of themselves as citizens of their states, rather than citizens of the capital. One of Britain's leading public-policy experts displayed the wrong attitude when he stated that economic developments anywhere in the empire that were "inconsistent with the Interest of the Mother State must be understood to be illegal and the practice of them unwarrantable. . . ."[820] The British thought that those in the hinterlands might agitate for fair play and might even threaten to secede, but one rule was essential to remember: "Every Act of a Dependent Provincial Government ought to Terminate in the Advantage of the Mother State. . . ."[821]

The American way was to let people go to work for their own advantage, and to emphasize production, not politics. The young United States grew not by planning but by pioneering, and it prospered when leaders in the capital practiced benign neglect. Early in the eighteenth century, Bolingbroke had written that the best way to increase governmental power is to accustom people to seeing it as on their side in the satisfaction of their lusts: "Disguise the fatal hook with baits of pleasure."[822] Two hundred years ago leaders discouraged the satisfaction of lusts; lusting did not cease, but it was neither trumpeted nor subsidized.

Christians who are Americans are double citizens; when the two citizenships come into conflict, our heavenly citizenship is the trump, first and last. But happy the time when the two citizenships can be in harmony. There was a time when this was often the case. Burgh, in 1774, contrasted the viciousness of English society with "the sobriety, and temperate way of living, practiced by the Dissenters retired to America." He praised "their thrift and regular manner of living," and noted that American society "if not entirely virtuous, has a show of virtue; and, if this were only an appearance, it is yet better for a people . . . than the open profession and practice of lewdness, which is always attended with national decay and poverty."[823]

What happens when we let it all hang out? As James Burgh wrote in 1774, "It is of great consequence to a kingdom, that religion and morals be considered as worthy the attention of persons of high rank." That is because

> the welfare of all countries in the world depends upon the morals of their people . . . when their manners are depraved, they will decline insensibly, and at least come to utter destruction. When a country is grown vicious, industry decays, the people become effeminate and unfit for labor. To maintain luxury, the great ones must oppress the meanest; and to avoid this oppression, the meaner sort are often compelled to seditious tumults or open rebellion.[824]

Now, we rarely comprehend the connections. May we do so again, and may a linking of governmental reform and personal virtue come again. Those who desire small government and those who yearn for holy government must hang together, or we will all hang separately.

Appendix

SOUNDBITES FROM THE 1780s FOR THE 1990s

Predictions of the Anti-Federalists

The Constitution will lead to "the consolidation of the States into one national government . . . the State sovereignties would be eventually annihilated, though the forms may long remain as expensive and burdensome remembrances of what they were. . . ." (*Philadelphia Independent Gazetteer*, April 22, 1788)

"The vast and important powers of the president [are a concern]. . . . He will be surrounded by expectants and courtiers . . . if the president is possessed of ambition, he has power and time sufficient to ruin his country." (*New York Journal*, November 8, 1787)

"The new constitution will prove finally to dissolve all the power of the several state legislatures, and destroy the rights and liberties of the people." (*New York Journal*, June 13, 1788)

"Certain characters now on the stage, we have reason to venerate, but though this country is now blessed with a Washington, Franklin, Hancock and Adams, yet posterity may have reason to rue the day when their political welfare depends on the decision of men who may fill the places of these worthies."([Boston] *Independent Chronicle*, December 6, 1787)

"Those who tell you that you safely may accept such a constitution and be perfectly at ease and secure that your rulers will always be so good, so wise, and so virtuous—such emanations of the deity—that they will never use their power but for your interest and your happiness, contradict the uniform experience of ages." (*Maryland Journal*, April 14, 1788)

"The direct tendency of the proposed system, is to consolidate the whole empire into one mass, and, like the tyrant's bed, to reduce all to one standard." (*Massachusetts Gazette*, December 11, 1787)

"Should the citizens of America, in a fit of desperation, be induced to commit this fatal act of political suicide, to which by such arguments they are simulated, the day will come when laboring under more than Egyption bondage; compelled to finish their quota of brick . . . you will, by sad experience, be convinced (when that conviction shall be too late) that there is a difference in evils and that the buzzing of gnats is more supportable than the sting of a serpent." (*Maryland Journal*, April 14, 1788)

"From the first history of government to the present time, if we begin with Nimrod and trace down the rulers of nations to those who are now invested with supreme power, we shall find few, very few, who have made the beneficent governor of the universe the model of their conduct, while many are they who, on the contrary, have imitated the demons of the darkness. . . . We have no right to expect that our rulers will be more wise, more virtuous, or more perfect than those of other nations have been." (*Maryland Journal*, March 28, 1788)

"[There is] an incontrovertible truth, that whatever by the constitution government even may do, if it relates to the abuse of power by acts tyrannical and oppressive, it some time or other will do. . . . Once power and authority are delegated to a government, it knows how to keep it, and is sufficiently and successfully fertile in expedients for that purpose . . . so far from parting with the powers actually delegated to it, government is constantly encroaching on the small pittance of rights reserved by the people to themselves, and gradually wresting them out of their hand. . . ." (*Maryland Journal*, March 28, 1788)

Predictions of the Federalists

"Allowing the utmost latitude to the love of power which any reasonable man can require, I am at a loss to discover what temptation the persons intrusted with the administration of the general government could ever feel to divest the States [of their authority over state and local issues]." (Alexander Hamilton, Federalist #17)

"The administration of private justice between the citizens of the same State, the supervision of agriculture and of other concerns of a similar nature, all those things, in short, which are proper to be provided for by local legislation, can never be desirable cares of a general jurisdiction. It is therefore improbable that there should exist a disposition in the federal councils to usurp the powers with which they are connected." (Alexander Hamilton, Federalist #17)

"Let it be admitted, for argument's sake, that mere wantonness and lust of domination would be sufficient to beget that disposition; still it may be safely affirmed that the sense of the constituent body of the national representatives, or, in other words, the people of the several States, would control the indulgence of so extravagant an appetite." (Alexander Hamilton, Federalist #17)

"It will always be far more easy for the State governments to encroach upon the national authorities than for the national government to encroach upon the State authorities." (Alexander Hamilton, Federalist #17)

"A disposition in the State governments to encroach upon the rights of the Union is quite as probable as a disposition in the Union to encroach upon the rights of the State governments. . . . [Conflicts] will be most apt to end to the disadvantage of the Union." (Alexander Hamilton, Federalist #31)

"The danger which most threatens our political welfare is that the State governments will finally sap the foundations of the Union." (Alexander Hamilton, Federalist #33)

"The number of individuals employed under the Constitution of the United States will be much smaller than the number employed under the particular States. [State and local officials] must exceed, beyond all proportion, both in number and influence, those of every description who will be employed in the administration of the federal system. . . . If the federal government is to have collectors of revenue, the State governments will have theirs also. And as those of the former will be principally on the seacoast, and not very numerous, the advantage in this view also lies on the same side." (James Madison, Federalist #45)

"The powers delegated by the proposed Constitution to the federal government are few and defined. Those which are to remain in the State governments are numerous and indefinite. The former will be exercised principally on external objects, as war, peace, negotiation, and foreign commerce; with which last the power of taxation will, for the most part, be connected. The powers reserved to the several States will extend to all the objects which, in the ordinary course of affairs, concern the lives, liberties, and properties of the people, and the internal order, improvement, and prosperity of the State." (James Madison, Federalist #45)

Troublesome Clauses

"The general government, when completely organized, will . . . [be] arrogating to itself the right of interfering in the most minute objects of internal police, and the most trifling domestic concerns of every state, by possessing a power of passing laws 'to provide for the general welfare of the United States,' which may affect life, liberty and property in every modification they may think expedient, unchecked by cautionary reservations. . . ." (*New York Daily Patriotic Register*, June 14, 1788)

Legislators have "authority to make all laws which they shall judge necessary for the common safety, and to promote the general welfare. This amounts to a power to make laws at discretion." (*New York Journal*, December 13, 1787)

"The legislature under this [general welfare clause] may pass any law which they may think proper. . . . This clause commits to the hands of the general legislature every conceivable source of revenue within the United States, [and will result in numerous laws that] may affect the personal rights of the citizens of the states, expose their property to fines and confiscation, and put their lives in jeopardy. (*New York Journal*, December 13, 1787)

"What ideas are included under the terms, to provide for the common defense and general welfare? Are these terms definite, and will they be understood, in the same cases by everyone? No one will pretend they will. It will then be matter of opinion, what tends to the general welfare and the Congress will be the only judges in the matter." (*Freeman's Oracle and New Hampshire Advertiser*, January 11, 1788)

The "necessary and proper" clause is so vast that "every law of the states may be controlled by this power. [It is] amply sufficient to carry the coup de grace to the state governments, to swallow them up in the grand vortex of general empire." (*Philadelphia Independent Gazetteer*, December 4, 1787)

The "general welfare" clause provides "undefined, unbounded and immense power. . . . Under such a clause as this, can anything be said to be reserved and kept back from Congress? . . . who shall judge for the legislature what is necessary and proper? Who shall set themselves above the sovereign?" (*Maryland Gazette and Baltimore Advertiser*, November 2, 1788)

"Few parts of the Constitution have been assailed with more intemperance than [the necessary and proper clause]. . . . If it be asked what is to be the consequence, in case the Congress shall misconstrue this part of the Constitution and exercise powers not warranted by its true meaning, I answer the same as if they should misconstrue or enlarge any other power vested in them . . . the success of the usurpation will depend on the executive and judiciary departments, which are to expound and give effect to the legislative acts; and in the last resort a remedy must be obtained from the people, who can, by the election of more faithful representatives, annul the acts of the usurpers." (James Madison, Federalist #44)

High Taxes

Federal power of direct and unlimited taxation eventually "will produce such dreadful oppression as the people cannot possibly bear . . . the whole of our property may be taken by this American government, by laying what taxes they please, giving themselves what salaries they please. . . ." (*New York Journal*, December 27, 1787)

"What can be more comprehensive than those words [general welfare]? . . . Whatever taxes, duties, and excises that the Congress may deem necessary to the general welfare may be imposed on the citizens of these states, and levied by their officers. The Congress are to be the absolute judges of the propriety of such taxes." (*Philadelphia Independent Gazetteer*, December 4, 1787).

It is unwise to "confer on so small a number the very important power of taking our money out of our pockets, and of levying taxes without control." (*Norfolk and Portsmouth Register*, March 5, 1788)

"If you anticipate what will be the enormous expense of this new government added also to your own, little will that portion be which will be left to you." (*New York Journal*, December 16, 1787)

America will face "appointment of a swarm of revenue and excise officers to prey upon the honest and industrious part of the community. . . . [Since] the authority to lay and collect taxes is the most important of any power that can be granted, [it will eventually] draw all others after it." (New York Journal, *December 13, 1787)*

"It is true that the Confederacy is to possess, and may exercise, the power of collecting internal as well as external taxes throughout the States; but it is probable that this power will not be resorted to, except for supplemental purposes of revenue." (James Madison, Federalist #45)

The Imperial Judiciary

"Most of the articles in this [Constitution], which convey powers of any considerable importance, are conceived in general and indefinite terms, which are either equivocal, ambiguous, or which require long definitions to unfold the extent of their meaning. [Given that ambiguity, federal judges] will give the sense of every article of the constitution, that may from time to time come before them. And in their decisions they will not confine themselves to any fixed or established rules, but will determine, according to what appears to them, the reason and spirit of the constitution." (*New York Journal*, January 31, 1788).

"The judicial power will operate to effect, in the most certain, but yet silent and imperceptible manner, what is evidently the tendency of the constitution: I mean, an entire subversion of the legislative, executive and judicial powers of the individual states. . . . Every adjudication of the supreme court, on any question that may arise upon the nature and extent of the general government, will affect the limits of the state jurisdiction. In proportion as the former enlarge the exercise of their powers, will that of the latter be restricted." (*New York Journal*, January 31, 1788)

"Every body of men invested with office are tenacious of power; they feel interested, and hence it has become a kind of maxim, to hand down their offices, with all its rights and privileges, unimpaired to their successors. The same principle will influence judges to extend their power, and increase their rights; this of itself will operate strongly upon the courts to give such a meaning to the constitution in all cases where it can possibly be done, as will enlarge the sphere of their own authority. Every extension of the power of the general legislature, as well as of the judicial powers, will increase the powers of the courts; and the dignity and importance of the judges, will be in proportion to the extent and magnitude of the powers they exercise." (*New York Journal*, January 31, 1788)

The Supreme Court will "be authorized to give the constitution a construction according to its spirit and reason, and not to confine themselves to its letter." (*New York Journal*, February 7 and 14, 1788)

The Supreme Court will "take cognizance of every matter, not only that affects the general and national concerns of the union, but also of such as relate to the administration of private justice, and to regulating the internal and local affairs of the different parts." (*New York Journal*, February 7 and 14, 1788)

The requirement "to establish justice [could come to] include not only the idea of instituting the rule of justice, or of making laws which shall be the measure or rule of right, [but also] the general distribution of justice between man and man." (*New York Journal*, February 7 and 14, 1788)

"This court will be authorised to decide upon the meaning of the constitution; and that, not only according to the natural and obvious meaning of the words, but also according to the spirit and intention of it. In the exercise of this power they will not be subordinate to, but above the legislature." (*New York Journal*, March 20, 1788)

"The supreme court then have a right, independent of the legislature, to give a construction to the constitution and every part of it, and there is no power provided in this system to correct their construction or do it away. If, therefore, the legislature pass any laws, inconsistent with the sense the judges put upon the constitution, they will declare it void." (*New York Journal*, March 20, 1788)

"The judges are supreme—and no law, explanatory of the constitution, will be binding on them. When great and extraordinary powers are vested in any man, or body of men, which in their exercise, may operate to the oppression of the people, it is of high importance that powerful checks should be formed to prevent the abuse of it. . . . The supreme judicial ought to be liable to be called to account, for any misconduct, by some body of men, who depend upon the people for their places. . . ." (*New York Journal*, April 10, 1788)

"The judges under this constitution will control the legislature, for the supreme court are authorised in the last resort, to determine what is the extent of the powers of the Congress. They are to give the constitution an explanation, and there is no power above them to set aside their judgement." (*New York Journal*, March 20, 1788)

"There is no authority that can remove them, and they cannot be contolled by the laws of the legislature. In short, they are independent of the people, of the legislature, and of every power under heaven. Men placed in this situation will generally soon feel themselves independent of heaven itself." (*New York Journal*, March 20, 1788).

Term Limits

Senators "should not be so long in office as to be likely to forget the hand that formed them, or be insensible of their interests . . . this is more likely to be the case with the senate, as they will for the most part of the time be absent from the state they represent, and associate with such company as will possess very little of the feelings of the middling class of people. For it is to be remembered that there is to be a federal city, and the inhabitants of it will be the great and the mighty of the earth." (*New York Journal*, April 10, 1788)

Legislators "become in some measure a fixed body, and often inattentive to the public good, callous, selfish, and the fountain of corruption. [Rotation of offices, a recognition that] even good men in office, in time, imperceptibly lose sight of the people, and gradually fall into measures prejudicial to them, [would] prevent these evils. . . ."(*New York Journal*, April 10, 1788)

"By this rotation, we may sometimes exclude good men from being elected. On the other hand, we guard against those pernicious connections, which usually grow up among men left to continue long periods in office."(*New York Journal*, April 10, 1788)

The rotation principle recognizes that "the useful information of legislators is not acquired merely in studies in offices, and in the meeting to make laws from day to day. They must learn the actual situation of the people by being among them, and when they have made laws, return home and observe how they operate." (*New York Journal*, April 10, 1788)

Bibliography

Newspapers

(Boston) *Independent Chronicle*
Boston Weekly News-Letter
The Craftsman
Freeman's Oracle and New Hampshire Advertiser
(London) *Independent Whig*
Maryland Gazette
Maryland Journal
Massachusetts Gazette
New England Courant
New York Daily Patriotic Register
New York Packet
New York Weekly Mercury
New York Weekly Post-Boy
New-York Weekly Journal
Norfolk and Portsmouth Register
Pennsylvania Chronicle
Pennsylvania Gazette
Pennsylvania Journal
Pennsylvania Packet
Philadelphia Independent Gazetteer
Providence Gazette
South Carolina Gazette

Books

Note: Bibliographical information for books since 1900 includes place of publication, publisher, and date; for books prior to 1900, publisher is omitted.

Abercromby, James. *An Examination of the Acts of Parliament Relative to the Trade and the Government of our American Colonies*. London, 1752.

Adams, Henry. *John Randolph*. New York, 1898.

Adams, James Truslow. *Revolutionary New England, 1691-1776.* Boston: Atlantic Monthly Press, 1921.
Adams, John. *Diary and Autobiography.* Edited by L. H. Butterfield, et al. Cambridge: Harvard University Press, 1961.
__________. *Novanglus*. Boston, 1775.
__________. *Works*. Boston, 1850-1856.
Adams, Samuel. *An Oration Delivered at the State-House in Philadelphia, to a very Numerous Audience, on Thursday the 1st of August, 1776.* Philadelphia, 1776.
__________. *First Book of the American Chronicles of the Times*. Boston, 1775.
__________. *Writings*. Edited by Harry Alonzo Cushing. New York: Putnam's, 1908.
Addison, Joseph. *The Freeholder*. Edited by James Leheny. Oxford: Clarendon, 1979.
Agresto, John. *The Supreme Court and Constitutional Democracy*. Ithaca, N.Y.: Cornell University Press, 1984.
Albanese, Catherine. *Sons of the Father: The Civil Religion of the American Revolution*. Philadelphia: Temple University Press, 1976.
Aldridge, Alfred Owen. *Benjamin Franklin and Nature's God*. Durham, N.C.: Duke University Press, 1967.
Alexander, James. *A Brief Narrative of the Case and Trial of John Peter Zenger*. New York, 1736.
Allen, John. *Oration Upon the Beauties of Liberty*. Boston, 1772.
Alley, Robert S., ed. *James Madison on Religious Liberty*. Buffalo: Prometheus, 1985.
Amos, Gary. *Defending the Declaration*. Nashville: Wolgemuth and Hyatt, 1989.
Anderson, Fred. *A People's Army*. Williamsburg, Vir.: University of North Carolina Press, 1984.
Andrews, Charles M. *The Colonial Period of American History*. New Haven: Yale University Press, 1934-1938.
A Narrative of a New and unusual American Imprisonment of two Presbyterian Ministers: And Prosecution of Mr. Francis Makemie, One of Them, for Preaching One Sermon at the city of New-York, By a Learner of Law, and Lover of Liberty. New York, 1707.
An Address to the Freeholders. Boston, 1751.
An Impartial Examination of the Conduct of the Whigs and Tories . . . London, 1763.
Archives of Maryland. Baltimore: Maryland Historical Society, 1936.
Atherton, Herbert M. *Political Prints in the Age of Hogarth: A Study of the Ideographic Representation of Politics*. London: Oxford University Press, 1974.
Axelrad, Jacob. *Patrick Henry*. New York: Random House, 1947.

Backus, Isaac. *An Appeal to the People*. Boston, 1780.
__________. *Government and Liberty Described*. Boston, 1778.
__________. *Policy as Well as Honesty*. Boston, 1779.
__________. *The Sovereign Decrees of God*. Boston, 1773.
__________. *Truth is Great and Will Prevail*. Boston, 1781.
Bacon, Thomas. *A Sermon Preached at the Parish Church of St. Peter's*. London, 1751.
Bailyn, Bernard. *Pamphlets of the American Revolution*. Cambridge: Harvard University Press, 1965.
__________. *The Ideological Origins of the American Revolution*. Cambridge: Harvard University Press, 1967.
__________. *The Origins of American Politics*. New York: Knopf, 1968.
Balch, Thomas, ed. *Letters and Papers Relating Chiefly to the Provincial History of Pennsylvania*. Philadelphia, 1855.
Baldwin, Alice M. *The New England Clergy and the American Revolution*. Durham, N.C.: Duke University Press, 1928.
Barton, Thomas. *Unanimity and Public Spirit*. Philadelphia, 1755.
Bayne-Powell, Rosamond. *Eighteenth-Century London Life*. New York: Dutton, 1938.
Becker, Carl L. *History of Political Parties in the Province of New York*. Madison: University of Wisconsin Press, 1909.
__________. *Benjamin Franklin*. Ithaca, N.Y.: Cornell University Press, 1946.
Beeman, Richard R. *The Old Dominion and the New Nation, 1788-1801*. Lexington, Ky.: The University Press of Kentucky, 1972.
Beer, George L. *The Old Colonial System, 1660-1754*. New York: Peter Smith, 1958.
__________. *British Colonial Policy, 1754-1765*. New York: Macmillan, 1907.
Bellamy, Joseph. *Works*. Boston, 1850.
Beloff, Max, ed. *The Debate on the American Revolution, 1761-1783*. London: Nicholas Kaye, 1949.
Belsham, William. *Memoirs of the Reign of George III*. London, 1795.
Beveridge, William. *Prices and Wages in England From the Twelfth to the Nineteenth Century*. London: Longmans, 1939.
Beverley, Robert. *The History and Present State of Virginia*. Edited by Louis B. Wright. Chapel Hill: University of North Carolina Press, 1947.
Beverly, Robert. *An Essay Upon the Government of the English Plantations on the Continent of America*. London, 1701.
Billikopf, David M, *The Exercise of Judicial Power, 1789-1864*. New York: Vantage, 1973.
Bining, Arthur C. *British Regulation of the Colonial Iron Industry*. Philadelphia: University of Pennsylvania Press, 1933.

Bloch, Ruth H. *Visionary Republic: Millennial Themes in American Thought, 1756-1800*. Cambridge: Cambridge University Press, 1985.

Bolingbroke, Henry St. John, Viscount. *Contributions to the Craftsman*. Edited by Simon Varey. Oxford: Clarendon Press, 1982.

Boller, Jr., Paul F. *George Washington & Religion*. Dallas: Southern Methodist University Press, 1963.

Bonomi, Patricia. *Under the Cope of Heaven: Religion, Society, and Politics in Colonial America*. New York: Oxford University Press, 1986.

Boorstin, Daniel J. *The Americans*. New York: Random House, 1958.

Borden, Morton, ed. *The Antifederalist Papers*. East Lansing: Michigan State University Press, 1965.

Bork, Robert. *The Tempting of America: The Political Seduction of the Law*. New York: Free Press, 1990.

Botsford, Jay. *English Society in the Eighteenth Century*. New York: Macmillan, 1924.

Boulton, William B. *The Amusements of Old London*. London: John C. Nimmo, 1901.

Boyd, George. *Elias Boudinot, Patriot and Statesman, 1740-1821*. Princeton: Princeton University Press, 1952.

Bradford, M.E. *Remembering Who We Are: Observations of a Southern Conservative*. Athens: University of Georgia Press, 1985.

__________. *A Worthy Company*. Wheaton, Ill.: Crossway, 1988.

Bridenbaugh, Carl. *Cities in Revolt: Urban Life in America, 1743-1776*. New York: Knopf, 1955.

__________. *Cities in the Wilderness: The First Century of Urban Life in America, 1625-1742*. New York: Knopf, 1960.

__________. *Early Americans*. New York: Oxford University Press, 1981.

__________. *Mitre and Sceptre*. London: Oxford University Press, 1962.

Brisco, Norman A., *The Economic Policy of Robert Walpole*. New York: Columbia University Press, 1907.

Brodie, Fawn. *Thomas Jefferson: An Intimate History*. New York: Norton, 1974.

Brown, John. *An Estimate of the Manners and Principles of the Times*. London, 1757.

Brown, Robert E., and B. Katherine Brown. *Virginia, 1705-1786: Democracy or Aristocracy*. East Lansing: Michigan State University Press, 1964.

Brown, Robert E. *Middle-Class Democracy and the Revolution in Massachusetts, 1691-1780*. Ithaca, N.Y.: Cornell University Press, 1955.

Brutus, Lucius Junius. *A Defence of Liberty Against Tyrants*. Gloucester, Mass.: Peter Smith, 1963.

Buck, Philip W. *Politics of Mercantilism*. New York: Holt, 1942.
Burgh, James. *Britain's Remembrancer . . . A Brief View, from History, of the Effects of the Vices Which Now Prevail in Britain, Upon the Greatest Empires and States of Former Times*. London, 1746.
__________. *Political Disquisitions*. London, 1774.
Burr, Sr., Aaron. *A Discourse Delivered at New-Ark*. New York, 1755.
Butterfield, Herbert. *George III and the Historians*. New York: Macmillan, 1959.
__________. *George III, Lord North, and the People, 1779-1780*. London: Bell, 1949.
Butts, R. Freeman. *The American Tradition in Religion and Education*. Boston: Beacon, 1950.
Buxbaum, Melvin H. *Benjamin Franklin and the Zealous Presbyterians*. University Park: Pennsylvania State University Press, 1975.
Buxbaum, Melvin H., ed. *Critical Essays on Benjamin Franklin*. Boston: G.K. Hall, 1987.
Byrd, II, William. *The Great American Gentleman: William Byrd of Westover in Virginia*. Edited by Louis B. Wright and Marion Tinling. New York: Putnam's, 1963.
__________. *The London Diary (1717-1721) and Other Writings*. Edited by Louis B. Wright and Marion Tinling. New York: Oxford University Press, 1958.
Calam, John. *Parsons and Pedagogues*. New York: Columbia University Press, 1971.
Carroll, Peter N. *Religion and the Coming of the American Revolution*. Waltham, Mass.: Ginn-Blaisdell, 1970.
Carson, Clarence. *The Colonial Experience, 1607-1774*. Wadley, Ala.: American Textbook Committee, 1983.
Cartwright, John. *American Independence, The Interest and Glory of Great Britain*. Philadelphia, 1776.
Chauncey, Charles, *Marvelous Things Done By the Right Hand and Holy Arm of God in Getting Him the Victory*. Boston, 1745.
__________. *The Idle-Poor secluded from the Bread of Charity by the Christian Law*. Boston, 1752.
Chinard, Gilbert. *Honest John Adams*. Boston: Little, Brown, 1933.
Chitwood, Oliver Perry. *Richard Henry Lee, Statesman of the Revolution*. Morgantown: West Virginia University Library, 1967.
Churchill, Charles. *Genuine Memoirs*. London, 1765.
__________. *Works*. London, 1774.
Clark, Charles E. *The Eastern Frontier*. New York: Knopf, 1970.
Clark, Dora Mae. *The Rise of the British Treasury: Colonial Administration in the Eighteenth Century*. New Haven: Yale University Press, 1960.
Clinton, Henry. *The American Rebellion: Sir Henry Clinton's Narrative of*

His Campaigns, 1775-1782. Edited by William Willcox. New Haven: Yale University Press, 1954.

Cobb, Sanford H. *The Rise of Religious Liberty in America*. New York: Macmillan, 1902.

Collins, Varnum Lansing. *President Witherspoon*. Princeton: Princeton University Press, 1925.

Conner, Paul W. *Poor Richard's Politics: Benjamin Franklin and His New American Order*. New York: Oxford University Press, 1965.

Cowing, Cedric B. *The Great Awakening and the American Revolution: Colonial Thought in the Eighteenth Century*. Chicago: Rand McNally, 1971.

Crane, Verner W. *Benjamin Franklin's Letters to the Press, 1758-1775*. Chapel Hill: University of North Carolina Press, 1950.

Craven, Wesley Frank. *The Colonies in Transition, 1660-1713*. New York: Harper & Row, 1968.

Cunliffe, Marcus, and Robin W. Wilkes. *Pastmasters*. New York: Harper & Row, 1969.

Cunningham, Noble E. *The United States in 1800: Henry Adams Revisited*. Charlottesville: University Press of Virginia, 1988.

Currey, Cecil B. *Road to Revolution: Benjamin Franklin in England, 1765-1775*. Garden City, N.Y.: Doubleday, 1968.

Dabney, Virginius. *The Jefferson Scandal: A Rebuttal*. New York: Dodd, Mead, 1981.

Daniels, Bruce C., ed. *Power and Status: Officeholding in Colonial America*. Middleton, Conn.: Wesleyan University Press, 1986.

Dashwood, Francis, and Benjamin Franklin. *An Abridgement of the Book of Common Prayers*. London, 1773.

Davenant, Charles. *Discourse on the Public Revenues and on the Trade of England*. London, 1698.

Davies, Samuel. *Religion and Patriotism, the Constituents of a Good Soldier*. Philadelphia, 1755.

__________. *Religion and Public Spirit*. Philadelphia, 1761.

__________. *Sermons on Important Subjects*. New York, 1845.

__________. *The Crisis; or, the Uncertain Doom of Kingdoms, at Particular Times*. London, 1757.

__________. *The Duty of Christians to Propagate Their Religion Among the Heathens*. London, 1758.

__________. *The State of Religion Among the Protestant Dissenters in Virginia*. Boston, 1751.

__________. *Virginia's Danger and Remedy*. Williamsburg, Va., 1756.

Davis, Burke. *The Campaign That Won America*. New York: Dial, 1970.

Defoe, Daniel. *The Complete English Tradesman*. London: Rivington, 1726-1732.

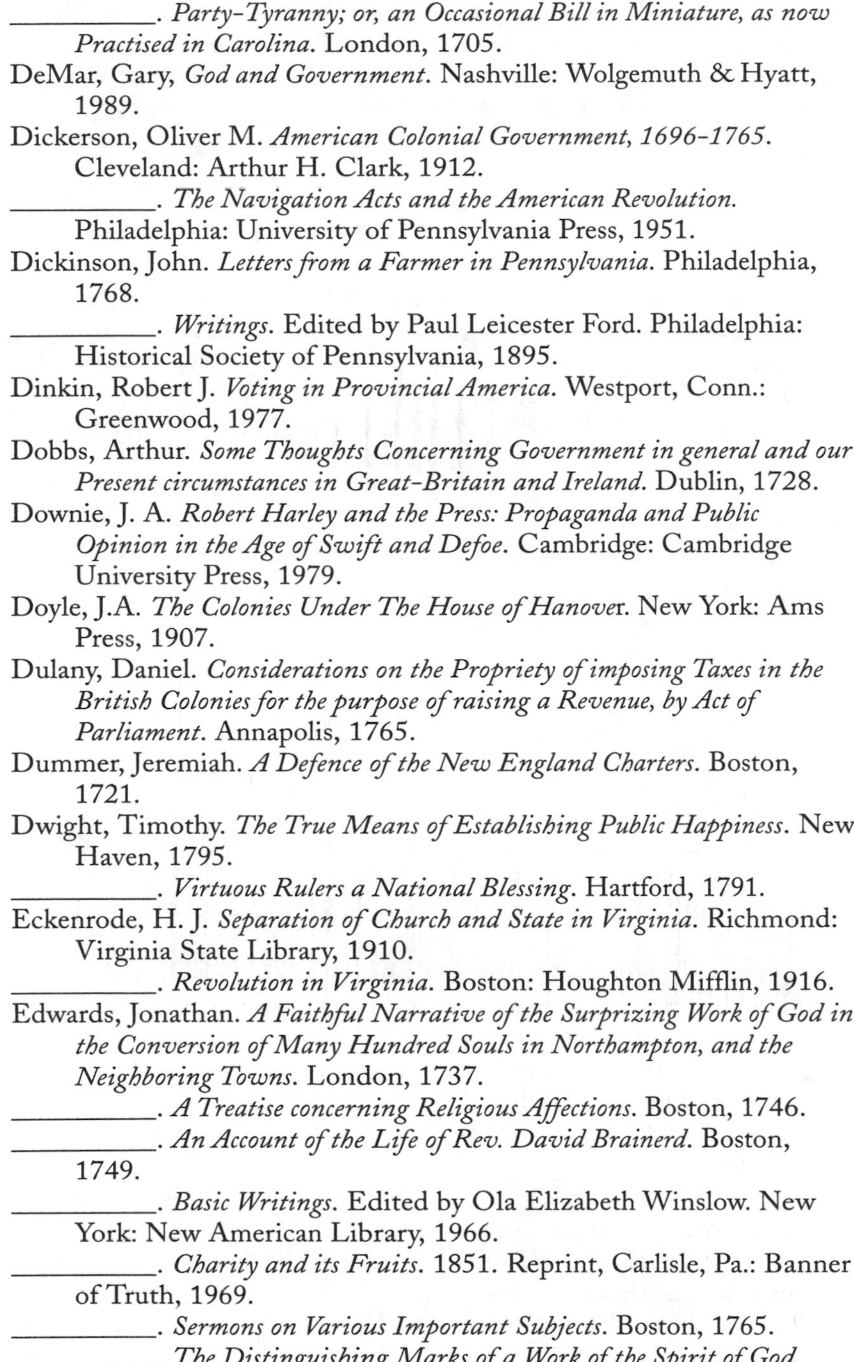

__________. *Party-Tyranny; or, an Occasional Bill in Miniature, as now Practised in Carolina*. London, 1705.

DeMar, Gary, *God and Government*. Nashville: Wolgemuth & Hyatt, 1989.

Dickerson, Oliver M. *American Colonial Government, 1696-1765*. Cleveland: Arthur H. Clark, 1912.

__________. *The Navigation Acts and the American Revolution*. Philadelphia: University of Pennsylvania Press, 1951.

Dickinson, John. *Letters from a Farmer in Pennsylvania*. Philadelphia, 1768.

__________. *Writings*. Edited by Paul Leicester Ford. Philadelphia: Historical Society of Pennsylvania, 1895.

Dinkin, Robert J. *Voting in Provincial America*. Westport, Conn.: Greenwood, 1977.

Dobbs, Arthur. *Some Thoughts Concerning Government in general and our Present circumstances in Great-Britain and Ireland*. Dublin, 1728.

Downie, J. A. *Robert Harley and the Press: Propaganda and Public Opinion in the Age of Swift and Defoe*. Cambridge: Cambridge University Press, 1979.

Doyle, J.A. *The Colonies Under The House of Hanove*r. New York: Ams Press, 1907.

Dulany, Daniel. *Considerations on the Propriety of imposing Taxes in the British Colonies for the purpose of raising a Revenue, by Act of Parliament*. Annapolis, 1765.

Dummer, Jeremiah. *A Defence of the New England Charters*. Boston, 1721.

Dwight, Timothy. *The True Means of Establishing Public Happiness*. New Haven, 1795.

__________. *Virtuous Rulers a National Blessing*. Hartford, 1791.

Eckenrode, H. J. *Separation of Church and State in Virginia*. Richmond: Virginia State Library, 1910.

__________. *Revolution in Virginia*. Boston: Houghton Mifflin, 1916.

Edwards, Jonathan. *A Faithful Narrative of the Surprizing Work of God in the Conversion of Many Hundred Souls in Northampton, and the Neighboring Towns*. London, 1737.

__________. *A Treatise concerning Religious Affections*. Boston, 1746.

__________. *An Account of the Life of Rev. David Brainerd*. Boston, 1749.

__________. *Basic Writings*. Edited by Ola Elizabeth Winslow. New York: New American Library, 1966.

__________. *Charity and its Fruits*. 1851. Reprint, Carlisle, Pa.: Banner of Truth, 1969.

__________. *Sermons on Various Important Subjects*. Boston, 1765.

__________. *The Distinguishing Marks of a Work of the Spirit of God*.

Applied to that uncommon Operation that has lately appeared on the Minds of many of the People of this Land. Boston, 1741.

__________. *The Works of President Edwards*. Edited by Sereno B. Dwight. New York, 1829-1830.

Eidsmoe, John. *Christianity and the Constitution*. Grand Rapids: Baker, 1987.

Elliot, Jonathan, ed. *The Debates in the Several State Conventions on the Adoption of the Federal Constitution*. Philadelphia: Lippincott, 1901.

Emery, Noemie. *Alexander Hamilton*. New York: Putnam's, 1982.

Emmons, Nathanael. *A Sermon preached before [the] governor . . . and House of Representatives . . . May 30, 1798, being the day of General Election*. Boston: Printed for the State, 1798.

Farrand, Max., ed. *The Records of the Federal Convention of 1787*. Rev. ed. New Haven: Yale University Press, 1966.

Fitzmaurice, Edmund George. *Life of William, Earl of Shelburne*. London: Macmillan, 1875.

Fleming, Thomas. *1776: Year of Illusions*. New York: Norton, 1975.

Flexner, James Thomas. *George Washington: Anguish and Farewell*. Boston: Little, Brown, 1972.

__________. *George Washington and the New Nation*. Boston: Little, Brown, 1969.

__________. *George Washington in the American Revolution*. Boston: Little, Brown, 1967.

Foner, Eric. *The New American History*. Philadelphia: Temple University Press, 1990.

Foner, Philip S., ed. *The Democratic-Republican Societies, 1790-1800*. Westport, Conn.: Greenwood, 1976.

Foote, William Henry. *Sketches of Virginia*. Richmond: John Knox Press, 1966.

Force, Peter, ed. *American Archives*. Washington, D.C., 1837-1853.

Ford, Paul Leicester, ed. *Pamphlets on the Constitution of the United States*. New York: Da Capo Press, 1968.

__________. *Essays on the Constitution of the United States*. Brooklyn: Historical Printing Club, 1892.

Fortescue, John, *A History of the British Army*. London: Macmillan, 1902.

Franklin, Benjamin. *Autobiography*. Edited by J. A. Leo Lemay and P. M. Zall. New York: Norton, 1986.

__________. *Autobiography*. Edited by Leonard W. Labaree. New Haven: Yale University Press, 1964.

__________. *Papers*. Edited by Leonard W. Labaree. New Haven: Yale University Press, 1959—.

__________. *The Political Thought of Benjamin Franklin*. Edited by Ralph Ketcham. Indianapolis: Bobbs-Merrill, 1965.
__________. *Writings*. Edited by Albert Henry Smyth. New York: Macmillan, 1905-1907.
Freeman, Douglas. *George Washington, a biography*. New York: Scribner's, 1948-57.
Fuller, Ronald. *Hell-Fire Francis*. London: Chatto & Windus, 1939.
Gales, Joseph, ed. *Debates and Proceedings in the Congress of the United States*. Washington, D.C.: Government Printing Office, 1934.
Gaustad, Edwin Scott. *A Religious History of America*. San Fransisco: HarperCollins, 1990.
Gee, Joshua. *Trade and Navigation of Great Britain Considered*. London, 1738.
Geissler, Suzanne. *Jonathan Edwards to Aaron Burr, Jr.: From the Great Awakening to Democratic Politics*. New York: Edwin Mellen, 1981.
Gelb, Norman. *Less Than Glory*. New York: Putnam's, 1984.
Gewehr, Wesley M. *The Great Awakening in Virginia, 1740-1790*. Durham, N.C.: Duke University Press, 1930.
Gillett, E. H. *History of the Presbyterian Church*. Philadelphia, 1864.
Gipson, Lawrence H. *The Coming of Revolution, 1763-1775*. New York: Harper, 1954.
Gordon, William. *A Discourse Preached December 15th, 1774*. Boston, 1775.
Green, Ashbel. *Obedience to the Laws of God: The Sure and Indispensable Defense of Nations*. Philadelphia, 1798.
Green, M. Louise. *The Development of Religious Liberty in Connecticut*. Boston: Houghton Mifflin, 1905.
Greene, Evarts B., and Virginia Harrington. *American Population before the Federal Census of 1790*. New York, 1932.
Greene, Jack P. *The Quest for Power: The Lower Houses of Assembly in the Southern Royal Colonies, 1689-1776*. Chapel Hill: University of North Carolina Press, 1963.
Harper, Lawrence A. *The English Navigation Laws*. New York: Columbia University Press, 1939.
Hart, Freeman H. *The Valley of Virginia in the American Revolution, 1763-1789*. Chapel Hill: University of North Carolina Press, 1942.
Hatch, Nathan O. *The Sacred Cause of Liberty*. New Haven: Yale University Press, 1977.
Headley, Joel T. *The Chaplains and Clergy of the Revolution*. New York, 1864.
Heimert, Alan. *Religion and the American Mind, from the Great Awakening to the Revolution*. Cambridge: Harvard University Press, 1966.

The Hellfire Club, kept by a Society of Blasphemers. London, 1721.
Hening, W. W., ed. *Laws of Virginia*. Richmond, 1823.
Henretta, James A. *"Salutory Neglect": Colonial Administration Under the Duke of Newcastle*. Princeton: Princeton University Press, 1972.
__________. et al., eds. *The Transformation of Early American History*. New York: Knopf, 1991.
Henry, Patrick. *Life, Correspondence, and Speeches*. Edited by William Wirth Henry. New York: Scribner's, 1891.
Hervey, Augustus. *Augustus Hervey's Journal*. Edited by David Erskine. London: William Kimber, 1953.
Higham, John. *History: Professional Scholarship in America*. Baltimore: Johns Hopkins University Press, 1989.
__________. *The Reconstruction of American History*. New York: Harper & Row, 1962.
Hoffer, Peter C., ed. *Commerce and Community*. New York: Garland, 1988.
__________. *Planters and Yeomen*. New York: Garland, 1988.
Humphrey, Edward Frank. *Nationalism and Religion in America, 1774-1789*. Boston: Chipman, 1924.
Hutchinson, Thomas. *The Diary and Letters of His Excellency, Thomas Hutchinson*. London, 1883-86.
__________. *The History of the Colony and Province of Massachusetts Bay*. Edited by Lawrence Shaw Mayo. Cambridge: Harvard University Press, 1936.
Illick, Joseph, ed. *America & England, 1558-1776*. New York: Appleton-Century, 1970.
Isaac, Rhys. *The Transformation of Virginia, 1740-1790*. Chapel Hill: University of North Carolina Press, 1982.
Jarrett, Derek. *England in the Age of Hogarth*. New York: Viking, 1974.
Jay, John. *Correspondence and Public Papers*. New York: Putnam's, 1893.
Jennings, Francis. *Empire of Fortune*. New York: Norton, 1988.
Jensen, Merrill. *The New Nation*. New York: Knopf, 1950.
Jenyns, Soames. *The Objections to the Taxation of Our American Colonies by the Legislature of Great Britain briefly consider'd*. London, 1765.
Johnson, Joan. *Princely Chandos: James Brydges, 1674-1744*. Gloucester, England: Alan Sutton, 1984.
Johnson, Samuel. *Taxation No Tyranny*. London, 1775.
Johnstone, Charles. *Chrysal, or the Adventures of a Guinea*. London, 1760.
Jones, Louis C. *The Clubs of the Georgian Rakes*. New York: Columbia University Press, 1942.
Journals of the Continental Congress. Edited by W. C. Ford and Gaillard Hunt. Washington, D.C.: Government Printing Office, 1904-1937.

Kalm, Peter. *The America of 1750: Peter Kalm's Travels in North America.* Edited by Adolph B. Benson. New York: Wilson-Erickson, 1937.
Kammen, Michael G. *Colonial New York: A History.* New York: Scribner's, 1975.
__________. ed. *Politics and Society in Colonial America: Democracy or Deference?* Hinsdale, Ill.: Dryden, 1973.
Kemp, Betty. *Sir Francis Dashwood: An Eighteenth-Century Independent.* New York: St. Martin, 1967.
Ketcham, Ralph, ed. *The Anti-Federalist Papers and the Constitutional Convention Debates.* New York: New American Library, 1986.
__________. *James Madison: A Biography.* New York: Macmillan, 1971.
Keteltas, Abraham. *The Religious Soldier.* New York, 1759.
Knight, George W. *History and Management of Land Grants for Education in the Northwest Territory.* New York, 1885.
Knollenberg, Bernhard. *Growth of the American Revolution: 1766-1775.* New York: Macmillan, 1975.
__________. *Origin of the American Revolution: 1759-1766.* New York: Macmillan, 1960.
Kraus, Michael, and Davis D. Joyce. *The Writing of American History.* Norman: University of Oklahoma Press, 1985.
Kronenberger, Louis. *Kings & Desperate Men.* New York: Knopf, 1942.
Labaree, Leonard Woods. *Conservatism in Early American History.* Ithaca, N.Y.: Cornell University Press, 1959.
__________. *Royal Government in America.* New Haven: Yale University Press, 1930.
Langdon, Samuel. *Government corrupted by Vice, and recovered by Righteousness*, Watertown, Mass., 1775.
Lauer, Paul E. *Church and State In New England.* Baltimore: Johns Hopkins University Press, 1892.
"Learner of Law, and Lover of Liberty, A." *A Narrative of a New and unusual American Imprisonment of two Presbyterian Ministers.* New York, 1707.
Leavenworth, Mark. *Charity Illustrated and Recommended.* New London, 1772.
Lecky, W. E. H. *A History of England in the Eighteenth Century.* London, 1882.
Lee, Richard Henry. *Letters from The Federal Farmer to the Republican. 1787-1788.* Reprint, Englewood Cliffs, N.J.: Prentice-Hall, 1962.
__________. *Letters.* Edited by James Ballagh. New York: Macmillan, 1914.
__________. *Memoir of the Life of Richard Henry Lee and His Correspondence.* Philadelphia, 1825.
Lewis, John D., ed. *Anti-Federalists versus Federalists.* San Francisco: Chandler, 1967.

Lewis, Paul. *The Man Who Lost America: A Biography of Gentleman Johnny Burgoyne*. New York: Dial, 1973.

Life, Adventures, Amours, and Intrigues of . . . Jeremy Twitcher. London, 1770.

Lincoln, Charles H., ed. *Correspondence of William Shirley*. New York: Macmillan, 1912.

__________. H. *The Revolutionary Movement in Pennsylvania, 1770-1776*. Philadelphia: University of Pennsylvania, 1901.

Lockridge, Kenneth A. *On the Sources of Patriarchal Rage*. New York: New York University Press, 1992.

Lord, Benjamin. *Religion and Government Subsisting Together in Society, Necessary to Their Compleat Happiness and Safety*. New London, 1751.

Macaulay, Catharine. *An Address to the People of England, Ireland, and Scotland on the Present Important Crisis of Affairs*. London, 1775.

Mackesy, Piers. *Could the British Have Won the War of Independence?* Worcester, Mass.: Clark University Press, 1976.

__________. *The Coward of Minden: The Affair of Lord George Sackville*. London: Allen Lane, 1979.

__________. *The War for America, 1775-1783*. Cambridge: Harvard University Press, 1964.

Madison, James. *Notes of Debates in the Federal Convention of 1787*. Athens, Ohio: Ohio University Press, 1966.

__________. *Papers*. Edited by Robert Rutland, et al. Chicago: University of Chicago Press, 1962-1973 .

__________. *The Writings of James Madison*. Edited by Gaillard Hunt. New York: Putnam's, 1900-1910.

Maier, Pauline. *The Old Revolutionaries*. New York: Knopf, 1980.

Main, Jackson Turner. *The Antifederalists: Critics of the Constitution, 1781-1788*. Chapel Hill: University of North Carolina Press, 1961.

__________. *The Social Structure of Revolutionary America*. Princeton: Princeton University Press, 1965.

Makemie, Francis. *A Good Conversation: A Sermon Preached at the City of New-York*. Boston, 1707.

__________. *Life and Writings*. Edited by Boyd S. Schleither. Philadelphia: Presbyterian Historical Society, 1971.

Malcolmson, Robert W. *Popular Recreations in English Society, 1700-1850*. London: Cambridge University Press, 1973.

Mannix, David. *The Hell Fire Club*. New York: Ballantine, 1959.

Marks, Frederick W. *Independence on Trial*. Baton Rouge: Louisiana State Press, 1973.

Marshall, Dorothy. *Eighteenth Century England*. New York: David McKay, 1962.

Marshall, Peter, and David Manuel. *The Light and the Glory*. Tarrytown, N.Y.: Revell, 1977.

Marshall, Peter, and Glyn Williams, eds. *The British Atlantic Empire before the American Revolution*. London: Frank Cass, 1980.

Mather, Cotton. *Diary of Cotton Mather, 1709-1712*. Boston: Massachusetts Historical Society, 1912.

__________. *Magnalia Christi Americana*. London, 1702.

Matthews, Richard K. *The Radical Politics of Thomas Jefferson*. Lawrence, Kan.: University Press of Kansas, 1984.

Mayo, Lawrence S. *John Wentworth, Governor of New Hampshire*. Cambridge: Harvard University Press, 1921.

McCants, David A. *Patrick Henry, The Orato*r. New York: Greenwood, 1990.

McClenachan, William. *The Christian Warrior*. Boston, 1745.

McColley, Robert. *Slavery and Jeffersonian Virginia*. Urbana: University of Illinois Press, 1973.

McCormick, Donald. *The Hell-Fire Club*. London: Jarrolds, 1958.

McDonald, Forrest, and Ellen McDonald, eds. *Confederation and Constitution, 1781-1789*. Columbia: University of South Carolina Press, 1968.

McDonald, Forrest. *We the People: The Economic Origins of the Constitution*. Chicago: University of Chicago Press, 1958.

McLoughlin, William. *New England Dissent, 1630-1833*. Cambridge: Harvard University Press, 1971.

__________. *Soul Liberty*. Hanover: University Press of New England, 1991.

McMahon, Marie P. *The Radical Whigs, John Trenchard and Thomas Gordon*. Lanham, Md.: University Press of America, 1990.

Meyer, Jacob X. *Church and State in Massachusetts from 1740 to 1833*. Cleveland: Western Reserve University Press, 1930.

Middleton, Richard. *Bells of Victory: The Pitt-Newcastle Ministry and the Conduct of the Seven Years' War, 1757-1762*. Cambridge: Cambridge University Press, 1985.

Miller, Helen Hill. *George Mason, Gentleman Revolutionary*. Chapel Hill: University of North Carolina Press, 1975.

Miller, John C. *Origins of the American Revolution*. Boston: Litle, Brown, 1943.

Miller, Lillian B. *"The Dye Is Now Cast": The Road to American Independence, 1774-1776*. Washington: Smithsonian Institution Press, 1975.

Miller, Perry, and Thomas H. Johnson, eds. *The Puritans*. New York: Harper & Row, 1963.

Miller, Perry, ed. *The American Puritans*. Garden City, N.Y.: Doubleday, 1956.

__________. *The New England Mind: From Colony to Province*. Boston: Beacon, 1961.

Moehlman, Conrad Henry, ed. *The American Constitutions and Religion*. Berne, Ind.: Moehlman, 1938.

Monaghan, Frank. *John Jay, Defender of Liberty*. New York: Bobbs-Merrill, 1935.

Monroe, James. *Writings*. Edited by Stanislaus Hamilton. New York, 1898.

Moore, Frank, ed. *The Diary of the American Revolution*. New York: Scribner's, 1860.

Morais, Herbert M. *Deism in Eighteenth Century America*. New York: Columbia University Press, 1934.

Morgan, Edmund S. *The Gentle Puritan: A Life of Ezra Stioles, 1727–1795*. New Haven: Yale University Press, 1962.

__________. *American Slavery, American Freedom: The Ordeal of Colonial Virginia*. New York: Norton, 1975.

Morgan, Edmund S., and Helen Morgan. *The Stamp Act Crisis: Prologue to Revolution*. Chapel Hill: University of North Carolina Press, 1953.

Morgan, Richard E. *The Supreme Court and Religion*. New York: Free Press, 1972.

Morris, Richard B. *Government Labor in Early America*. New York: Columbia University Press, 1945.

Morse, Jedediah. *Annals of the American Revolution*. Hartford, 1824.

Morton, Richard L. *Colonial Virginia*: Chapel Hill: University of North Carolina Press, 1960.

Mulder, John M., and John F. Wilson. *Religion in American History: Interpretive Essays*. Englewood Cliffs, N.J.: Prentice-Hall, 1978.

Murray, Iain H. *Jonathan Edwards*. Edinburgh: Banner of Truth, 1987.

Myers, Albert V., ed. *Narratives of Early Pennsylvania, West Jersey, and Delaware*. New York: Scribner's, 1912.

Noll, Mark A. *A History of Christianity in the United States and Canada*. Grand Rapids: Eerdmans, 1992.

__________. *Princeton and the Republic, 1768–1822*. Princeton: Princeton University Press, 1989.

North, Gary. *Political Polytheism: The Myth of Pluralism*. Tyler, Tex.: Institute for Christian Economics, 1989.

Oberg, Barbara B., and Harry S. Stout, eds. *Benjamin Franklin, Jonathan Edwards, and the Representation of American Cultur*e. New York: Oxford University Press, 1993.

Olasky, Marvin. *Central Ideas in the Development of American Journalism*. Hillsdale, N.J.: Lawrence Erlbaum, 1991.

__________. *The Tragedy of American Compassion*. Wheaton, Ill.: Crossway Books, 1992.

Osgood, Herbert L. *The American Colonies in the Eighteenth Century.* New York: Columbia University Press, 1924-1925.
Oswald, Richard. *Memorandum On the Folly of Invading Virginia.* Charlottesville: University of Virginia Press, 1953.
Otis, James. *The Rights of the British Colonies Asserted and Proved.* Boston, 1764.
Paine, Thomas. *Common Sense.* Philadelphia, 1776.
Pargellis, Stanley M. *Lord Loudon in North America.* New Haven: Yale University Press, 1933.
Parkman, Francis. *A Half-Century of Conflict.* New York: Collier, 1962.
Parrington, Vernon Louis. *The Colonial Mind.* New York: Harcourt, Brace and Company, 1927.
Parson, Jonathan. *Freedom from Civil and Ecclesiastical Slavery.* Newburyport, 1774.
Pellew, George. *John Jay.* Boston: Houghton, Mifflin, 1891.
Penn, William. *Primitive Christianity Revived in the Faith and Practice of the People Called Quakers.* London: 1696.
Percy, Hugh. *Letters . . . 1774-1776.* Edited by Charles K. Bolton. London, 1902.
Peterson, Merrill D. *Adams and Jefferson.* Athens: University of Georgia Press, 1976.
Petty, William. *Economic Writings.* New York: Kelley, 1964.
Phelps, Glenn A. *George Washington and American Constitutionalism.* Lawrence: University Press of Kansas, 1993.
Phillips, Ulrich. *Life and Labor in the Old South.* Boston: Little, Brown, 1929.
Pilcher, George William. *Samuel Davies: Apostle of Dissent in Colonial Virginia.* Knoxville: University of Tennessee Press, 1971.
"Plebian, A." *An address to the People of the state of New York.* New York, 1788.
Plumb, J. H. *Sir Robert Walpole.* London: Cresset, 1956.
__________. *Georgian Delights.* Boston: Little, Brown, 1980.
Pollock, John. *George Whitefield and the Great Awakening.* Tring, England: Lion, 1972.
Poore, ed. *Federal and State Constituions.* Washington, 1878, 2nd edition.
Potts, Louis W. *Arthur Lee.* Baton Rouge: Louisiana State Press, 1981.
Powell, Milton, ed. *The Voluntary Church:.* New York: Macmillan, 1967.
Pownall, Thomas. *The Administration of the Colonies.* London, 1764.
Proud, Robert. *The History of Pennsylvania.* Philadelphia, 1797.
Ramsay, David. *The History of the American Revolution.* Philadelphia, 1789.
Randall, Willard. *A Little Revenge: Benjamin Franklin and His Son.* Boston: Little, Brown, 1984.

Robinson, Henry. *Certain Considerations* . . . London, 1651.

Robinson-Morris, Matthew. *Considerations on the Measures Carrying on With Respect to the British Colonies in North America*. Philadelphia, 1774.

Rodger, N. A. M. *The Insatiable Earl: A Life of John Montagu, Fourth Earl of Sandwich, 1718–1792*. London: HarperCollins, 1993.

Rodick, Burleigh. *American Constitutional Custom*. New York: Philosophical Library, 1953.

Rogers, Alan. *Empire and Liberty*. Berkeley: University of California Press, 1974.

Root, E. Merrill. *Brainwashing in the High Schools*. New York: Devin-Adair, 1959.

Rothbard, Murray. *Conceived in Liberty*. New York: Arlington House, 1975.

Royster, Charles. *A Revolutionary People at War: The Continental Army and American Character, 1775–1783*. Chapel Hill: University of North Carolina Press, 1979.

Rushdoony, Rousas John. *The Nature of the American System*. Nutley, N.J.: Craig Press, 1965.

__________. *This Independent Republic*. Fairfax, Va.: Thoburn Press, 1978.

Rutherford, Livingston. *John Peter Zenger, His Trial and a Bibliography of Zenger Imprints*. New York: Dodd, Mead, 1904.

Sachs, William S., and Ari Hoogenboom. *The Enterprising Colonials*. Chicago: Argonaut, 1965.

Saussure, Cesar. *A Foreign View of England in the Reigns of George I and George II*. London: Murray, 1902.

Saye, Albert Berry. *New Viewpoints in Georgia History*. Athens: University of Georgia Press, 1943.

Schlesinger, Arthur M. *Prelude to Independence: The Newspaper War on Britain, 1764–1776*. New York: Random House, 1957.

Schneider, David M. *History of Public Welfare in New York State*. Chicago: University of Chicago Press, 1938.

Schutz, John A. *Thomas Pownall, British Defender of American Liberty*. Glendale, Ca.: Arthur H. Clark, 1951.

__________. *William Shirley, King's Governor of Massachusetts*. Chapel Hill: University of North Carolina Press, 1961.

Selby, John D. *The Revolution in Virginia, 1775–1783*. Williamsburg: Colonial Williamsburg Foundation, 1988.

Shipley, Jonathan. *A Sermon Preached Before the Incorporated Society for the Propagation of the Gospel in Foreign Parts*. London, 1773.

Singer, C. Gregg. *A Theological Interpretation of American History*. Phillipsburg, N.J.: Presbyterian and Reformed, 1964.

Skotheim, Robert Allen. *American Intellectal Histories and Historians*. Princeton, N.J.: Princeton University Press, 1966.

Smith, Charlotte Watkins. *Carl Becker: On History & the Climate of Opinion*. Ithaca, N.Y.: Cornell University Press, 1956.

Smith, Elwyn A., ed. *The Religion of the Republic*. Philadelphia: Fortress Press, 1971.

Smith, Jeffery A. *Franklin and Bache: Envisioning the Enlightened Republic*. New York: Oxford University Press, 1990.

Smith, Page. *A New Age Now Begins*. New York: McGraw-Hill, 1976.

__________. *John Adams*. Garden City, N.Y.: Doubleday, 1962.

Smith, Paul, comp. *English Defenders of American Freedoms, 1774–1778*. Washington: Library of Congress, 1972.

Smith, William. *History of the Province of New York*. (Cambridge, MA: Harvard University Press, 1972; Philadelphia, 1792).

Some Remarks on Mr. President Clap's History and Vindication, of the Doctrines of the New-England Churches &c. New Haven, 1756.

Sosin, Jack M., *English America and Imperial Inconstancy*. Lincoln: University of Nebraska Press, 1985.

__________. *Agents and Merchants*. Lincoln: University of Nebraska Press, 1965.

Spaulding, W. Wilder, *New York in the Critical Period*. New York: Columbia University Press, 1932.

Speck, W. A. *Stability and Strife*. Cambridge, Mass.: Harvard University Press, 1977.

Steele, Ian K. *Betrayals: Fort William Henry and the 'Massacre.'* New York: Oxford University Press, 1990.

Stiles, Ezra. *Literary Diary*. Edited by Franklin B. Dexter. New York: Scribner's, 1901.

Stille, Charles J. *The Life and Times of John Dickinson*. Philadelphia: Historical Society of Pennsylvania, 1891.

Stohlman, Martha Lou Lemmon. *John Witherspoon: Parson, Politician, Patriot*. Philadelphia: Westminister, 1976.

Stokes, Anson Phelps. *Church and State in the United States*. New York: Harper, 1950.

Stokes, Anthony. *A View of the Constitution of the British Colonies . . . at the Time the Civil War Broke Out on the Continent of America*. London, 1783.

Stout, Harry S. *The New England Soul*. New York: Oxford University Press, 1986.

Strout, Cushing. *The New Heavens and New Earth: Political Religion in America*. New York: Harper & Row, 1974.

Sweet, William Warren. *Religion in the Development of American Culture, 1765-1840*. New York: Scribner's, 1952.

Sydnor, Charles S. *Gentlemen Freeholders: Political Practices in*

Washington's Virginia. Chapel Hill: University of North Carolina Press, 1952.

Symmes, Thomas. *Lovewell Lamented*. Boston, 1725.

Szatmary, David. *Shays' Rebellion: The Making of an Agrarian Insurrection*. Amherst: University of Massachusetts Press, 1980.

Tennent, Gilbert. *A Persuasive to the Right Use of the Passions in Religion*. Philadelphia, 1760.

__________. *The Necessity of Praising God for Mercies Received*. Philadelphia, 1745.

Tilley, John A. *The British Navy and the American Revolution*. Columbia: University of South Carolina Press, 1987.

Trask, Kerry A. *In the Pursuit of Shadows*. New York: Garland, 1989.

Trenholme, Louise. *The Ratification of the Federal Constitution in North Carolina*. New York: Columbia University Press, 1932.

Tuchman, Barbara. *The First Salute*. New York: Knopf, 1988.

Tuveson, Ernest Lee. *Redeemer Nation: The Idea of America's Millennial Role*. Chicago: University of Chicago Press, 1968.

Tyler, Moses Coit. *History of American Literature During the Colonial Period*. New York: Putnam's, 1898.

__________. *The Literary History of the American Revolution*. New York: Putnam's, 1897.

Valentine, Alan. *Lord George Germain*. London: Oxford University Press, 1962.

Vinal, William. *A Sermon on the Accursed Thing That Hinders Success and Victory in War*. Newport, 1755.

Walpole, Horace. *Corespondence*. New Haven: Yale University Press, 1937-1980.

Ward, Henry M. *"Unite or Die."* Port Washington, N.Y: Kennikat Press, 1971.

Washington, George. *Writings*. Edited by John C. Fitzpatrick. Washington, D.C.: Government Printing Office, 1931-1944.

Wells, William. *The Life and Public Services of Samuel Adams*. New York, 1865-1868.

Wenger, Mark R., ed. *The English Travels of Sir John Percival and William Byrd II*. Columbia: University of Missouri Press, 1989.

White, T. H. *The Age of Scandal*. New York: Putnam's, 1950.

Wigglesworth, Samuel. *An Essay for Reviving Religion*. Boston, 1733.

Will, George F. *Restoration*. New York: Free Press, 1992.

Willcox, William B. *The Age of Aristocracy 1688-1830*. Lexington, Mass.: Heath, 1971.

Williams, Elisha. *The Essential Rights and Liberties of Protestants, a Seasonable Plea for Liberty of Conscience and the Right of Private Judgment in matters of Religion, without any control from Human Authority*. Boston, 1744.

Williams, John. *God in the Camp*. Boston, 1707.
Williamson, Chilton. *American Suffrage, from Property to Democracy, 1760–1860*. Princeton: Princeton University Press, 1960.
Willison, George F. *Patrick Henry and His World*. Garden City, N.Y.: Doubleday, 1969.
Wills, Gary. *Inventing America*. Garden City, N.Y.: Doubleday, 1978.
Wilson, James. *Considerations on the Authority of Parliament*. Philadelphia, 1774.
Wirt, William. *The Life of Patrick Henry*. Hartford, 1847, 10th edition.
Wise, Gene. *American Historical Explanations*. Minneapolis: University of Minneapolis, 1980.
Witherspoon, John. *Ecclesiastical Characteristics*. London, 1753.
Wood, W. J. *Battles of the Revolutionary War*. Chapel Hill, N.C.: Algonquin, 1990.
Wright, Louis B. *The Cultural Life of the American Colonies: 1607–1763*. New York: Harper, 1957.
Zuckerman, Michael. *Peaceable Kingdoms: New England Towns in the Eighteeenth Century*. New York: Knopf, 1970.

Endnotes

Introduction

1. John Brown, *An Estimate of the Manners and Principles of the Times* (London, 1757), 24.
2. Ibid.,18.
3. Ibid.
4. Scriptural passages (such as those from Romans 13) about submitting to governing authorities did not lead most Bible-honoring patriots to desist from their efforts, since most of the local governing authorities were in rebellion against those of England.

Dual Governments

5. Carl Bridenbaugh, *Cities in the Wilderness* (New York: Knopf, 1960), 223, 239.
6. Ibid., 267.
7. Francis Makemie, *Life and Writings*, ed. Boyd S. Schleither (Philadelphia: Presbyterian Historical Society, 1971), 38.
8. *Premier Projet pour L'Expedition contre la Nouvelle Angleterre*, quoted in Francis Parkman, *A Half-Century of Conflict* (New York: Collier, 1962), 22.
9. In the 1690s, New York had almost fallen into civil war: A faction that held an eleven-seat-to-ten edge in the New York Assembly seized control of the courts and sentenced some opponents to death. The other faction refused to give in, however, and its elected leaders met in a second, dueling legislature; both sides stockpiled muskets.
10. See "The Watch-Tower" essays in the *New York Weekly Mercury*, April 7-July 15, 1755, for an early journalistic review of Cornbury's rise and fall.
11. Comparative pricing over time is very hazardous, but there are several ways to proceed. First, in the eighteenth century a pound sterling was literally that: It could be traded for sixteen ounces of silver. Today, with an ounce of silver selling in the $5 range, one

pound of silver is worth $80. So, a quick way to approximate a current equivalent of salaries and costs then is to multiply pounds by eighty. (Then there were twenty shillings to the pound and twelve pence to the shilling; now, there are just one hundred pence to the pound.) A more thorough way is to compare commodity prices of basic foodstuffs such as bread, milk, beef, and eggs. William Beveridge, in his classic work *Prices and Wages in England From the Twelfth to the Nineteenth Century* (London: Longmans, Green, 1939), did just that over the centuries in England, charting inflation and deflation by using the records of hospitals, boarding schools, and other institutions. His statistics (see particularly pp. 698-741) suggest that in England during the quarter-century from 1720 to 1744 (a period of stable prices), one pound sterling on the average could buy about 65 pounds of beef, 180 pounds of bread, 150 quarts of milk, 40 pounds of candles, or 30 pounds of butter; comparing that to current bulk prices, one pound then may have been worth about $70. (Commodity prices in the colonies may have varied somewhat, of course.) Prices from 1745 to 1775 apparently rose by about 20 percent, which would make one pound of silver worth about $84 on the eve of the Revolution.

12. Herbert L. Osgood, *The American Colonies in the Eighteenth Century* (New York: Columbia University Press, 1924-1925), 2:76. Cornbury's bill for the conference alone was £2,194.
13. William Smith, *History of the Province of New-York* (Cambridge, Mass: Harvard University Press, 1972), 130.
14. Michael G. Kammen, *Colonial New York: A History* (New York: Scribner's, 1975), 156.
15. Osgood, *The American Colonies in the Eighteenth Century*, 2:69-71.
16. House members concerned about French intentions wanted a larger military force and were willing to appropriate additional money for defense, but they concluded that Cornbury was billing them for ten times as many candles for the military garrison as were actually used, with each candle purchased at a cost many times higher than the going rate.
17. William Smith, 122. When the assembly voted £1,800 for the maintenence of about 180 men, it coupled that grant with the demand that the legislature have the same powers within New York that the House of Commons had in England: among these was the power to examine accounts. See also Osgood, *The American Colonies in the Eighteenth Century*, 2:84, and Spencer, 316.
18. William Smith, 122-23, *History of the Province of New-York*, notes that Cornbury's reaction to these checks was not positive: "His Lordship, who had hitherto been treated with great complaisance,

took offence at this parsimonious scrutiny, and ordered the assembly to attend him . . . he made an angry speech."

19. See Sosin, *Jack Sosin, English America and Imperial Inconstancy* (Lincoln: University of Nebraska Press, 1985), 218, and Osgood, *The American Colonies in the Eighteenth Century*, 2:73-74.
20. Cornbury also had been made governor of New Jersey in a British cost-cutting endeavor; his popularity in that colony, except among those who were beholden to him, also plunged. By 1705, the assembly there was so sick of him that it took the dangerous step of petitioning the queen for her cousin's removal and charging Cornbury with arbitrary collection of fees, granting of a monopoly of trade on the road from Amboy to Burlington, interference with private businesses, and acceptance of a large bribe to exclude three members from the assembly. The Queen, however, was not amused by the legislative initiative, and her cousin played on.
21. The assembly promptly appropriated special funds for fortifying New York City and defending the northern frontier.
22. *Public Advertiser*, 25 January 1770.
23. The Duke of Newcastle was also responsible for the appointment of William Shirley as governor of Massachusetts Bay at that time; he apparently responded to the personal solicitations of Mrs. Shirley.
24. Leonard Labaree, *Royal Government in America* (New Haven: Yale University Press, 1930), 50: "Buying and selling of offices was looked upon in England at this time as a legitimate form of business transaction. . . ."
25. Charles E. Clark, *The Eastern Frontier* (New York: Knopf, 1970), 301; see Charles H. Lincoln, ed., *Correspondence of William Shirley* (New York: Macmillan, 1912), 1:6-43.
26. In theory, England did have a separation of powers, and William Blackstone in his *Commentaries* made favorable comments about the country's governmental organization chart, as did Montesquieu in his *Spirit of the Laws*. Both books influenced American polittcal theory.
27. Dorothy Marshall, *Eighteenth Century England* (New York: David McKay, 1962), 155.
28. Ibid., 156: "Walpole was not over-concerned with men's morality as long as he got their votes. His use of patronage was efficient and ruthless. Only friends, relations and those who could serve him received his favours."
29. See "Cato's Letters," nos. 17, 20, 32, 37, 70; 144 columns in all were published in the *Independent Whig* between 1720 and 1723.
30. The *Craftsman*, 17 August 1728, and Henry St. John, Viscount

Bolingbroke, *Contributions to the Craftsman*, ed. Simon Varey (Oxford: Clarendon Press, 1982), 51.

31. Jack P. Greene, *The Quest for Power: The Lower Houses of Assembly in the Southern Royal Colonies, 1689-1776* (Chapel Hill: University of North Carolina Press, 1963), 8.
32. *New York Weekly Journal*, April 10, 1740, p.4.
33. John Locke's *Second Treatise of Government* and other works had developed the theoretical basis for this.
34. Bernard Bailyn, *The Origins of American Politics* (New York: Knopf, 1968), 76.
35. See Lawrence A. Harper, *The English Navigation Laws* (New York: Columbia University Press, 1939), 216. Those who knew the ropes could play the calendar. Ships did not sail on their own, generally; those whose captains wished to go to Virginia generally sailed with the tobacco fleet each spring, and correct timing could give skillful colonial political players six months to a year's head start. For example, early in the century, Governor Nicholson of Virginia was a firm partisan of the royal prerogative, and he had some support in London. When six of the nine members of the governor's council determined to have him removed, they dispatched James Blair and Stephen Founce to London in the fall of 1703 to present formal protests against Nicholson—but Blair and Founce waited until the tobacco fleet left for the Chesapeake Bay area in the spring of 1704 to press their charges. This meant that the governor would not learn of the official charges against him until the arrival of the next fleet, probably the next year—and by then, with the rumor mill churning and political favors being flashed, it was too late: The Earl of Orkney received the position.
36. See Richard V. W. Buel, Jr., "Political Thought Before the Revolution, in Michael G. Kammen, ed., *Politics and Society in Colonial America:: Democracy or Deference?* (Hinsdale, Ill.: Dryden, 1973), 111.
37. Robert J. Dinkin, *Voting in Provincial America* (Westport, Conn.: Greenwood, 1977), 64.
38. Thomas Balch, ed., *Letters and Papers Relating Chiefly to the Provincial History of Pennsylvania* (Philadelphia, 1855), 63-64; cited in Dinkin, *Voting in Provincial America*, 64.
39. John Adams, *Diary and Autobiography*, ed. L. H. Butterfield, et al. (Cambridge: Harvard University Press, 1961), 3:294.
40. See Dinkin, *Voting in Provincial America*, 50-71. Later, Madison based his plea for a six-year term for senators in part on the assumption that turnover would remain high.
41. As Cornbury continued to lose popularity, he also declared his commitment to public service by issuing decrees such as one

against air pollution: "sundry persons," it seems, had been burning great quantities of dead oysters and oyster shells, causing considerable smoke and nauseous odors. Although one historian (Kammen, *Colonial New York*, 158) has thought it "curious . . . that this passion for public rectitude and civic order reached its peak during Cornbury's regime, for he was despised," it became typical in America for those profiting from public gullibility to declare ever more loudly their concern for the public interest.

42. Makemie (1658-1708), a Scotch-Irish minister, had come to Maryland as a Presbyterian missionary in 1683. For other biographical information see Makemie, *Life and Writings*, ed. Boyd S. Schleithe (Philadelphia: Presbyterian Historical Society, 1971).
43. Francis Makemie, *A Good Conversation: A Sermon Preached at the City of New-York* (Boston, 1707), 31.
44. Ibid.
45. Ibid.
46. See *A Narrative of a New and unusual American Imprisonment of two Presbyterian Ministers: And Prosecution of Mr. Francis Makemie, One of Them, for Preaching ONE SERMON at the city of NEW-YORK, By a Learner of Law, and Lover of Liberty* (New York, 1707).
47. Ibid., 3-6; Cornbury claimed that Parliament had forbidden "strowling Preachers, and you are such, and shall not Preach in my Government." Makemie responded, "There is not one word, my Lord, mentioned in any part of the Law, against Travelling or Strowling Preachers, as Your Excellency is pleased to call them; and we are to judge that to be the true end of the Law, which is specifyed in the Preamble thereof, which is for the satisfaction of Scrupulous Consciences . . . ."
48. Ibid.; Osgood, *The American Colonies in the Eighteenth Century*, 2:18; Kammen, *Colonial New York*, 158.
49. William Smith, 310.
50. See Osgood, *The American Colonies in the Eighteenth Century*, 2:81, and Sosin, *English America* 219. The letter, written soon after the Makemie trial (and for safety's sake dispatched from Connecticut) also presented other specific detail of Cornbury's monetary misfeasance, violation of rights, and reprehensible habits.
51. William Smith, 128; Osgood, *The American Colonies in the Eighteenth Century*, 2:85, 94.
52. Sosin, *English America*, 219.
53. Scc William Smith, 181. Queen Anne also gave Cornbury funds for his future livelihood. He returned to English society, yet was not forgotten by citizens of New York who remembered him with

"universal contempt" even half a century later for his "freaks of low humour" (cross-dressing) and his "despotick rule, savage bigotry, insatiable avarice, and injustice."

54. Quoted in Osgood, *The American Colonies in the Eighteenth Century*, 2:105.
55. Cotton Mather, *Diary of Cotton Mather, 1709-1712* (Boston: Massachusetts Historical Society 1912), 639.
56. Litigation especially increased in commercial centers such as Salem, where wealth and property began to be prized more highly than knowledge and piety, as those involved with local shipping and processing industries became far more concerned with fishing for saleable seafood than with fishing for men.
57. See William Penn, *Primitive Christianity Revived in the Faith and Practice of the People Called Quakers* (London: 1696); his hopes were in accordance with Quaker belief that the "Light Within" outshone original sin.
58. Robert Proud, *The History of Pennsylvania* (Philadelphia, 1797), 1:307; Albert V. Myers, ed., *Narratives of Early Pennsylvania, West Jersey, and Delaware* (New York: Scribner's, 1912), 202-15.
59. Robert Beverly, *The History and Present State of Virginia*, ed. Louis B. Wright (Chapel Hill: University of North Carolina Press, 1947), 312.
60. Sosin, op. cit., 64. Each colony in 1700 could present a similar rendition of disputes and disappointment.
61. Each would be paid a stipend of £250 (perhaps $20,000) annually.
62. Sosin, op. cit., 73.
63. Spotswood quoted in *Journal of Burgesses*, 1712-26, pp. 166-70, cited in Osgood, *The American Colonies in the Eighteenth Century*, 2:236-37.
64. Osgood, *The American Colonies in the Eighteenth Century*, 2:228-43. Spotswood fought back for several years with loose biblical allusions: He told the assembly in 1720 (*Journal of Burgesses*, 254) that he looked upon Virginia "as a Rib taken from Britain's Side . . . this Eve must thrive so long as her Adam flourishes, and if she allowed any serpent to tempt her to go astray it would but multiply her sorrow and quicken her husband to rule more strictly over her."
65. Spotswood's replacement, a court favorite, was more laid-back.
66. See J. A. Doyle, *The Colonies under the House of Hanover* (New York: Ams Press, 1907), 113.
67. *Boston Weekly News Letter*, 18-25 July 1728.
68. Thomas Hutchinson, *The History of the Colony and Province of Massachusetts Bay*, ed. Lawrence Shaw Mayo (Cambridge: Harvard University Press, 1936), 2:333-34.

69. Doyle, *The Colonies under the House of Hanover*, 118.
70. Hutchinson, *The History of the Colony*, 2:364.
71. Ibid., 47.
72. Ibid., 372.
73. Doyle, *The Colonies under the House of Hanover*, 122. Belcher became disappointed in his Massachusetts income and later tried to be appointed governor of South Carolina on the grounds that he had lost money while governor of Massachusetts. Others of greater influence had a leg up in the South Carolina race, but after two years of letter-writing Belcher was given the governorship of New Jersey (by then separated from the New York position) as a consolation prize.
74. See Charles M. Andrews, *The Colonial Period of American History* (New Haven: Yale University Press, 1934-1938), 386. The colonists did derive some protection from Parliamentary jealousies of royal officials. Since leaders of the House of Commons were working to restrict executive power in England so as to gain more authority for themselves, they were reluctant to grant more power to crown officials in the colonies. This was apparent in 1715, for example, when the Board of Trade again entertained notions of setting up a central colonial government under its control, and introduced a measure to that effect; House of Commons leaders stopped the bill in committee.
75. In one instance, a certain devotion to principle within the House of Commons is apparent. In 1734, the House of Lords resolved that every colony had to send over a complete collection of its laws, with any law found to cut into the king's authority or the trade of Great Britain to be disallowed, regardless of what various colonial charters said. But the House of Commons would not go along, probably because of its desire to maintain the sanctity of contracts: Nothing in the charters of Maryland, Connecticut, or Rhode Island obliged those colonies to send over their laws for review.
76. See Calendar State Papers [British governmental records], Colonial, 1701, §§286, 420, 422, and Andrews, *The Colonial Period of American History*, 377, 380.
77. Beverly (probably), *An Essay*, 10.
78. Most of England, of course, was under virtual representation; this plan would put America under actual representation.
79. See Andrews, *The Colonial Period of American History*, 383.
80. *An Address to the Freeholders* (Boston, 1751), 6.
81. *New York Weekly Journal*, 5 March 1739. Some men out of social ambition coveted assembly posts; although social life in Williamsburg or other provincial capitals bored those used to

London, others thought highly of gatherings along the James River.

82. Lawrence A. Harper, *The English Navigation Laws* (New York: Columbia University Press, 1939), 16.
83. William Petty, *Economic Writings* (New York: Kelley, 1964), 1:60. Today, government and the practice of medicine are similar: both are interventionist.
84. Robinson, ii-iii, cited in Harper, *The English Navigation Laws*, 17.
85. The debate about extending the franchise went on for decades, and John Adams summarized the most freqent conclusion among the colonists when he wrote, "If you give to every man who has no property, a vote, will you not make a fine encouraging provision for corruption, by your fundamental law? Such is the frailty of the human heart, that very few men who have no property have any judgment of their own. They talk and vote as they are directed by some man of property, who has attached their minds to his interest." (Letter to James Sullivan, May 26, 1776, in John Adams, *Works* [Boston, 1850-56], 9:376.)
86. Chilton Williamson, *American Suffrage, from Property to Democracy, 1760-1860* (Princeton: Princeton University Press, 1960), 11.
87. Robert J. Dinkin, *Voting in Provincial America* (Westport, Conn.: Greenwood, 1977), 33-49; Richard B. Morris, *Government and Labor in Early America* (New York: Columbia University Press, 1945), 503-6; Robert E. Brown, and B. Katherine Brown, *Virginia, 1705-1786: Democracy or Aristocracy* (E. Lansing: Michigan State University Press, 1964), 143-44.
88. Michael G. Kammen, ed., *Politics and Society in Colonial America: Democracy or Deference?* (Hinsdale, Ill.: Dryden Press, 1973), 80.
89. Ibid., 43.
90. Ibid.
91. Dinkin, *Voting in Provincial America*, 30.
92. Ibid.
93. Karl Marx would write, "Is not private property as an idea abolished when the non-owner becomes legislator for the owner?" For further discussion see Rousas John Rushdoony, *The Nature of the American System* (Nutley, N.J.: Craig Press, 16.
94. Dinkin, *Voting in Provincial America*, 32.
95. Ibid., 33.
96. Edmund Morgan's *American Slavery, American Freedom* lays out the path of history; the book's subtitle, *The Ordeal of Colonial Virginia*, notes the pathos (New York: Norton, 1975).
97. Richard Henry Lee, *Memoir of the Life of Richard Henry Lee and His Correspondence* (Philadelphia, 1825), 17-19, reports his first speech in the assembly, in 1759; Lee attacked the slave trade and

concluded by saying, "I have seen it observed by a great writer, that Christianity, by introducing into Europe the truest principle of humanity, universal benevolence, and brotherly love, had happily abolished civil slavery. Let us, who profess the same religion, practice its precepts; and by agreeing to this duty, convince the world that we know and practice our true interests, and that we pay a proper regard to the dictates of justice and humanity!"

98. John Dickinson, *Letters from a Farmer in Pennsylvania* (Philadelphia, 1768), Letter 9.
99. John Agresto, *The Supreme Court and Constitutional Democracy* (Ithaca, N.Y.: Cornell University Press, 1984), 43.
100. Dickinson, *Letters from a Farmer in Pennsylvania*, Letter 9.
101. Ibid.

Golden Chains

102. This is how America appeared to British officers; see John A. Tilley, *The British Navy and the American Revolution* (Columbia: University of South Carolina Press, 1987), 5.
103. The diaries, mouldering in library archives, were discovered, deciphered, transcribed, and published beginning in 1939. There are three portions: one from 1709 through 1712, when Byrd was in Virginia; the second from 1717 to 1721, showing his activities while in London; the third from 1729 to 1741, with Byrd back in Virginia.
104. March 31-April 9, 1709, in William Byrd II, *The Great American Gentleman: William Byrd of Westover in Virginia*, ed. Louis B. Wright and Marion Tinling (New York: Putnam's, 1963), 13-15.
105. Ibid., 59, 78, 103, 119.
106. Ibid., 109, 120, 147, 148.
107. Ibid., 73, 147, 186.
108. Ibid., 80.
109. Ibid., 110.
110. Ibid., 137-38.
111. Ibid., 136.
112. Ibid., 241.
113. William Byrd II, *The London Diary (1717-1721) and Other Writings*, ed. Louis B. Wright and Marion Tinling (New York: Oxford University Press, 1958), 68, 71, 77, 85. "I kissed the maid till my seed ran from me" or "I kissed the maid till I committed uncleanness" are refrains in his diary of 1718.
114. Ibid., 118.
115. Ibid., 146, 162; see also pp. 141, 161, 168, 221, 223, 225, 232, 233, 339. "I went to Will's Coffeehouse and drank a dish of

chocolate, and about ten went to the bagnio and bathed and then lay all night with Annie Wilkinson and rogered her twice. I neglected my prayers. . . . In the evening I went to visit Mrs. A–l–n, a mistress of mine, and she treated me with a bottle of Rhenish wine and I rogered her well and gave her a guinea. About 11 o'clock I went home and neglected to say my prayers."

116. Ibid., 243; see also pp. 269, 272, 341.
117. Ibid., 136.
118. Ibid., 263.
119. Ibid., 121. Similarly, "I picked up a woman and set down in a coach and committed uncleanness. . . . I picked up a young girl and carried her to the tavern and gave her some mutton cutlets and committed uncleanness with her, and then walked home and neglected my prayers." pp. 143, 168; see also pp. 127, 128, 135, 146, 156, 161, 274, 282, 285, 288.
120. Ibid., 157.
121. Ibid., 236. The food for wealthy men like Byrd also was varied and plentiful: at a typical London outing, "we ate some ham and chicken and ate some salmon . . . ate some lobster and tongue and drank Burgundy and champagne." (p. 121)
122. Ibid., 291-92, 317. And the frequent conclusion: "In going home I picked up a gentlewoman, carried her to the tavern where we ate lobster, and then went to the bagnio". . . . "Met Molly and had some oysters for supper and about eleven we went to bed and I rogered her."
123. Ibid.,"Then my friend sent for the widow J-n-s who came and we went to bed and I rogered her twice and about ten we had a broiled chicken for supper and about twelve we parted and I went home and neglected my prayers." (p. 182) "I picked up a woman and carried her to the tavern and gave her a broiled chicken for supper but she could provoke me to do nothing because my roger would not stand with all she could do. About ten I went home and said my prayers." (p. 231)
124. Ibid., 228-29. "Went to meet Mrs. C-r-t-n-y at Mrs. Smith's . . . we went to bed and I rogered her once and gave her a guinea"
125. Ibid., 240.
126. Ibid., 476, 482, 484: He did find a cooperative maid at one house on December 4, and on December 9 "felt the breasts of the Negro girl which she resisted a little."
127. Ibid., 513.
128. Ibid., p. 374.This happened repeatedly: "I said my prayers and made Annie feel about my person. . . . I committed uncleanness with Annie and then prayed to God to forgive me." (pp. 409, 410)

see also pp. 377, 404, 406, 408, 412, 416, 431, 433, 434, 437, 438, 443.

129. Ibid., 446, 447.
130. Ibid., 491; see also pp. 448, 468, 490, 491, 499, 502, 505, 506, 508, 509, 514, 515, 518, 526, 527. Byrd sometimes would note that "Annie lay down with me but I only kissed her," and would sometimes add a postscript: "committed uncleanness with Annie, for which God forgive me, and I was very sorry for it."
131. Ibid., 38. A diary fragment from Byrd's old age does record that he "played the fool" then several times.
132. Donald McCormick, *The Hell-Fire Club* (London: Jarrolds, 1958), 14.
133. *Weekly Journal*, 20 February 1720, 380-81; cited in Louis C. Jones, *The Clubs of the Georgian Rakes* (New York: Columbia University Press, 1942), 37.
134. See Plumb, *Georgian Delights* (Boston: Little, Brown, 1980), 4, 8. In Plumb's words, "The placid exteriors of Georgian houses, the well-kept lawns, the restfully contrived vistas, the distant folly and unruffled lake breed of themselves a sense of expansive well being. . . ."
135. See Collins and Baker, 128, 185. Chandos had attained the lucrative position of British postmaster general early in the century and made a fortune that he invested throughout the British empire: building projects in London, oyster fisheries, copper mines, land in New York State, investment in the Africa Company, and so on.
136. Cesar Saussure, *A Foreign View of England in the Reigns of George I and George II* (London: Murray, 1902), 217. As Plumb (op. cit., chapter one) notes, great merchants also had political power: an oligarchy of wealth had authority in London; the economic lords of sugar, tobacco, and slave-trading dominated Bristol; coal magnates controlled Newcastle.
137. *Oxford Magazine*, May 1772, 186; cited in Jones, *The Clubs of the Georgian Rakes*, 26.
138. Bostonians in 1702 did find it necessary to form a Society for the Suppression of Disorders. Carl Bridenbaugh, *Cities in the Wilderness: The First Century of Urban Life in America, 1625-1742* (New York: Knopf, 1960), 226-27, quotes several reports from Philadelphia, and refers to problems elsewhere but mixes up Cotton and Increase Mather.
139. See Louis Kronenberger, *Kings & Desperate Men* (New York: Knopf, 1942), 26.
140. See McCormick, *The Hell-Fire Club*, 21-22. Later in the century some of the annotations became particularly florid; for example,

John Wilkes (p. 22) recommended one "Effie" to his friend Charles Churchill, praising her ability for "translating the language of love into a rich, libidinous and ribald phraseology which lends enchantment to her amoristic acrobatics."

141. McCormick, *The Hell-Fire Club*, 23.
142. *Weekly Journal*, 20 February 1720, 380-81; cited in Louis C. Jones, *The Clubs of the Georgian Rakes*, 37.
143. *The Hellfire-Club, kept by a Society of Blasphemers* (London, 1721), 19; cited in Ronald Fuller, *Hell-Fire Francis* (London: Chatto & Windus, 1939), 25. It was said that at club meetings "Each man strives who in Sin shall most abound,/And fills his Mouth with Oaths of dreadful sound."
144. Ronald Fuller, *Hell-Fire Francis* (London: Chatto & Windus, 1939), 27.
145. Ibid., 36.
146. Print reproduced in Jones, T*he Clubs of the Georgian Rakes*, 22.
147. *Oxford Magazine*, May 1772, 186. A woman alone on the street after dark, and sometimes even one accompanied by a man, could be subject to gang rape.
148. James Burgh, *Political Disquisitions* (London, 1774), 3:105.
149. *Whitehall Evening Post*, 1 May 1773.
150. Bishop Burnet quoted in Burgh, 3:32.
151. Ibid.
152. Louis Kronenberger, *Kings & Desperate Men* (New York: Knopf, 1942), 176, 178. The universities were reformed during the Victorian era.
153. See Fuller, *Hell-Fire Francis*, 45, 58.
154. See Rosamond Bayne-Powell, *Eighteenth-Century London Life* (New York: Dutton, 1938), 192. Government lotteries were popular among the lower classes, and Bayne-Powell notes that "In the upper ranks, card playing was often the chief occupation of the day." Bayne-Powell (p. 46) quotes Lady Hertford's remark that it was "a mortifying sight, that playing should become the business of the nation, from the age of fifteen to four-score."
155. William B. Boulton, *The Amusements of Old London* (London: John C. Nimmo, 1901), 202.
156. Claret and port were the most popular table wines; rum and whiskey were not commonly drunk in England until the end of the century.
157. Bayne-Powell, *Eighteenth-Century London Life*, 52. Bayne-Powell adds, "Many, perhaps we must say the majority, of the men in the upper classes and a large number of women, lived a life of habitual immorality. The men took their pleasure where they pleased. They

would keep a mistress until they were tired of her, and would then cast her out into the street."

158. By 1700 the basic Navigation Act was already forty years old. It was originally aimed to protect British shipping from Dutch competition, and did so by providing that only English-owned vessels, of which the master and at least three-fourths of the crew were English, could ship goods to or transport goods from any English colony. These provisos helped many American colonists, since they were also defined as English, but the nuances were abundant: Lawrence A. Harper, *The English Navigation Laws* (New York: Columbia University Press, 1939), 388-89, explains well the different classes of ships that were English-built but foreign-owned, English-owned but foreign-built, etc.
159. In Oliver M. Dickerson's summary (*American Colonial Government, 1696-1765* [Cleveland: Clark, 1912], 32), "Instead of being oppressive the shipping clauses of the Navigation Act had become an important source of colonial prosperity which was shared by every colony."
160. For basic developments, see the following Acts: 13 and 14 Charles II, c. 11; 5 William and Mary, c. 5; 3 and 4 Anne, c. 10; 12 Anne, c. 9; 8 George I, c. 12; 11 George II, c. 26; 24 George II, c. 57; 4 George III, c. 26. For acts concerning wood products, see 5 George III, c. 45; and 9 George III, c. 50.
161. See George L. Beer, *The Old Colonial System, 1660-1754* (New York: P. Smith, 1958), 2:240-41. Dickerson, *American Colonial Government*, 14, has statistics on bounty payments; see also pp. 17-18, 36.
162. Act of 5 George II, c. 22.
163. For additional background on the hat industry see Herbert L. Osgood, *The American Colonies in the Eighteenth Century* (New York: Columbia University Press, 1924-1925), 2:346; for the state of the industry in 1791 see Alexander Hamilton's Report on Manufactures. Concerning woolen goods, the prohibition on water export did not affect household and community production, and distribution of goods within a particular colony was unrestricted. The American textile industry remained small for economic, not political reasons; the proof of that proposition is that during the half-century following the Revolution, Americans continued to import woolen goods, which made up 30 percent of all imports in 1821.) As long as textile-industry wages in England were very poor, and as long as American laborers had the option of readily available land, American labor was overpriced in comparison.
164. For further discussion, see Arthur C. Bining, *British Regulation of*

the Colonial Iron Industry (Philadelphia: University of Pennsylvania Press, 1933); neither Bining's intensive research into the eighteenth-century iron industry, nor Victor S. Clark's on manufacturing generally, found any American iron works that were discontinued, steel furnaces destroyed, or iron-works operators prosecuted. Even after liberty was achieved, progress in steel was slow: In 1810, over a third of a century after independence, Tench Coxe's report showed only four steel furnaces in the entire United States. For additional information see Dickerson, *The Navigation Acts and the American Revolution*, 48.

165. See Charles M. Andrews, *The Colonial Period of American History* (New Haven: Yale University Press, 1934-1938), 347.
166. Joshua Gee, *Trade and Navigation of Great Britain Considered* (London, 1738), 149.
167. That figure was given by James Otis, in his book *The Rights of the British Colonies Asserted and Proved* (Boston, 1764); in New York the customary rate was a fourth to a halfpenny per gallon.
168. Ibid., 135.
169. (Bernhard Knollenberg, *Origin of the American Revolution: 1759-1766* [New York: Macmillian, 1960], 139).The multi-volumed works by Andrews, *The Colonial Period of American History*, and Osgood, *The American Colonies in the Eighteenth Century*, provide useful information on the Navigation Acts' effect, but the most incisivie analysis of American reaction to the Acts is Dickerson's, *The Navigation Acts and the American Revolution*; he notes (pp. 31, 33) that "by 1760 all opposition had disappeared." Dickerson's search of contemporary newspapers, pamphlets, and other publications discovered no evidence of anti-Navigation agitation, "nor did prominent Americans express any desire for a general relaxation of its major requirements."
170. January 9, 1712, in Byrd, *The Great American Gentleman*, 1:205, 206, 207.
171. Ibid., 209, 214.
172. Correspondence of Governor Horatio Sharpe in *Archives of Maryland*, 3:3. Royal governors, however, did not have as much wherewithal for bribery as did their masterful practitioners in London. Bailyn, *The Origins of American Politics*, 72, quotes British officials in America, often hamstrung by colonial legislatures, as saying that they had insufficient gifts to bestow, and thus were "without the means of stopping the mouths of the demagogues." See also Dinkin, *Voting in Provincial America*, 67.
173. *An Impartial Examination of the Conduct of the Whigs and Tories . . . (London, 1763), 63.*
174. See Plumb, *Sir Robert Walpole*, 59-61, and Herbert M. Atherton,

Political Prints in the Age of Hogarth: A Study of the Ideographic Representation of Politics (London: Oxford University Press, 1974). As Plumb and others have pointed out, campaigning was expensive, since voters generally demanded bribes, and governing even more so, since constitutents needed stroking. Members of Parliament who wished reelection typically provided their districts with a piped water supply, a new town hall, or a new school building, and made sure that the relatives of aldermen and other local influentials received government jobs.

175. Osgood, *The American Colonies in the Eighteenth Century*, 3:324, 327.
176. Dorothy Marshall, 164.
177. Ibid., 164-66. It should be noted, however, that during this entire period structural changes in colonial administration provided the opportunity for more control from London. Colonies that were under proprietary rather than direct royal control had certain protections and privileges, and the goal of the Board of Trade in London was generally to supplant charter and proprietary government by royal government. In 1685, only two provinces had royal government, but one by one, as British centralizers took advantage of local upheavals, plums fell into the basket: by 1763 only Pennsylvania and Maryland remained as proprietary governments, and Connecticut and Rhode Island were the only colonies enjoying elected governors by charter.
178. Charles Davenant, "On the Planation Trade," pt. 2, disc. 3 of *Discourse on the Public Revenues and on the Trade of England* (London, 1698), 207.
179. Quoted in "The Irregular and Disorderly State of the Plantations," Report, American Historical Association, 1892, 39; cited in Andrews, *The Colonial Period of American History* (New Haven: Yale University Press, 1934-1938), 336.
180. See Osgood, *The American Colonies in the Eighteenth Century*, 2:319-20.
181. Davenant, *Discourse on the Public Revenues and on the Trade of England*, 207. Davenant also worried about what might happen should the colonies become rebellious teenagers: "Colonies are the strengh of the kingdom, while they are under good discipline, while they are made to observe the fundamental laws of this original country, and while they are kept dependent upon it. But otherwise they are worse than members lopp'd from the body politic, being indeed like offensive arms wrested from a nation to be turned against it as occasion shall serve."
182. *The Craftsman*, 28 December 1728.
183. Andrews, *The Colonial Period of American History*, 342.

184. See, for example, Arthur Dobbs, *Some Thoughts concerning Government in general and our Present circumstances in Great-Britain and Ireland* (Dublin, 1728); cited in Andrews, *The Colonial Period of American History*, 335-36
185. Henry St. John, Viscount Bolingbroke, *Contributions to the Craftsman*, ed. Simon Varey (Oxford: Clarendon Press, 1982), 170-72.
186. Ibid.
187. Dorothy Marshall, 155.
188. Ibid., 156: "Walpole was not over-concerned with men's morality as long as he got their votes. His use of patronage was efficient and ruthless. Only friends, relations and those who could serve him received his favours."
189. Bolingbroke, op. cit., 170-72.
190. Ibid., 96-97.
191. James Burgh, *Britain's Remembrancer . . . A Brief View, from History, of the Effects of the Vices Which Now Prevail in Britain, Upon the Greatest Empires and States of Former Times* (London, 1746), 15. Burgh particularly disliked "English Traders burlesqued into French dancing masters, their clothes bepatched with Lace, their hands unfitted for Business by being muffled up in Cambrick to the Finger-ends."
192. Ibid., 16.
193. Ibid.
194. Ibid.
195. Ibid.
196. Ibid., 6.
197. John Brown, 2:239.
198. Ibid., 240.
199. Ibid., 219-20. The political result would be, "The People would be easily persuaded, that they have nothing left, but an expensive Shadow of their former Constitution: That the greatest Part of their Property is spent in supporting a new System, built on the Ruins of their former Privileges. . . ."
200. Frankin engaged in "any manner of pleasant Exercises" with any manner of pleasing women. See, for example, Cecil B. Currey, *Road to Revolution: Benjamin Franklin in England, 1765-1775* (Garden City, N.Y.: Doubleday, 1968), 109, and many other accounts. Franklin's own list of virtues, contained in his autobiography, included "chastity" as the twelfth. He gave an interesting definition of the word: "Rarely use venery but for health and offspring, never to dullness, weakness, or the injury of your own or another's peace or reputation."
201. Benjamin Franklin, *Papers* , ed. Leonard W. Labaree, 2:411.

Theological Battles

202. See Herbert L. Osgood, *The American Colonies in the Eighteenth Century* (New York: Columbia University Press, 1924-1925), 2:4 and Labaree, *Royal Government*, 15. In the colonies, royal governors were to support the established denomination, and ministers were to support the government. Each new crown-appointed governor was responsible for overseeing religious and moral life as well as political and economic life. Governors—with the exception of those appointed to head Massachusetts and New Hampshire—were directed to see that the Book of Common Prayer was read every Sunday and holy day; that the sacraments were administered in all Anglican churches according to the established rites; that Anglican parishes had clergymen who were not acting scandalously and that the clergymen were paid.
203. Daniel Defoe, *Party-Tyranny; or, an Occasional Bill in Miniature, as now Practised in Carolina* (London, 1705).
204. See Sosin, *English America* . . . 95, 101.
205. Osgood, *The American Colonies in the Eighteenth Century*, 2:29.
206. Daniel J. Boorstin, *The Americans* (New York: Random House, 1958), 129.
207. George F. Willison, *Patrick Henry and His World* (Garden City, N.Y.: Doubleday, 1969), 64. Their counterparts in England displayed the same talents.
208. Ronald Fuller, *Hell-Fire Francis* (London: Chatto & Windus, 1939), 34.
209. Ibid., 33 provides a good summary analysis: "Rationalism in the Church encouraged laziness in the cleric: and the opposite of Enthusiasm is Indifference. 'Above all No Enthusiasm' is the motto of a bell in a midland church."
210. Reynolds quoted by Rosamond Bayne-Powell, *Eighteenth-Century London Life* (New York: Dutton, 1938), 291-92.
211. John Brown, 1:34.
212. Ibid., 51: "Bare and impudent Obscenity" formerly was "confined to Brothels, [but] the *Double-Entendre*, like a modern fine Lady, is now admitted into the best Company."
213. Ibid., 54-55.
214. Ibid., 74: "The Man of Fashion is indeed cut off from the very Means of Solid Instruction. His late Hours occasion a late Rising; and thus the Morning, which should be devoted to the Acquisition of Knowledge, is devoted to Sleep, to Dress, and Ignorance."
215. Ibid., 84-85.
216. Ibid., 118-19.

217. Churchill, *Works*, 149.
218. Bayne-Powell, *Eighteenth-Century London Life*, 290.
219. John Brown, *An Estimate of the Manners and Principles* 1:34.
220. W. A. Speck, *Stability and Strife* (Cambridge: Havard University Press, 1977), 98; he notes, "Owing their translations from one see to another more to active service on the whig side in parliamentary elections and voting for the government in the House of Lords than to exemplary piety or to theological scholarship; publishing pamphlets in defence of the ministry rather than treatises in defence of the faith; spending all their time in London in attendance at debates in the upper house or at ministerial levees rather than in their dioceses taking care of souls, ordaining priests or confirming laymen—no wonder they did not seem an exemplary episcopate."
221. *Acts and Resolves of Province of Massachusetts Bay*, 1:62.
222. Lord Cornbury showed how personal arrogance could lead to conflict—but, even if governors were angels, the colony's church-state rules virtually guaranteed tensions.
223. William Smith, 118-19. In addition, a fractured New York Assembly in 1693 had passed a law giving no special status to the Church of England, but simply specifying that six towns in the four southern counties of the colony should have a public tax to support "a good, sufficient, Protestant Minister." The particular denomination was up for grabs.
224. Presbyterians over the years won some court battles and lost others. Disputes were hottest in 1710, from 1719 through 1732, and again during the 1760s, as inhabitants of Jamaica kept refusing to pay Anglican salaries and kept trying to repossess their own building. The experience showed that letting the majority of residents decide a town's tenured theology was not going to work. Presbyterian stirring up of public opinion against the Anglicans eventually led to denominational disestablishment. For additional perspective, see R. Freeman Butts, *The American Tradition in Religion and Education* (Boston: Beacon Press, 1950), 27-28.
225. In T. H. White's words, *The Age of Scandal* (New York: Putnam's, 1950, 189-90) "Successful clergymen constituted a monied aristocracy who ate and drank well."
226. Once Spotswood was no longer governor, he and Byrd became friends.
227. Jones quoted in Daniel J. Boorstin, *The Americans* (New York: Random House, 1958), 127-28.
228. In 1748, soon after Thomas Sherlock was made bishop of London, he told the king about his concerns with vestry independence. Sherlock complained that the Virginia system as it

had developed was "a great blow to the Kings Supremacy and right of Patronage"; he recognized that as "the People has got this power, they will not easily part with it," but he suggested that subtle ways be found "to qualify it."

229. Samuel Wigglesworth's father was Michael Wigglesworth, author in 1662 of the long poem, "God's Controversy with New England."
230. Ibid.
231. Mark A. Noll, *A History of Christianity in the United States and Canada* (Grand Rapids: Eerdmans, 1992), 97.
232. Jonathan Edwards, "God's Awful Judgment (1748)," in *The Works of President Edwards*, ed. Sereno B. Dwight (New York, 1829-30), 2:37-39.
233. Ibid.
234. Jonathan Edwards, "Thoughts on the Revival," in *Works*, 1:366.
235. Gilbert Tennent, *The Necessity of Praising God for Mercies Received* (Philadelphia, 1745), 7.
236. Benjamin Lord, *Religion and Government Subsisting Together in Society, Necessary to Their Compleat Happiness and Safety* (New London, 1751), 42.
237. Mark Leavenworth, *Charity Illustrated and Recommended* (New London, 1772), 31.
238. Patricia Bonomi, *Under the Cope of Heaven* (New York: Oxford University Press, 1986), 186.
239. Ibid., 152, 157, 186.
240. See Ruth H. Bloch, *Visionary Republic: Millennial Themes in American Thought, 1756–1800* (Cambridge: Cambridge University Press, 1985), 42.
241. *Pennsylvania Gazette*, 22 November 1739.
242. Osgood, *The American Colonies in the Eighteenth Century*, 3:471.
243. Samuel Davies, *Sermons on Important Subjects* (New York, 1845), 100.
244. Ryder quoted in Osgood, *The American Colonies in the Eighteenth Century*, 3:475.
245. George William Pilcher, *Samuel Davies: Apostle of Dissent in Colonial Virginia* (Knoxville: University of Tennessee Press, 1971), 83.
246. Davies, Samuel, *The Duty of Christians to Propagate Their Religion Among the Heathens* (London, 1758). Davies did not attack slavery and himself owned slaves, but he frequently spoke of the need for humane treatment within that institution, noting that slaves should be treated as members of the master's family.
247. Pilcher, *Samuel Davies: Apostle of Dissent in Colonial Virginia*, 108; Noll, *A History of Christianity in the United States and Canada*, 106-7. Davies also argued that slaveowners' neglect of their

responsibility to teach slaves about Christ was one of the sins for which the French and Indian War was punishment: "Thousands of poor slaves [were] almost as ignorant of Christianity as when they left the wilds of Africa." (*Religion and Patriotism, the Constituents of a Good Soldier* [Philadelphia, 1755], 57.)

248. See *A True State of the Present Difference between the Royal African Company and the Separate Traders* (London, 1717) quoted in Charles M. Andrews, *The Colonial Period of American History* (New Haven: Yale University Press, 1934-1938), 346.
249. *Virginia Gazette*, 15 August 1771; see also Wesley M. Gewehr, *The Great Awakening in Virginia, 1740-1790* (Durham, N.C.: Duke University Press, 1930), 116. In the mind of one observer, "Some of them were hare-lipped, others were blear eyed, or hump-backed, or bow legged, or clump footed; hardly any of them looked like other people."
250. A charge against five Baptists in Spottsylvania County was that "they cannot meet a man on the road but they must ram a text of Scripture down his throat."
251. See Gewehr, *The Great Awakening in Virginia*, 120, 122, 130.
252. Alan Heimert, *Religion and the American Mind, from the Great Awakening to the Revolution* (Cambridge: Harvard University Press, 1966), 303.
253. Increase Mather, *An Essay for the Recording of Illustrious Providences* (Boston, 1684), preface.
254. Cotton Mather, *Magnalia Christi Americana* (London, 1702) 2:341.
255. *New-York Weekly Journal*, 31 December 1773, 2.
256. During the post-Cornbury years, legislative vigilance had slackened. Since Cosby commanded the garrison and was thus responsible for administering military appropriations, he could underpay soldiers and gain for himself an extra £2000 annually. The governor ordinarily took a percentage of appeasement presents for Indians that the assembly allocated, and he could and did also file well-padded expense accounts for his trips to Albany.
257. James Alexander, *A Brief Narrative of the Case and Trial of John Peter Zenger* (New York, 1736), n.p.
258. See Marvin Olasky, *Central Ideas in the Development of American Journalism* (Hillsdale, N.J.: Lawrence Erlbaum, 1991), chs. 3 and 4.
259. See Osgood, *The American Colonies in the Eighteenth Century*, 3:95.
260. J. A. Doyle, *The Colonies Under The House of Hanover* (New York: Ams Press, 1907), 164. Bradley also anticipated that London arrogance would snicker at the possibility of revolt: "It may be

thought impractical at present for any of these provinces or places alone to attempt anything of that kind."

261. Whitefield, *Works*, 3:163.
262. Elisha Williams, *The Essential Rights and Liberties of Protestants, a Seasonable Plea for Liberty of Conscience and the Right of Private Judgment in matters of Religion, without any control from Human Authority* (Boston, 1744), 26.
263. Ibid., 27.
264. *Some Remarks on Mr. President Clap's History and Vindication, of the Doctrines of the New-England Churches &c.* (New Haven, 1756), 109.
265. *New-York Weekly Journal*, 12 March 1739. *New-York Gazette*, 11-18 March 1734 cited in Bonomi, *Under the Cope of Heaven* 87. Under press pressure the New York Assembly took action similar to that of other colonies. In 1739, it began requiring that salaries to public officials be listed by name and individual amounts, rather than appropriated in a gross sum; that measure curtailed the governor's appointment power, for if the Assembly did not like his appointees it would not pay their salaries. In 1741, it eliminated the garrison stipend, and in 1742, it began to refuse to make grants for a longer period than one year. The effect of such measures was to curtail the governor's influence and also make the post less economically desirable. By 1753, the governor's salary was probably only three-fourths as large as Cornbury's in 1703 had been and ancillary sources of income were stripped away. For additional information see Michael G. Kammen, *Colonial New York: A History* (New York: Scribner's, 1975), 202.
266. Peter Kalm, *The America of 1750: Peter Kalm's Travels in North America*, ed. Adolph B. Benson (New York: Wilson-Erickson, 1937), 1:139-40.
267. James Abercromby, *An Examination of the Acts of Parliament Relative to the Trade and the Government of our American Colonies* (London, 1752). Abercromby argued that rules passed when the colonies "were only commencing and taking birth" were inadequate, and that steps must be taken to ensure the colonists' "reverence, respect and obedience." He wanted statuatory limitations on colonial power and increased subservience to Great Britain so as to have an economy "conducive to the general and particular state of the British people." For additional perspective see Charles M. Andrews, *The Colonial Period of American History* (New Haven: Yale University Press, 1934-1938), 411.
268. See also Osgood, *The American Colonies in the Eighteenth Century*, 2:330, for an early assessment of economic trends by a deputy surveyor: He glumly noted that colonists were learning how to

make woolen, linen, iron, and copper products, and "in a few years they will set up for themselves independent of England." A work from the 1720s, Jeremiah Dummer's *Defence of the New England Charters* (Boston, 1721), stressed the courage and suffering that underlay the founding of the northern colonies, juxtaposed that with the advantages Great Britain gained from them, and hinted that they could go their own way if the English were obdurate. Dummer also emphasized the usefulness of the colonies as a market for English exports and the importance of northern products—particularly lumber, provisions, and horses sent from New England to the island colonies, and ship-building supplies provided to the British navy—for the continuation of the imperial system. But none of these writings advocated independence.

269. See Butts, *The American Tradition in Religion and Education*; and Daniel J. Boorstin, *The Americans* (New York: Random House, 1958), 130.
270. Boorstin, *The Americans*, 131.
271. Charles Chauncey, 16-17.
272. Bacon, Thomas, *A Sermon Preached at the Parish Church of St. Peter's* (London, 1751); for additional discussion, see Olasky, *The Tragedy of American Compassion* (Wheaton, Ill.: Crossway Books, 1992), chapter 1.
273. John Brown, *An Estimate of the Manners and Principles of the Times* (London, 1757), 1:55.
274. Donald McCormick, *The Hell-Fire Club* (London: Jarrolds, 1958), 132; see also Fuller, *Hell-Fire Francis*; Louis C. Jones, *The Clubs of the Georgian Rakes* (New York: Columbia University Press, 1942); and other accounts.
275. McCormick, *The Hell-Fire Club*, 33. Dashwood was born in 1708 and died on December 11, 1781, sixteen days after news of the British surrender at Yorktown arrived in London.
276. *Town and Country Magazine*, 1769, 1:122.
277. See Fuller, *Hell-Fire Francis*; McCormick, *The Hell-Fire Club*; Jones, *The Clubs of the Georgian Rakes*; Cecil B. Currey, *Road to Revolution: Benjamin Franklin in England, 1765-1775* (Garden City, N.Y.: Doubleday, 1968); David Mannix *The Hell Fire Club* (New York: Ballantine, 1959); Barbara Jones, *Follies and Grottoes*.
278. McCormick, *The Hell-Fire Club*, 87.
279. Charles Johnstone, *Chrysal, or the Adventures of a Guinea* (London, 1760), 384, 387.
280. Evidently trying to give himself cover in case a libel action was brought, Johnstone placed the Abbey not in its actual location but on an island in the middle of a lake at West Wycombe Park.
281. See McCormick, *The Hell-Fire Club*, 90.

282. Ibid., 74.
283. Potter quoted in Fuller, *Hell-Fire Francis*, 137.
284. Benjamin Franklin, *Writings*, ed. Albert Henry Smyth (New York: Macmillan, 1905-1907), 6:111, and Currey, *Road to Revolution*, 105-7.
285. Melvin H. Buxbaum, *Benjamin Franklin and the Zealous Presbyterians* (University Park: Pennsylvania State University, 1975), 138-51, discussed the Franklin-Whitefield connection and suggests that the wily Franklin may have publicized Whitefield's controversial speaking in order to encourage a civil war within the theologically Reformed camp, and thus undermine his political enemies.
286. Benjamin Franklin, *Papers*, ed. Leonard W. Labaree (New Haven: Yale University Press, 1959-), 102-4. Franklin speculated, "It may be that these created Gods are immortal, or it may be that after many Ages, they are changed, and Others supply their Places."
287. Ibid. Franklin was not inclined to worship the God of the Bible, but he argued that "since there is in all Men something like a natural Principle which enclines them to DEVOTION or the Worship of some unseen Power . . . it seems required of me, and my Duty, as a Man, to pay Divine Regards to SOMETHING."
288. Ibid. Franklin sometimes sounded like an eighteenth-century New Ager.
289. Franklin, *Writings*, 6:111.
290. McCormick, *The Hell-Fire Club*, 107.
291. Mannix, *The Hell Fire Club*, 91.
292. Ibid. They are noted as having attended a religious service together at a Unitarian chapel in London on April 17, 1774. Franklin and Dashwood also shared business interests: Dashwood for a time was England's Postmaster General, and Franklin, with a similar role in America, was pleased that Dashwood "has re-organized the postal services of England." (McCormick, *The Hell-Fire Club*, 43)
293. Francis Dashwood, and Benjamin Franklin, *An Abridgement of the Book of Common Prayers* (London, 1773). See also Betty Kemp, *Sir Francis Dashwood: An Eighteenth-Century Independent* (New York: St. Martin's, 1967), 137.
294. Franklin, *Writings*, 9:358.
295. Franklin would only make oblique mentions of such matters, however: He did not write much about his venery or his veneration of an idol from the pantheistic pantheon. See Franklin, *Papers*, 7:294-95, for advice to one writer on why not to come clean about controversial beliefs that might damage public standing: "tho' your Reasonings are subtle, and may prevail with

some Readers, you will not succeed so as to change the general Sentiments of Mankind on that subject, and the Consequence of printing this Piece will be a great deal of Odium drawn upon your self . . . He that spits against the Wind, spits in his own Face."

296. Franklin, *Papers*, 10:167-68, 232-33, 320
297. Franklin, *Writings*, 7:186.
298. Franklin, *Papers*, 2:113, 115. For this and other attacks on Presbyterianism by Franklin, also see Buxbaum, *Benjamin Franklin*, 1, 37, 89, 96-109, 112, and 214. Franklin so feared Presbyterian influence in Pennsylvania that he advocated royal government: see Buxbaum, 13-14, 155, 177, 192, 199, and 205-19.
299. Franklin, *Papers*, 2:91-126. See also Alfred Owen Aldridge, *Benjamin Franklin and Nature's God* (Durham: Duke University Press, 1967). Aldridge praised Franklin for how he "spoke out boldly in the first person against the fundamentalist position—the obligation of literal interpretation."

The War to End Wars

300. Osgood, *The American Colonies in the Eighteenth Century* (New York: Columbia University Press, 1924-1925), 2:524-25.
301. On the other hand, Rhode Island hawks and doves debated so long that the 150 men eventually dispatched arrived in Canada too late to fight.
302. Douglass a quarter-century before had fought smallpox inoculation, arguing that the procedure was not approved by London experts.
303. Buxbaum, *Benjamin Franklin*, 149.
304. English forces had failed in an attempt to seize the fort at St. Augustine five years before; in Osgood's words, the conquest of Louisbourg "was the only important victory, and certainly the most dramatic one, which had yet been won by the British in the colonial wars." (*The American Colonies in the Eighteenth Century*, 2:533).
305. Thomas Hutchinson, *The History of the Colony and Province of Massachusetts Bay*, edited by Lawrence Shaw Mayo (Cambridge: Harvard University Press, 1936), 3:50.
306. Britain and France officially declared war in 1756.
307. Davies, Samuel, *Sermons on Important Subjects* (New York, 1845), 365. The same reasons would apply a century later, during the War Between the States.
308. Ibid.
309. Francis Jennings, *Empire of Fortune* (New York: Norton, 1988), 142.

310. Ibid., 143.
311. Alan Rogers, *Empire and Liberty* (Berkeley: University of California Press, 1974), 63.
312. Jennings, *Empire of Fortune*, 157.
313. Benjamin Franklin, *Autobiography*, ed. Leonard W. Labaree (New Haven: Yale University Press, 1964), 226.
314. See Thomas Barton, *Unanimity and Public Spirit* (Philadelphia, 1755), 10.
315. Davies, Samuel, *Virginia's Danger and Remedy* (Williamsburg, Va., 1756), 12-19.
316. Davies united dissent with wartime patriotism, typified by his famous sermon following the defeat of General Braddock's force in 1755: Frightened Virginians should "cry aloud to God for help" but also show God's spirit within them by helping themselves: "Christians should be patriots. What is that religion good for that leaves men cowards upon the appearance of danger?" (Davies, "On the Defeat of General Braddock" in *Sermons on Important Subjects*, 3:100).
317. Davies made this prescient observation in a footnote to his published sermon, "Religion and Patriotism" (also included in *Sermons*, 3:47).
318. Stanley M. Pargellis, *Lord Loudon in North America* (New Haven: Yale University Press, 1933), 57-82; see also Jennings, *Empire of Fortune*, 285.
319. Rogers, *Empire and Liberty*, 54.
320. Historians still disagree on the number of persons killed after the surrender: estimates range from 200 to 1,300. The Indians' scalping of hospital patients and disarmed prisoners had an ironic aftermath: many were victims of smallpox, and the Indians took not only scalps but the disease as well home to their friends and relations. The resultant massacre by disease probably left more fatalities among the Indians than there had been among the whites. (Jennings, *Empire of Fortune*, 319, 320.)
321. John Brown., 1:79-80.
322. Ibid., 95.
323. Ibid., 101.
324. Ibid., 2:175-76.
325. *Pennsylvania Gazette*, 16 March 1758, 1.
326. See Fred Anderson, *A People's Army* (Williamsburg, Va.: University of North Carolina Press, 1984), 14.
327. Perry's recollections quoted in Anderson, *A People's Army*, 11-12.
328. Jennings, *Empire of Fortune*, 220. Jennings notes, "Perhaps Wolfe planned to clean the site on which he would fall dead."
329. Rogers, *Empire and Liberty*, 55. Forbes told the Pennsylvania

Assembly that unless it provided him with the wagons he demanded, British troops would leave the frontier "and sweep the whole Country indiscriminately of every Waggon, Cart, or Horse." Forbes succeeded in breaking the gridlock, but only by raising more opposition to British demands.

330. See the *Pennsylvania Magazine of History and Biography*, 3 (1879): 14; colonists complained that "as arrogance unchecked knows no bounds, the military soon silenced the civil power, [and] property became dependent on the moderation of a licentious soldiery."
331. See Jennings, *Empire of Fortune*, 226, 298.
332. Rogers, *Empire and Liberty*, 61. British generals averaged fifty-five years of age in 1755, and colonels fifty; American generals averaged forty-three years of age, and colonels twenty-seven. English officers were gentlemen, while American officers typically were small businessmen or farmers.
333. Rogers, *Empire and Liberty*, 72.
334. Ibid.
335. See chapter 4 of Anderson, *A People's Army*.
336. See Jennings, *Empire of Fortune*, and Rogers, *Empire and Liberty*.
337. Jennings, *Empire of Fortune*, 303. Army procurers sometimes resorted to kidnapping, a procedure seen as equivalent to naval impressment.
338. See Jesse Lemisch, "Jack Tar in the Streets: Merchant Seamen in the Politics of Revolutionary America," *William and Mary Quarterly*, 3d ser., 25 (1968): 383.
339. Wolfe's force had sat before Quebec for two and a half months. His artillery could not shoot far and high enough to reach the French citadel on the heights of Quebec.
340. Jennings' analysis of the war (*Empire of Fortune*, 211) is good and succinct: "By maintaining massive armies in the field, however ineptly led, the British drained New France of men and resources, and eventually overwhelmed the French by sheer weight. When the breakthrough came, the regulars took Quebec and Montreal. In that sense they 'won' the war."
341. Rogers, *Empire and Liberty*, 67. Of course, the master-slave relationship that appalled Americans when they looked at the British was perpetuated in their attitudes toward blacks. The difference was that on this side of the Atlantic the sharpest distinctions were along racial rather than class lines.
342. Anderson, *A People's Army*, 191.
343. In some colonies the councils were rubber-stamps, but in others they fought for some independence.
344. See William Lawon Grant, "Canada versus Guadeloupe," *American Historical Review*, 17 (July 1912): 735-43.

345. See *Boston Gazette*, 5 May and 12 May 1760, with its reports on town meetings and the British desire to eliminate them because they were "popular and mobish"; see also Robert E. Brown, *Middle-class Democracy and the Revolution in Massachusetts*, 1691-1780 (Ithaca: Cornell University Press, 1955), 191-92.
346. John C. Miller, *Origins of the American Revolution* (Boston: Little, Brown, 1943), 73.
347. Comptroller Weare, "Observations on the British Colonies on the Continent of America," in Massachusetts Historical Society, *Collections*, 1st ser., 1:67-82; cited in Robert E. Brown, *Middle-Class Democracy*, 179.
348. Ibid.
349. Charles Royster, *A Revolutionary People at War: The Continental Army and American Character, 1775-1783* (Chapel Hill: University of North Carolina Press, 1979), 10. Another London calculation went like this: If the decentralizing tendencies of the prewar years continue, the colonies will be lost: England might as well make a stand now before the colonies became stronger.
350. James Thomas Flexner, *George Washington and the New Nation* (Boston: Little, Brown, 1969), 69.
351. Ibid.
352. See Jack Greene's essay in Peter Marshall, and Glyn Williams, eds., *The British Atlantic Empire before the American Revolution* (London: Frank Cass, 1980), 98.
353. The British Museum houses a painting, done in 1742 by George Knapton, of Sandwich in Turkish dress.
354. See Louis C. Jones, *The Clubs of the Georgian Rakes* (New York: Columbia University Press, 1942), 91.
355. Sandwich's spin doctors later passed around the story that he had started eating sandwiches because he worked so hard that he could not leave his desk.
356. N. A. M. Rodger, *The Insatiable Earl: A Life of John Montagu, Fourth Earl of Sandwich, 1718-1792* (London: HarperCollins, 1993), 71-72, 75, 318.
357. Ronald Fuller, *Hell-Fire Francis* (London: Chatto & Windus, 1939), 63.
358. The British government had two secretaries of state at that time, and would shortly add a third (for the American colonies).
359. See Rodger, *The Insatiable Earl: A Life of John Montagu, Fourth Earl of Sandwich, 1718-1792*, 80, 115-16. George III did at one point indicate his disapproval of Sandwich's cavorting by turning him down for a position he wanted, but apparently political as much as personal considerations were involved.
360. Jones, *The Clubs of the Georgian Rakes*, 116-17.

361. Wilkes, Dashwood, and Sandwich all had been members of the Society of Beefsteaks, a rollicking club for rakes.
362. See Donald McCormick, *The Hell-Fire Club* (London: Jarrolds, 1958), 97-102. Sandwich evidently thought it amusing to hold burlesque services at times. There is a story of Sandwich's once asking the baboon to "say grace," and a clergyman guest who responded, "I was intending to say grace myself, but I had no idea you had a near relative for a chaplain."
363. McCormick, *The Hell-Fire Club*, 132; Fuller, *Hell-Fire Francis*, 162-63; many other accounts. Charles Johnstone, *Chrysal, or the Adventures of a Guinea* (London, 1760), 163, has Sandwich saying, "Spare me, gracious Devil. I am as yet but half a sinner. I never have been half so wicked as I pretended." There are obvious inaccuracies in Johnstone's storytelling; Rodger, who is extraordinarily sympathetic to Sandwich, discounts such accounts and all of Wilkes' attacks—but Rodger's decidedly amoral analysis (declaring moral questions to be nonissues) is itself suspect. Reports of abbey activities did circulate contemporaneously in publications such as *Town and Country*, March 1769, 122, and May 1773, 245.
364. *New Foundling Hospital for Wits*, 4,106; Fuller, *Hell-Fire Francis*, 63, 190. Wilkes inspired the publication and selling of other caricatures as well, and went after Sandwich personally, writing that "His name is a shame—and his eyes are so lewd!"
365. Sandwich was effective in party councils but had little popular appeal; as Horace Walpole wrote, "Sandwich can never get rid of the smell of brimstone." For additional background, see McCormick, *The Hell-Fire Club*, 96.
366. Jones, *The Clubs of the Georgian Rakes*, 136, writes that Wilkes had read the poem to Sandwich and Dashwood, who enjoyed it and encouraged Wilkes to have a copy printed for each Medmenham member. This would make Sandwich's action an even more hypocritical set-up, but there is insufficient evidence on this point.
367. Warburton, like many other prelates of the period, apparently led a graceless life.
368. McCormick, *The Hell-Fire Club*, 141.
369. Bernard Knollenberg, *Origin of the American Revolutionary*: 1759-1766 (New York: Macmillan, 1960), 37.
370. Charles Churchill, "The Candidate," in *Works* (London, 1774), 3:105.
371. *In limine*: an eighteenth-century Latin expression referring to the vagina.
372. Buxbaum, *Benjamin Franklin*, 105: Franklin "was the first man in the Middle Colonies to carry on a sustained and open attack on

Calvinism and the Presbyterian Establishment, just as he and his fellow Couranteers had been the first to perpetrate an open and sustained assault on New England Calvinism and its supporters."

373. Franklin, Benjamin, *Papers*, ed. Leonard W. Labaree, 11:332.
374. Bernhard Knollenberg, *Origin of the American Revolution: 1759-1766* (New York: Macmillian, 1960), 155; see also Murray Rothbard's discussion of Franklin in *Conceived in Liberty* (New York: Arlington House, 1975), 3:44.
375. Buxbaum, *Benjamin Franklin*, 207-19. Most Pennsylvanians desired less royal power in their commonwealth, not more. Franklin's allies gained 3,500 signatures on a petition for royal government, but opponents gathered 15,000 and won a crucial election.
376. Adams' letter to Tudor, June 5, 1817, quoted in *American Historical Review*, 47 (July 1942): 806-7.

Coalition Building

377. Cecil B. Currey, *Road to Revolution: Benjamin Franklin in England, 1765-1775* (Garden City, N.Y.: Doubleday, 1968), 5.
378. John Adams, *Works* (Boston, 1850-1856), 4:6,21.
379. Buxbaum, *Benjamin Franklin*, 206.
380. Ibid. Desperate Quaker leaders tried to put the colony under direct royal control, in the belief that they could dominate a governing council to be appointed by the king. Pennsylvania Presbyterians in turn attacked attempts to have their rights "greatly abridged."
381. Gilbert Tennent, *A Persuasive to the Right Use of the Passions in Religion* (Philadelphia, 1760), 21.
382. Thomas Pownall, *The Administration of the Colonies* (London, 1764), 93-94.
383. Murray Rothbard, *Conceived in Liberty* (New York: Arlington House, 1975), provides a favorable portrayal of Walpole and his policies.
384. See Edwin Scott Gaustad, *A Religious History of America* (San Fransico: Harper & Row, 1990), 183.
385. Bernhard Knollenberg, *Origin of the American Revolution, 87.*
386. Ibid.
387. Jack P. Greene, "The Seven Years' War and the American Revolution: The Causal Relationship Reconsidered," in Peter Marshall, and Glyn Williams, eds., *The British Atlantic Empire before the American Revolution* (London: Frank Cass, 1980), 98.
388. See Joseph B. Felt, "Statistics of Taxation in Massachusetts," in American Statistical Association, *Collections*, (1847), 1:211-581,

and Lawrence H. Gipson, *The Coming of Revolution, 1763-1775* (New York: Harper, 1954), 121-53.

389. Quoted in Oliver M. Dickerson, *The Navigation Acts and the American Revolution* (Philadelphia: University of Pennsylvania Press, 1951), 54.
390. Ibid. Britain's Sir Charles Dalrymple told Americans in 1775 that "eight millions of us pay ten millions of taxes, which amounts to twenty-five shillings on each person, three millions of you pay only seventy-five thousand pounds, or six pence on each person, and this in a country where a labouring man gets three times the wages that he does in England, and yet may live on half the expense." (One pound contained 240 pence.)
391. Knollenberg, *Origin of the American Revolution*, 1:144.
392. Anyone who wished to make out a will, obtain a mortgage or lease agreement, buy land or an insurance policy, publish a newspaper or pamphlet, or even purchase dice or playing cards, had to pay.
393. David Ramsay, *The History of the American Revolution* (Philadelphia, 1789), 61-62.
394. Rothbard, *Conceived in Liberty*, 3:73.
395. Knollenberg, *Origin of the American Revolution*, 79-80.
396. *An Appeal to the Public*, quoted in Gaustad, *A Religious History of America*, 88.
397. See Carl Bridenbaugh, *Mitre and Sceptre* (London: Oxford University Press, 1962), 138-68.
398. Quoted in Bonomi, 200.
399. Bridenbaugh, *Mitre and Sceptre*, 323.
400. Ibid: "Republicanism in religion existed in all of the colonies, not just in New England."
401. Joseph Bellamy, *Works* (Boston, 1850), 1:590-96.
402. Of the major historians, only Carl Bridenbaugh (*Mitre and Sceptre*, 207) has seen this clearly; he wrote, "For us of the twentieth century, it is very, very difficult to recover imaginatively a real understanding of the enormous effect of this controversy on the opinions and feelings of a pious, dissenting people grown accustomed to ecclesiastical self-government."
403. Adams' statement in Jedediah Morse, *Annals of the American Revolution* (Hartford, 1824), 198, 200.
404. *New-York Gazette*, 16 May 1768.
405. *Pennsylvania Journal*, beginning March 24, 1768; cited in Arthur M. Schlesinger, *Prelude to Independence: The Newspaper War on Britain, 1764-1776* (New York: Random House, 1957), 123. The articles apparently were written by Francis Alison, a Presbyterian who was vice-provost of the College of Philadelphia, and by John Dickinson.

406. *Boston Gazette*, 4, 11, 18 April 1768.
407. See William Wirt Henry's edited biography of Patrick Henry, (*Life, Corespondence, and Speeches*, [New York: Scribner's, 1891]), 1:13-16; and also Richard R. Beeman, *The Old Dominion and the New Nation, 1788-1801* (Lexington, Kentucky: University Press of Kentucky, 1972), 17; George William Pilcher, *Samuel Davies: Apostle of Dissent in Colonial Virginia* (Knoxville: University of Tennessee Press, 1971), 83-88; and Meade, 1:69-70.
408. Quoted in Charles C. Cohen, "The 'Liberty or Death' Speech: A Note on Religion and Revolutionary Rhetoric," *William and Mary Quarterly*, 38 (1981): 712.
409. Rhys Issac, "Religion and Authority: Problems of the Anglican Establishment in Virginia in the Era of the Great Awakening and the Parsons' Cause," *William and Mary Quarterly*, 3d ser., 30 (1973): 13.
410. Ibid., 12.
411. Bridenbaugh, *Mitre and Sceptre*, 100.
412. Henry, *Life, Corespondence, and Speeches*, 1:41.
413. Ibid., see also George F. Willison, *Patrick Henry and His World* (Garden City, N.Y.: Doubleday, 1969), 69; Jacob Axelrad, *Patrick Henry* (New York: Random House, 1947), 26.
414. Knollenberg, *Origin of the American Revolution*, 83.
415. *Virginia Gazette*, 6, 20 June 1771, and Isaac, "Religion and Authority," 185. The incident occurred after a group of Anglican clergymen agreed to circulate a petition for the establishment of an American episcopate, but four of them dissented and made their case publicly in the pages of the Gazette.
416. Samuel Adams, *Writings*, ed. Harry Alonzo Cushing (New York: Putnam's, 1908), 1:33, and 3:220.
417. Pauline Maier, *The Old Revolutionaries* (New York: Knopf, 1980),47.
418. *Boston Gazette*, 4 April 1768.
419. Samuel Adams, *Writings*, 2:232.
420. Ibid.
421. The Stamp Act required the affixing of stamps on not only civil documents but all documents "in ecclesiastical matters in any court of probate, court of the ordinary, or other court exercising ecclesiastical jurisdiction within said colonies."
422. Bridenbaugh, *Mitre and Sceptre*, 237.
423. Ibid., 259. Bridenbaugh among all conventional historians has most clearly seen the culture-war aspects of the revolutionary struggle. Bernard Bailyn, while underestimating the role of Awakened understanding in the prerevolutionary crises, also observed the concern, writing (*The Ideological Origins of the*

American Revolution [Cambridge: Harvard University Press, 1967], 95) that colonists "saw about them, with increasing clarity, not merely mistaken, or even evil, policies violating the principles upon which freedom rested, but what appeared to be evidence of nothing less than a deliberate assault launched surreptitiously by plotters against liberty in both England and America."

424. John Adams, *Works*, 3:450-51.
425. Ibid., 3:464.
426. Ibid., 10:85.
427. Alan Heimert, *Religion and the American Mind, from the Great Awakening to the Revolution* (Cambridge: Harvard University Press, 1966), 351-52.
428. Bridenbaugh, *Mitre and Sceptre*, 311-12.
429. Alice M. Baldwin, *The New England Clergy and the American Revolution* (Durham: Duke University Press, 1928), 113. The theologically conservative were crucial to the Revolutionary effort; Heimert (*Religion and the American Mind*, 290-93) demolishes the legend that Jonathan Mayhew and other theological liberals were central to the Revolutionary effort. Mayhew's attacks on the Anglican church's "enormous hierarchy ascending by various gradations from the dust to the skies" were useful to the patriotic course. He also posed the right questions concerning the Angelican church: "Will they never let us rest in peace? . . . Is it not enough, that they persecuted us out of the old world? Will they pursue us into the new to convert us here?—compassing sea and land to make us proselytes?" Mayhew also was suspicious of Anglican attempts to dispel concern by saying that bishops were to be dispatched not to rule but simply for administrative ease: Mayhew saw a slippery slope, noting that "people are not usually deprived of their liberties all at once, but gradually, by one encroachment after another, as it is found they are disposed to bear them." And yet, Mayhew's dislike for Calvinists such as Samuel Adams was so strong (a true son of the Arminian preacher Experience Mayhew, Mayhew drank in deism and Lockean philosophy at Harvard) that he could not coalesce with them against the British.
430. Mark A. Noll, *A History of Christianity*, 122. See Alice Baldwin's documentation in *The New England Clergy and the American Revolution* of how Calvinist ministers explained to their congregations that resistance to a tyrannical king was obedience to God.
431. Morgan, *The Stamp Act Crisis*, 254.
432. Heimert, *Religion and the American Mind*, 21.
433. John Witherspoon *Ecclesiastical Characteristics* (London, 1753), 10.

434. Witherspoon did not dwell on which came first, knowledge of God's truth or liberty; over time, the latter depends on the former.
435. James Witherspoon walked the talk; in 1776, when he was twenty-five, he was killed by a cannonball during the Battle of Germantown.
436. Ralph Ketcham, *James Madison* (New York: Macmillan, 1971), 37.
437. Jarnum Collins, *President Witherspoon* (Princeton: Princeton University Press, 1925), 112.
438. Articles in *Gazetteer and New Daily Advertiser*, quoted in Buxbaum, *Benjamin Franklin*, 32-33; other polite terms included "scum and refuse" who deserved a return "to their inferior rank. . . ."
439. *American Historical Review*, 4 (1906): 498.
440. Cushing Strout, *The New Heavens and New Earth: Political Religion in America* (New York: Harper & Row, 1974), 74.
441. Jonathan Parson, *Freedom from Civil and Ecclesiastical Slavery* (Newburyport, 1774), 11-15.
442. See Collins op. cit., and Martha Lou Lemmon Stohlman, *John Witherspoon: Parson, Politician, Patriot* (Philadelphia: Westminister, 1976).
443. William A. Gordon, *Discourse Preached December 15th, 1774* (Boston, 1775), n.p.
444. Edward Frank Humphrey, *Nationalism and Religion in America, 1774-1789* (Boston: Chipman, 1924), 410. Adams was making a motion that Jacob Duche, an Anglican rector, open with prayer the September 7, 1774, session of the First Continental Congress. Duche did so, and was appointed chaplain of Congress; ironically, he defected to the British side in 1777.
445. *Newport Mercury*, 22 March 1773.
446. James Burgh, *Political Disquisitions* (London, 1774), title page.
447. Ibid., 3:130. One reason for the problem, the patriotic Burgh argued (p. 148), was that young noblemen "set out to visit foreign countries before they have acquired any knowledge of their own, and get their minds infected with foreign vices before they have established in them any good and virtuous habits."
448. Ibid., 130.
449. Ibid., 141.
450. Ibid., 1:v.
451. Ibid.
452. Ibid., 175. Burgh did not see rotation of offices as a silver bullet capable of slaying sin; he wanted to contain it. As Burgh wrote on pp. 267-68, "It is difficult to exclude corruption. . . . But the difficulty of excluding corruption is no reason for giving over all endeavors to abolish it; any more than the difficulty of living a virtuous life amidst the various temptations, to which our frail

nature is exposed, is a reason for our giving over all endeavors to regulate our conduct by the strict laws of morality."

453. John Adams' letter (1775) to Burgh, quoted in Joseph Illick, ed., *America & England, 1558-1776* (New York: Appleton-Century, 1970), 260.
454. See William Wells, *The Life and Public Services of Samuel Adams* (New York, 1865-1868), 1:10.
455. John Cartwright, *American Independence, the Interest and Glory of Great Britain* (Philadelphia, 1776), letter 9.
456. Ibid.
457. *Journals of the Continental Congress*, ed. W. C. Ford and Gaillard Hunt (Washington, D.C.: Government Printing Office, 1904-37), 1:6.
458. Richard Henry Lee, *Memoir*, 78.
459. Catharine Macaulay, *An Address to the People of England, Ireland, and Scotland on the Present Important Crisis of Affairs* (London, 1775), 2. She noted that the treaty extended the boundaries of Quebec, thus "enlarging the bounds where despotism is to have its full sway . . . so as to comprehend those vast regions that lie adjoining to the northerly and westerly bounds of our colonies."
460. Ibid., 5.
461. Ibid.
462. Ibid. She also complained vigorously that the Stamp Act and other measures should have been fought in England by those who knew the history of English rights—but "with the same guilty acquiescence, my countrymen, you have seen the last Parliament finish their venal course, with passing two acts for shutting up the Port of Boston . . . and changing their chartered constitution of government."
463. Burgh, *Political Disquisitions*, 313. Such measures, Burgh claimed, "would have brought into the treasury ten times more than could have ever been expected from taxing, by force and authority, the unrepresented Colonies."
464. Dickinson, *Writings*, 16.
465. Ibid., 19.
466. John Dickinson, *Letters from a Farmer in Pennsylvania* (Philadelphia, 1768), 3.
467. Cecil B. Currey, *Road to Revolution: Benjamin Franklin in England, 1765-1775* (Garden City, N.Y.: Doubleday, 1968), 52-53.
468. See "The Reasons on Which Were Founded the Protest . . . Concerning the Sending of Mr. Franklin . . . ," *Pennsylvania Journal* (November 1, 1764), and *An Answer to the Plot* (Philadelphia, 1764).

469. Currey, *Road to Revolution: Benjamin Franklin in England*, 386: "He was a satisfied place holder in the imperial bureaucracy, and a supporter of the new king."
470. Ibid., 92-99.
471. Verner W. Crane, *Benjamin Franklin's Letters to the Press*, 1758-1775 (Chapel Hill: University of North Carolina Press, 1950), 195.
472. Benjamin Franklin, *Writings*, ed. Albert Henry Smyth (New York: Macmillan, 1905-1907), 5:362-63.
473. Ibid., 6:311-12.
474. Ibid. See also Franklin's 1773 piece, "Rules by Which a Great Empire May be Reduced to a Small One"; it and other revealing tidbits may be found in Franklin, *Papers*, ed. Leonard W. Labaree, 13:20, 47-48, 55-58, 79-81; 14:64-71, 129-35, 228-32; and 15:81, 181-82.
475. See Currey, *Road to Revolution: Benjamin Franklin in England*, 382-83.
476. Currey details Franklin's involvement with land speculation and disappointment with British policies that affected his investments.
477. Max Beloff, ed., *The Debate on the American Revolution, 1761-1783* (London: Nicholas Kaye, 1949), 225-28. Burke elegantly noted that "America, gentlemen say, is a noble object . . . an object well worth fighting for. Certainly it is, if fighting a people be the best way of gaining them."
478. Ibid.
479. William Safire, ed., *Lend Me Your Ears: Great Speeches in History* (New York: Norton, 1992).
480. Samuel Johnson, *Taxation No Tyranny*, 3d ed. (London, 1775); cited in Lillian B. Miller, *"The Dye Is Now Cast": The Road to American Independence*, 1774-1776 (Washington: Smithsonian Institution Press, 1975), 163.
481. Famous letter-writer Horace Walpole asked (Miller, *"The Dye Is Now Cast": The Road to American Independence*, 167), "What is England now?" and proceeded to answer his own question: "A gaming, robbing, wrangling, railing nation, without genius, character, or allies."
482. William Wirt, *The Life of Patrick Henry* (Hartford, 1847), 138.
483. Ibid., 140, 141.
484. Jeremiah 6:14, 14:15, 39:8, cited in Cohen, "The 'Liberty or Death' Speech: A Note on Religion and Revolutionary Rhetoric."
485. Some historians have asked whether Patrick Henry really said these words, because the speech was first published in 1816, forty-one years after the event, in Wirt's biography of Henry; Wirt based the text on a reconstituted transcript produced by federal

judge St. George Tucker, a spectator at the church when Henry gave his speech. The most comprehensive analysis, Stephen T. Olsen's *A Study in Disputed Authorship: The 'Liberty or Death' Speech* (Ph.D. diss., Pennsylvania State University, 1976), concludes on the basis of market word tests (which measure habits of word selection) that Tucker wrote the speech. Cohen, however, points out that the Scriptural citations in the speech show that while Tucker may have produced many of the specific fill-in words, he was largely a secularized writer and "was an unlikely figure to couch Revolutionary rhetoric in biblical language." Cohen concludes that the heart of the speech, the biblical emphasis, and the most quotable lines, are Henry's. Certainly, the speech made a remarkable impact at the time, and the flag of the militia that served under him carried the slogan, "Liberty or Death." See also Safire's discussion in *Lend Me Your Ears: Great Speeches in History*, 84-86.

486. Samuel Adams, *First Book of the American Chronicles of the Times* (Boston, 1775), 1.
487. Adams, writing anonymously but acknowledging authorship to his friends, noted in the pamphlet the role of "Jeremiah, to-wit, Samuel Adams."
488. Ibid., 8.
489. Ibid., 1-14.

Vice, Virtue, and the Battlefield

490. Speech of February 2, 1775, in Peter Force, ed., *American Archives* (Washington, D.C.: 1837-1853), 1:1542.
491. Hugh Percy, *Letters . . .* 1774-1776, ed. Charles K. Bolton (London, 1902), 28-29; cited in Bernhard Knollenberg, *Growth of the American Revolution: 1766-1775* (New York: Macmillan, 1975), 11-12.
492. Speech of March 16, 1775, in Force, *American Archives*, 1681.
493. *Dictionary of National Biography* (London, 1882), 13:701.
494. N. A. M. Rodger, *The Insatiable Earl: A Life of John Montagu, Fourth Earl of Sandwich, 1718-1792* (London: HarperCollins, 1993), 163.
495. Ibid., 162.
496. Willliam Wilberforce was the leader of these activities.
497. Rodger, *The Insatiable Earl: A Life of John Montagu, Fourth Earl of Sandwich, 1718-1792*, 161, 163.
498. David Hume, *Letters*, 3:319.
499. The British government then had three Secretaries of State: Essentially, one was for northern Europe, one for points south and east, and one for points west.

500. Piers Mackesy's *The Coward of Minden: The Affair of Lord George Sackville* (London: Allen Lane, 1979); and Alan Valentine's *Lord George Germain* (London: Oxford University Press, 1962); are informative biographies of Sackville; memoirs by Cumberland, Stockdale, and Wraxall also are useful, as is Edmund George Fitzmaurice's *Life of William, Earl of Shelburne* (London: Macmillan, 1875) and the Balderston-edited diaries of Hester Thrale.
501. Mackesy, *The Coward of Minden*, 34, 254.
502. Letter to Lord Hertford, November 18, 1763, in Horace Walpole, *Corespondence* (New Haven: Yale University Press, 1937-1980), 38:232. Walpole's letter to Horace Mann, 20:315, repeated one savage ditty of the day: "Religion is now become a mere farce/ Since the head of the church is in Cunningham's arse."
503. Ibid., 20:254.
504. Mackesy, *The Coward of Minden*, 255.
505. Ibid., 257. Thompson later entered the service of the Elector of Bavaria, achieved a reputation in science, and was created Count Rumford.
506. Mackesy, *The Coward of Minden*, 35.
507. Thomas Hutchinson, *The Diary and Letters of His Excellency, Thomas Hutchinson,* (London, 1883-86), 1:289; (entry of October 18, 1779); also in Mackesy, *The Coward of Minden*, 257. Mackesy is apologetic for bringing up issues of sexual leanings, but writes, "I have dwelt on Sackville's homosexual reputation in the belief that it was his Achilles' heel. It may help to explain the strangely hostile reaction which he aroused in many people . . . his difficulty in forming happy working relationships with some of his colleagues, and the recurring hints of instability which flit through his life."
508. Valentine, *Lord George Germain*, 474.
509. Edmund Fitzmaurice, *Life of William, Earl of Shelburne*, (London, 1875), 1:360, 362-63.
510. Valentine, *Lord George Germain*, 380.
511. See contemporary accounts summarized in Valentine, *Lord George Germain*, 127-28.
512. W. J. Wood, *Battles of the Revolutionary War* (Chapel Hill: Algonquin, 1990), xxxi.
513. Ibid., xxviii.
514. "Vagrants, smugglers, and criminals of various kinds might thus escape such legal penalties as had been adjudged them," Edward Curtis wrote in *The Organization of the British Army in the American Revolution*. "In this way every gaol served as a recruiting depot." (Cited in Wood, *Battles of the Revolutionary War*, xxviii.)

515. Samuel Langdon, *Government corrupted by Vice, and recovered by Righteousness*, (Watertown, Mass., 1775). His text was Isaiah 1:2b.
516. Ibid.
517. Patrick Henry, *Life, Corespondence, and Speeches*, ed. William Wirth Henry (New York: Scribner's, 1891), 1:280.
518. Ibid.
519. *Pennsylvania Evening Post*, 27 June 1775.
520. *Norwich Packet*, 6 November 1775.
521. Catherine Albanese, *Sons of the Father: The Civil Religion of the American Revolution* (Philadelphia: Temple University Press, 1976), 24.
522. Samuel Spring: "The soldiers stacked their arms all over the aisles, and I preached to the army and to the citizens who crowded the galleries." Quoted in Joel T. Headley, *The Chaplains and Clergy of the Revolution* (New York, 1864), 100; cited in Suzanne Geissler, *Jonathan Edwards to Aaron Burr, Jr.: From the Great Awakening to Democratic Politics* (New York: Edwin Mellen, 1981), 138.
523. Albanese, *Sons of the Father: The Civil Religion of the American Revolution*, 86.
524. A working guide to determine the probability of God's special providence might be, "If a dog bites a man, that's not news. If a man bites a dog, that's news. If a man bites a lion and the lion does not eat him up, that's a miracle."
525. Albanese, 87.
526. Ibid.
527. The bitter Lee later said, "I desire most earnestly that I may not be buried in any church or church yard . . . I have had so much bad company while living, that I do not choose to continue it when dead." Norman Gelb, *Less Than Glory* [New York: Putnam's, 1984], 122.
528. General Orders, August 3, 1776, in George Washington, *Writings*, ed. John C. Fitzpatrick (Washington, D.C.: Government Printing Office, 1931-1944), 5:367.
529. General Orders, July 9, 1776, in Washington, *Writings*, 245. The reverence of Washington and other revolutionary leaders kept the American Revolution from becoming French-like. In Cushing Strout's words (*The New Heavens and New Earth: Political Religion in America* [New York: Harper & Row, 1974],. 54), "No rebels have been more saturated with respect for traditional morality and civil order, yet without calling for dictatorship or terror; and no enthusiasts for the millennial prospects of the revolutionary future can ever have been as troubled as the Americans were by the special guilts of those who considered themselves a chosen people,

addicted to declaring occasions for public fasts and national humiliation."

530. Henry, *Life, Corespondence, and Speeches*, 1:451. The convention on June 25, 177,6 also resolved "that the practice of gaming and profane swearing will ever be considered as an exclusion from all public offices or employments."
531. Gelb, *Less Than Glory*, 79.
532. Flexner, *George Washington in the American Revolution*, 176; Wood, *Battles of the Revolutionary War*, 65.
533. Flexner, 171. Contemplation of Washington's character moved even the deistic Paine to discuss God's blessings: "I reckon it among those kind of public blessings which we do not immediately see that God hath blessed him with uninterrupted health and given him a mind that can even flourish upon care."
534. Ibid., 183.
535. F. J. Hudleston, *Warriors in Undress* (London: Castle, 1925), 100.
536. Gelb, *Less Than Glory*, 91-92.
537. John Calvin, *Institutes of the Christian Religion*, ed. John T. McNeill, trans. Ford Lewis Battles (Philadelphia: Westminster, 1960), 2:1504 (bk. 4, ch. 20, sec. 16).
538. Quoted in Gary Amos, *Defending the Declaration* (Nashville: Wolgemuth and Hyatt, 1989), 43, 47.
539. Blackstone, *Commentaries on the Laws of England* (1765), ed. St. George Tucker (1803; reprint, South Hackensack, N.J.: Rothman Reprints, 1969), 1:39.
540. Ruth H. Bloch, *Visionary Republic: Millennial Themes in American Thought, 1756-1800* (Cambridge: Cambridge University Press, 1985), 62.
541. Ibid.
542. Albanese, *Sons of the Father: The Civil Religion of the American Revolutio*n, 120; see also Amos, *Defending the Declaration*, 157.
543. Calvin, *Institutes*, 1:202 (bk. 1, ch. 16, sec. 4).
544. The Westminister Confession (1646) was (and is) the defining creedal document of Reformed churches in the Puritan and Presbyterian tradition.
545. Calvin, *Institutes*, 1:197 (bk. 1, ch. 16, sec. 1). Calvin observed that "to make God a momentary Creator, who once for all finished his work, would be cold and barren, and we must differ from profane men especially in that we see the presence of divine power shining as much in the continuing state of the universe as in its inception."
546. The Declaration of Independence throughout emphasized the temple of royalty, not that of the British parliament: There was no need for the colonies to declare themselves independent from that

to which they never had been subject, as they understood the imperial relationship.

547. Samuel Adams, *An Oration Delivered at the State-House in Philadelphia, to a very Numerous Audience, on Thursday the 1st of August, 1776* (Philadelphia, 1776).
548. Ibid.
549. Albanese, *Sons of the Father: The Civil Religion of the American Revolution*, 22.
550. Ibid., 25.
551. See one of Shaw's most popular plays, *The Devil's Disciple*, in which "Gentleman Johnny" Burgoyne appears; see also Paul Lewis, *The Man Who Lost America: A Biography of Gentleman Johnny Burgoyne* (New York: Dial, 1973), 272-73.
552. Lewis, 97-102.
553. See Valentine, *Lord George Germain*, 429-30.
554. Lewis, op. cit., 101.
555. Letter of November 20, 1776, in Force, *American Archives*, 3:928.
556. Fitzmaurice, 1:358-59. William Knox, Germain's under secretary, gave a slightly different version of the story: Sackville, Knox wrote, was leaving, and Knox told him "that there was no letter to Howe to acquaint him with the plan or what was expected of him . . . 'So,' says Lord Sackville, 'my poor horses must stand in the street all the time, and I shan't be to my time anywhere.'" According to Knox, Sackville's deputy secretary D'Oyly promised to write to Howe, and "with this his Lordship was satisfied as it enabled him to keep his time, for he would never bear delay or disappointment." D'Oyly then neglected to write Howe, and Sackville, preoccupied with his own affairs, never checked. (See Lewis, *The Man Who Lost America: A Biography of Gentleman Johnny Burgoyne*, 106, and Valentine, *Lord George Germain*, 284.)
557. John Fortescue, *A History of the British Army* (London: Macmillan, 1902), part 2, volume 3, notes that Howe's letters show that he knew of the Burgoyne campaign plans but was also planning a campaign to take Philadelphia; since that also had removed London approval, he believed that's where he was to go. Fortescue (p. 210) is astounded at what Sackville had wrought: "Howe was left with directions to attack Philadelphia, and Burgoyne with positive and unconditional commands to advance to Albany and there place himelf under Howe's orders. . . . Never was there a finer example of the art of organizing disaster."
558. *The Parliamentary History of England* (London, 1810), 19:534.
559. Ibid., 19:1224.
560. W. E. H. Lecky, *A History of England in the Eighteenth Century* (London, 1882), 4:72.

561. Freeman, *George Washington, a biography* (New York: Scribner's, 1948-57), 4:570.
562. Barbara Tuchman, *The First Salute* (New York: Knopf, 1988), 183.
563. Flexner, *George Washington in the American Revolution,* 319.
564. Ibid; see Paul F. Boller, Jr., *George Washington & Religion* (Dallas: Southern Methodist University Press, 1963), 92-115, for more quotations from Washington concerning Providence.
565. Flexner op. cit.
566. Ronald Fuller, *Hell-Fire Francis* (London: Chatto & Windus, 1939), 247-51. Hackman was hanged at Tyburn.
567. Rodger, *The Insatiable Earl: A Life of John Montagu, Fourth Earl of Sandwich, 1718-1792*, 189.
568. See John A. Tilley, *The British Navy and the American Revolution* (Columbia: University of South Carolina Press, 1987), 117; Tilley notes that "in the winter of 1777-1778 innocuous Tory admirals willing to serve in North America under the earl of Sandwich were becoming rare."
569. Rodger, loc. cit.
570. For an account of the Parliamentary attacks on Sandwich during 1779 and Sandwich's defense, see Tilley, *The British Navy and the American Revolution*, 131-32.
571. Daniel A. Baugh, "The Politics of British Naval Failure, 1775-1777," *American Neptune*, 52 (1992): 246.
572. *Dictionary of National Biography*, 13:704.
573. Valentine, *Lord George Germain*, 337-40.
574. William Belsham, *Memoirs of the Reign of George III* (London, 1795), 2:134.
575. Ibid., 409.
576. Ibid,. 408.
577. See Valentine, *Lord George Germain*, 116, 129, for examples of Sackville-Sandwich quarrels.
578. Walpole, *Corespondence*, to Sir Horace Mann, January 17, 1782, 25:238; letter of Edmund Malone to the Earl of Charlemont, June 18, 1781, quoted in Valentine, *Lord George Germain*, 396.
579. Fuller, *Hell-Fire Francis*, 245.
580. *Dictionary of National Biography*, 13:701.
581. Fuller, *Hell-Fire Francis*, 245.
582. See Walpole's letter to Lady Ossory, June 7, 1780, in *Corespondence*, 33:184.
583. *Memoirs of the Life of Sir Samuel Romilly* (London, 1840), 1:123; cited by editor in Walpole, *Corespondence*, 29:62.
584. *Dictionary of National Biography*, 13:703. According to the dictionary's summary, "It is not therefore to be wondered at that when war with France broke out in 1778 the number of ships in

the navy was inadequate, and that of what there were many were not seaworthy. . . ." The *DNB* account was written by the great naval historian Sir John Knox Laughton.

585. See Tilley, *The British Navy and the American Revolution*, 238: Rodney "found the opportunity to rest more or less comfortably ashore and acquire an unimaginable sum in prize money. . . ."
586. Valentine, *Lord George Germain*, 144, 363, 367; he notes (p. 363) that "no arrangement could have been better calculated to shake Clinton's confidence in Lord George and in himself, or more likely to set him at odds with Cornwallis. It was one thing to resign voluntarily and with honour, but quite another to have one's junior officer conscious that at any moment he might become one's successor. It was not long before Clinton had convinced himself that Cornwallis was playing his cards to replace him."
587. Sackville to Clinton, May 2, 1781, in Henry Clinton, *The American Rebellion: Sir Henry Clinton's Narrative of His Campaigns, 1775-1782*, ed. William Willcox (New Haven: Yale University Press, 1954), 519.
588. Clinton also spent time moving around four homes and a farm he royally maintained in Manhattan and Long Island, and writing many letters complaining about other commanders, such as Admiral Marriot Arbuthnot.
589. See Burke Davis, *The Campaign That Won America* (New York: Dial, 1970), 38. Clinton, viewing himself as moral because he had only one mistress, complained that General James Robertson, military governor of New York, was forever "smelling after every giddy girl that will let him come nigh her." Others said that Robertson and Oliver Delancey, the Adjutant General of New York, took money that could have been used for the military effort and lavished it "upon favorites, upon little misses, upon strumpets, panderers, and hangers-on."
590. Horace Walpole, 3 November 1781, *Last Journals*, 2:377.
591. Davis, *The Campaign That Won America*, 63.
592. Ibid, 102.
593. Ibid., and many other accounts. As Barbara Tuchman, *The First Salute* (p. 245), notes, "Miraculous is a term often applied to the Yorktown campaign. . . . It required a decision as bold as Hannibal's to cross the Alps by elephant. . . . The junction in Virginia had to be coordinated by two different national demands separated across an ocean without benefit of telephone, telegraph or wireless. That this was carried out without a fault seems accountable only by a series of miracles."
594. See Valentine, *Lord George Germain*, 127.
595. See Tilley, *The British Navy and the American Revolution*, 235-75.

596. Tuchman, *The First Salute*, 267. There were other tales of cut-off heads and an unborn baby hanged from a tree. Cornwallis' troops were instructed to destroy everything in their path.
597. Davis, *The Campaign That Won America*, 241-89; Wood, *Battles of the Revolutionary War*, 257-93.
598. Albanese, *Sons of the Father: The Civil Religion of the American Revolution*, 84.
599. Ibid., 83. Some recent historians have been similarly awestruck. Barbara Tuchman, *The First Salute* (p. 245), described the complications of the Yorktown expedition and observed, "That this was carried out without a fault seems accountable only by a series of miracles."
600. Washington, *Writings*, 26:496.
601. Ibid.
602. Ibid. Washington biographer Douglas Freeman (5:493) pointed out that some of Washington's letters and papers during the Revolution were drafted by assistants Jonathan Trumbull, Jr. and David Humphreys, who enjoyed "accentuating and enlarging with their pens the place that Providence had in the mind of Washington. Washington *Papers* editor John Fitzpatrick noted, however, that Washington sometimes gave his aides memos concerning his intentions, sometimes dictated to them, and sometimes wrote out letters himself, but in all cases Washington "dominated his correspondence, and cannot be denied complete responsibility for it." (*Writings*, 1:xliii-xlv.)

Agitated Peace

603. Article 5. The Articles of Confederation and other useful documents are readily available in paperback in Ralph Ketcham, ed., *The Anti-Federalist Papers and the Constitutional Convention Debates* (New York: New American Library, 1986).
604. *Providence Gazette*, 10 May 1783.
605. Article by Abraham Yates, Jr., in the *New York Packet*, 21 April 1785.
606. W. W. Hening, ed., *Laws of Virginia* (Richmond, 1823), 11:171.
607. Burnett, 401.
608. Gary Wills, *Inventing America* (Garden City, N.Y.: Doubleday, 1978), 37.
609. Jackson Turner Main, *The Antifederalists: Critics of the Constitution, 1781-1788* (Chapel Hill: University of North Carolina Press, 1961), 15.
610. Maryland Constitution of 1776, in Poore, *Federal and State Constitutions*, 819. Protection at that time was for Christians; "all persons, professing the Christian religion, are equally entitled to

protection in their religious liberty." Protection was extended to all persons in 1851.

611. Ibid. The Pennsylvania constitution the same year stated that "no man ought or of right can be compelled to attend any religious worship, or erect or support any place of worship, or maintain any ministry, contrary to, or against, his own free will and consent." Section 45 of that constitution, however, showed the desire to have government maintain social order: "Laws for the enforcement of virtue, and prevention of vice and immorality shall be made and constantly kept in force, and provision shall be made for their due execution." (Poore, 1541).
612. There were 500 Jews in Charleston, South Carolina in 1773; they comprised the largest Jewish community in America at that time.
613. Article 2, in Poore, 956.
614. Ibid. Amendments to the Massachusetts constitution in 1833 disestablished all churches.
615. Catherine Albanese, *Sons of the Father: The Civil Religion of the American Revolution* (Philadelphia: Temple University Press, 1976), 83-85.
616. Some editors were self-conscious in such reporting, though. The *Pennsylvania Evening Post*, reporting a battle in 1775, noted that the British cannon "raked the whole length of the street, and absolutely threw double-headed shot as far as the church; and afterwards, as our troops approached, cannonaded them heavily with grape-shot"—and yet, while the British had thirty-one killed and wounded, the Americans had "no more than a slight wound in a soldier's hand." The newspaper's conclusion: The report "will scarcely appear credible, except to such as acknowledge a Providence over human affairs." (Cited in Albanese, 82-84.)
617. Albanese, 87.
618. Ibid., 88.
619. Records of the Presbyterian Church (Philadelphia, 1904), 362.
620. Flexner, *George Washington and the New Nation*, 491.
621. Governeur Morris wrote in 1782 that if the war soon ended, "I have no hope that our union can subsist except in the form of an absolute monarchy."
622. See Evarts B. Greene, and Virginia Harrington, *American Population Before the Federal Census of 1790* (New York, 1932).
623. There were problems in developing a new marketing system without British mercantile expertise, but Merrill Jensen (*The New Nation* [New York: Knopf, 1950], 235) notes that the average price for tobacco was higher in the 1780s than in the 1760s.
624. See Low, 84-85.
625. *Pennsylvania Packet*, 29 April 1785.

626. Tench Tilghman to Washington, July, 1784, quoted in Jensen, *The New Nation*, 123.
627. *Pennsylvania Gazette*, 28 July 1784.
628. Ibid., 22 February 1786; cited in Jensen, *The New Nation*, 221.
629. Oliver M. Dickerson, *American Colonial Government, 1696-1765* (Cleveland: Arthur H. Clark, 1912), 42.
630. Agrippa [Winthrop] in *The Massachusetts Gazette*, 30 November 1787.
631. Jensen, *The New Nation*, 25 and 162. Farmers particularly were not accustomed to a cash economy; as James Swan explained in his book *National Arithmetick*, "When a farmer brings his produce to market, he is obliged to take up with the buyer's offer, and is forced, not infrequently, to take merchandise in exchange, which is totally insufficient to discharge his taxes."
632. By 1786 the economy apparently was improving, and Benjamin Franklin wrote, with his typical exaggeration, that "America never was in higher prosperity, her produce abundant and bearing a good price, her working people all employed and well paid, and all property in lands and houses of more than treble the value it bore before the war." (*Works*, 9:300.)
633. Richard Henry Lee, *Letters from The Federal Farmer to the Republican* (1787-88; reprint, Englewood Cliffs, N.J.: Prentice-Hall, 1962), 91. Lee argued that the trend, after several years of "repairing houses and estates, restoring industry," and reestablishing fisheries, was upward.
634. Letter of 27 October 1783, in the *Warren-Adams Letters*, 2:232, 249; cited in Jensen, *The New Nation*, 187, 188.
635. Agrippa [Winthrop] in *The Massachusetts Gazette*, 27 November 1787.
636. See David Szatmary, *Shays's Rebellion: The Making of an Agrarian Insurrection* (Amherst: University of Massachusetts Press, 1980) for more detail.
637. For a brief summary of the extent of rebellion and reactions to it, see Glen A. Phelps, *George Washington and American Constitutionalism* (Lawrence, Kansas: University Press of Kansas, 1993), 85-90.
638. Letter to Henry Lee, October 31, 1786, in George Washington, *Writings*, ed. John C. Fitzpatrick (Washington, D.C.: Government Printing Office, 1931-1944), 29:33.
639. Letter to James Madison, 5 November 1786, in Washington, *Writings*, 52.
640. Ibid., 26 December 1786, 123.
641. Ibid.

642. Letter to David Humphreys, 26 December 1786, Washington, *Writings*, 126.
643. Letter to Henry Knox, 3 February 1787, Washington, *Writings*, 153.
644. Letter to Madison, 31 March 1787, Washington, *Writings*, 190-91. Washington also was doing some thinking about slavery during this period: He wrote to John Francis Mercer on 9 September 1786 (ibid., 5), "I never mean (unless some particular circumstance should compel me to it) to possess another slave by purchase; it being among my first wishes to see some plan adopted, by which slavery in this country may be abolished by slow, sure, and imperceptible degrees."
645. "A PLEBIAN," *An address to the People of the state of New York: showing the Necessity of Making Amendments to the Constitution, proposed for the United States, previous to its adoption* (New York, 1788): "We are told, that agriculture is without encouragement; trade is languishing; private faith and credit are disregarded, and public credit is prostrate; that the laws and magistrates are condemned. . . ."
646. Letter of 15 May 1787, in Richard Henry Lee, *Letters*, ed. James Ballagh (New York: Macmillan, 1914), 419. Despite his concern, Lee did not accept appointment to the Constitutional Convention for three reasons: his health, his position as a member of Congress which created a conflict of interest (although other Congressmen did not see it that way), and his initial confidence in those who were going to the convention. When Lee declined his nomination, he wrote to Virginia governor Edmund Randolph, "There are so many gentlemen of good hearts and sound heads appointed to the Convention, at Philadelphia, that I feel a disposition to repose with confidence in their determinations." (26 March 1787; Lee, *Letters*, 415) His repose soon was shattered.
647. The Philadelphia writer Centinel [pseud.] gave the typical incrementalist argument: Americans should not "impute the temporary and extraordinary difficulties that have hitherto impeded the execution of the confederation, to defects in the system itself." He wrote that "the harpies of power have been industriously inculcating the idea that all our difficulties proceed from the impotency of Congress, and have at length suceeded to give to this sentiment almost universal currency and belief. The devastations, losses and burdens occasioned by the late war; the excessive importation of foreign merchandise and luxuries, which have drained the country of its specie and involved it in debt, are all overlooked, and the inadequacy of its powers of the present confederation is erroneously supposed to be the only cause of our

difficulties." (Morton Borden, ed., *The Antifederalist Papers* [East Lansing: Michigan State Univ. Press, 1965], 51)

648. Brutus, Jr. [pseud.], in *New York Journal*, 8 November 1787.
649. Agrippa [Winthrop] in the *Massachusetts Gazette*, 27 November 1787.
650. See Jensen, *The New Nation*, 247-48, for other economic discussions, and Lee's letter to Mason of 15 May 1787, in Lee, *Letters*, 419.
651. Candidus [pseud.] in the [Boston] *Independent Chronicle*, 6 December 1787.
652. Mason's wording, in Jonathan Elliot, ed., *The Debates in the Several State Conventions on the Adoption of the Federal Constitution* (Philadelphia: Lippincott, 1901), 3:30. Luther Martin's formal proposal, which the Constitutional Convention did not accept, was as follows: "and whenever the legislature of the United States shall find it necessary that revenue should be raised by direct taxation, having apportioned the same by the above rule, requisitions shall be made of the respective states to pay into the Continental treasury their respective quotas within a time in the said requisition to be specified; and in case of any of the states failing to comply with such requisition, then, and then only, to have power to devise and pass acts directing the mode and authorizing the collection of the same." (Elliot, *The Debates in the Several State Conventions on the Adoption of the Federal Constitution*, 1:369.)
653. Lee, *Letters from The Federal Farmer to the Republican*, 171. Lee extended this principle but was not adament about it: He proposed "requiring that certain important laws of the federal head—as a requisition or a law for raising monies by excise—shall be laid before the state legislatures, and if disapproved of by a given number of them, say by as many of them as represent a majority of the people, the law shall have no effect. Whether it would be advisable to adopt both, or either of these checks, I will not undertake to determine." (Ibid.; also see Borden, *The Antifederalist Papers*, 117.)
654. Lee, *Letters from The Federal Farmer to the Republican*, 171, and Elliot, *The Debates in the Several State Conventions on the Adoption of the Federal Constitution*,3:214. Lee saw requirements for supermajorities on other key issues as useful in "raising checks, and guarding against undue combinations and influence in a federal system."
655. Elliot, *The Debates in the Several State Conventions on the Adoption of the Federal Constitution*, 3:275.

656. See Main, *The Antifederalists: Critics of the Constitution, 1781-1788*, 83.
657. "A Farmer," *Freeman's Oracle and New Hampshire Advertiser*, 11 January 1788: "As to the foreign debt, they have the promise of more interest from us than they can anywhere else, and we shall be able to pay them both interest and principal shortly."
658. Letter to his brother, Francis Lightfoot Lee, 14 July 1787; Lee, *Letters*, 424.
659. Agrippa [Winthrop] in *The Massachusetts Gazette*, 30 November 1787. He continued, "The Congress lands are full adequate to the redemption of the principal of their debt, and are selling and populating very fast. The lands of this state, at the west, are, at the moderate price of eighteen pence an acre, worth near half a million pounds in our money. They ought, therefore, to be sold as quick as possible. An application was made lately for a large tract at that price, and continual applications are made for other lands in the eastern part of the state. Our resources are daily augmenting."
660. Samuel Bryan, in Borden, *The Antifederalist Papers*, 53. Bryan proposed that debts could be paid through "imposts on commerce, which all agree to vest in Congress, together with the immense tracts of lands at their disposal . . . Congress have lately sold land to the amount of eight millions of dollars, which is a considerable portion of the whole debt."
661. Candidus [pseud.] in the [Boston] *Independent Chronicle*, 6 December 1787.
662. William Paterson introduced the New Jersey plan at the Constitutional Convention on June 15; on June 19 the Convention voted, seven states to three, with one divided, to table the New Jersey plan and work once again from the Virginia plan. See, among other records, James Madison, *Notes of Debates in the Federal Convention of 1787* (Athens, Ohio: Ohio University Press, 1966), 118-48.
663. See, for example, Jackson Turner Main, *The Antifederalists: Critics of the Constitution, 1781-1788*, 72-76.
664. Quoted in Main, *The Antifederalists: Critics of the Constitution, 1781-1788*, 178. In New York, Brutus Junior argued that the "immediate danger of anarchy and commotions" was something emphasized by "wicked and ambitious men. . . . Those who are anxious to precipitate a measure will always tell us that the present minute must be seized. Tyrants have always made use of this plea; but nothing in our circumstances can justify it."
665. Samuel Adams and Patrick Henry—"I smell a rat," Henry said—

did not attend the Constitutional Convention. See chapter eight for more on Hamilton.

666. Lee, *Letters*, 464. He added, "With such people, obedience resulting from fear, the offspring of force, is preferable to obedience flowing from esteem and confidence."
667. Elliot, *The Debates in the Several State Conventions on the Adoption of the Federal Constitution*, 4:192.
668. Main, *The Antifederalists*, 147.
669. See J. Budziszewski, "Politics of Virtue, Government of Knaves," *First Things* (June/July 1994): 38-44.
670. *The Federalist Papers*, 353.
671. Ibid., 286.
672. Alfred [Winthrop], *The New-York Journal*, 25 December 1787: "When I see we are sending great quantities of tobacco, wheat and flour to England and other parts of the globe beyond the Atlantic . . . I cannot be brought to believe that America is in that deplorable ruined condition which some designing politicians represent. . . ."
673. Elliot, *The Debates in the Several State Conventions on the Adoption of the Federal Constitution*, 3:137-76.
674. Lee, October 1, 1787, *Letters*, 438. Lee continued to acknowledge that the Articles of Confederation had defects, but they were but "a feather in the balance against a mountain, compared with those which would infallibly be the result of the loss of general liberty, and that happiness men enjoy under a frugal, free, and mild government." (See also his *Letters from the Federal Farmer to the Republican,* 156.)
675. Elliot, *The Debates in the Several State Conventions on the Adoption of the Federal Constitution*, 3:46.
676. Ibid.
677. Lee, *Letters from the Federal Farmer to the Republican*, Letter 3, 111
678. Ibid.
679. Ibid., additional letters.
680. Ibid., 291
681. Ibid.
682. Ibid., 352.
683. See the appendix for examples of predictions by Madison and Hamilton. For an analysis that faults the common sense "realism" taught by John Witherspoon that underlay Madison's approach, see Gary North, *Political Polytheism: The Myth of Pluralism* (Tyler, Tex.: Institute for Christian Economics, 1989), 318-20.
684. *The Federalist Papers*, 196.
685. Borden, ed., *The Antifederalist Papers*, 42: "It is true this government is limited to certain objects, or to speak more

properly, some small degree of power is still left to the States; but a little attention to the powers vested in the general government, will convince every candid man, that if it is capable of being executed, all that is reserved for the individual States must very soon be annihilated, except so far as they are barely necessary to the organization of the general government."

686. Ibid., 44-45. The elastic clause was particularly dangerous because it could "operate to do away with all idea of confederated States, and to effect an entire consolidation of the whole into one general government." It could "receive a construction to justify the passing almost any law. . . . By such a law, the government of a particular State might be overturned at one stroke."
687. Lee, Letter 3, *Letters from the Federal Farmer to the Republican*, 110-11. Lee proposed restricting federal tax power to import duties, because they could "usually be collected in a few seaport towns, and of a few individuals, though ultimately paid by the consumer; a few officers can collect them, and they can be carried no higher than trade will bear, or smuggling permit—that in the very nature of commerce, bounds are set to them. But internal taxes, as poll and land taxes, excises, duties on all written instruments, &c. may fix themselves on every person and species of property in the community; they may be carried to any lengths, and in proportion as they are extended, numerous officers must be employed to assess them, and to enforce the collection of them."
688. Ibid.
689. Elliot, *The Debates in the Several State Conventions on the Adoption of the Federal Constitution*, 3:30.
690. Cato [George Clinton], *New York Journal*, 16 December 1787.
691. Quoted in Paul Leicester Ford, ed., *Pamphlets on the Constitution of the United States* (New York: Da Capo Pess, 1968), 9.
692. Quoted in Paul Leicester Ford, ed., *Essays on the Constitution of the United States* (Brooklyn: Historical Printing Club, 1892), 329-30, and in Elliot, *The Debates in the Several State Conventions on the Adoption of the Federal Constitution*, 1:495.
693. Borden, *The Antifederalist Papers*, 234.
694. Ibid., 184.
695. A Columbian Patriot [probably Elbridge Gerry], in John D. Lewis, ed., *Anti-Federalists versus Federalists* (San Francisco: Chandler, 1967), 184. The critic noted that life tenure "by a little well timed bribery, will probably be done, to the exclusion of men of the best abilities from their share in the offices of government."
696. Ford, *Pamphlets on the Constitution of the United States*, 10-11. Gerry particularly feared that senators would go on and on: "A

Senate chosen for six years will, in most instances, be an appointment for life. . . ."

697. Lewis, *Anti-Federalists versus Federalists*, 135.
698. Elliot, *The Debates in the Several State Conventions on the Adoption of the Federal Constitution*, 3:405.
699. Brutus [pseud.], in the *New York Journal*, 10 April 1788.
700. Brutus [pseud.], for example, recommended four-year terms for senators, with a maximum of three terms or twelve years of service.
701. Elliot, *The Debates in the Several State Conventions on the Adoption of the Federal Constitution*, 3:275.
702. [Philadelphia] *Independent Gazetteer*, 16 January 1788. Bryan also argued that the Federalists were moving too fast. "To rush at once into despotism because there is a bare possibility of anarchy ensuing from the rejection, or from what is yet more visionary, the small delay that would be occasioned by a revision and correction of the proposed system of government is so superlatively weak, so fatally blind."
703. Ibid. Both sides early in 1788 also grabbed onto economic news that seemed to be suggesting either a deepening crisis or an economic turnaround. For example, early in 1788 anti-Federalist Agrippa [Winthrop] reported that Massachusetts shipowners were sending over twelve vessels to countries around the Indian Ocean; he concluded that the economy was recovering, for "we are now rising fast above our difficulties; everything at home has the appearance of improvements, government is well established, manufactures increasing rapidly, and trade expanding." (*Massachusetts Gazette*, 5 February 1788.)
704. Elliot, *The Debates in the Several State Conventions on the Adoption of the Federal Constitution*, 4:313.
705. Minority/Dissent statement in Lewis, *Anti-Federalists versus Federalists*, 131-32.
706. Main, *The Antifederalists: Critics of the Constitution, 1781-1788*, 202-3.
707. Hellen Hill Miller, *George Mason, Gentleman Revolutionary* (Chapel Hill: University of North Carolina Press, 1975), 278.
708. Publicly, though, the Federalists continually emphasized that concern was unnecessary because all powers not specifically granted to the central government were reserved to the states.
709. James Madison, *The Writings of James Madison.*, ed. Gaillard Hunt (New York: Putnam's, 1900-1910), 5:100.
710. For example, the problem of western lands, instead of leading to civil war, was becoming part of the solution. James Monroe noted at the Virginia ratifying convention that "causes of war between

the states have been represented in all those terrors which splendid genius and brilliant imagination can so well depict, but, sir, I conceive they are imaginery—mere creatures of fancy. . . . Territorial claims may now be said to be adjusted. Have not Virginia, North Carolina, and other states, ceded their claims to Congress? The dispute between Virginia and Maryland are also settled; nor is there an existing controversy between any of the states at present. Thus, sir, this great source of public calamity has been terminated without the adoption of this government."

711. Elliot, *The Debates in the Several State Conventions on the Adoption of the Federal Constitution*, 3:32.
712. Ibid., 214.
713. Ibid., 59.
714. Ibid., 53; compare with chapter eight of 1 Samuel. To continue the Old Testament imagery, anti-Federalists noted that some Americans who had benefited from the British regulatory system still yearned for the fleshpots of that Egypt. Merchants wanted shipping preferences from the federal government, artisans wanted tariffs, and farmers wanted agrarian relief.
715. Ibid., 214
716. Ibid., 661, 665. This was clearly the goal of the convention: When a motion was made to delete this article from the proposed amendments, it was defeated 85-65.
717. Ibid., 2:249c.
718. Borden, *The Antifederalist Papers*, 193.
719. Elliot, *The Debates in the Several State Conventions on the Adoption of the Federal Constitution*, 3:50.
720. Ibid., 3:159.
721. Freeman H.Hart, *The Valley of Virginia in the American Revolution, 1763-1789* (Chapel Hill: University of North Carolina Press, 1942), 187.
722. Main, *The Antifederalists: Critics of the Constitution, 1781-1788*, 192.
723. Ibid., 230.
724. Monroe, *Writings* (New York, 1898), 1:186.
725. Elliott, *The Debates in the Several State Conventions on the Adoption of the Federal Constitution*, 3:616.
726. Max Farrand, ed., *The Records of the Federal Convention of 1787*, rev. ed. (New Haven: Yale University Press, 1966), 3:302.

Tempests to Come

727. Poore, 1280. Local tax money could be used "for the support and maintenance of public Protestant teachers of piety, religion, and morality." But "no person of any one particular religious sect or

denomination shall ever be compelled to pay towards the support of the teacher or teachers of another persuasion, sect, or denomination."

728. Edwin Scott Gaustad, *A Religious History of America* (San Fransico: Harper & Row, 1990), 48.
729. Local vestries were allowed to continue taxing parishes for poor relief.
730. See Patrick Henry, *Life, Corespondence, and Speeches*, ed. William Wirth Henry (New York: Scribner's, 1891), 1:431, for insight into his understanding of toleration; Eckenrode, *Separation of Church and State in Virginia* (Richmond, 1910), 58-61, has the early bill's language.
731. Although the bill was not explicit about the rights of non-Christians, this is evidently where their tax money would go. The county schools generally had a broadly Christian base.
732. Quoted in Eckenrode, op. cit., 75. Mason added, "Among us a depravity of manners and morals prevails, to the destruction of all confidence between man and man." It was in the public interest to reduce depravity and improve confidence by whatever methods worked.
733. Henry, Madison's letter to Jefferson, 9 January 1785, in *Life, Corespondence, and Speeches*, 1:495; and "Remonstrance," in Madison, 8:229, 298-304.
734. This idea had been discussed in America at least since Roger Williams.
735. Eckenrode, op. cit., 72-116, provides a solid summary.
736. Baptists particularly were suspicious of the ability of governments to be fair in their certification that particular denominations were acting "peaceably and faithfully." They did not agree with the critique that total religious disestablishment would benefit atheism.
737. See de Tocqueville, *Democracy in America*, available in many editions.
738. For more information about this early American style of compassion, see Marvin Olasky, *The Tragedy of American Compassion* (Wheaton, Ill.: Crossway Books, 1992), chapter 1.
739. Frank Monaghan, *John Jay, Defender of Liberty* (New York: Bobbs-Merrill, 1935), 233-34.
740. Ibid., 422.
741. Scripture restricts slavery and tells Christian masters that their slaves are their brothers, and that in Christ the master-slave distinction is irrelevant. Yet, while Scripture makes defense of slavery in some modes impossible and in other modes difficult, it does not simply ban all of its modes.

742. Mark A. Noll, *A History of Christianity in the United States and Canada* (Grand Rapids: Eerdmans, 1992), 201.
743. Allen went on to become in 1816 the first bishop of a new denomination, the African Methodist Episcopal Church (Bethel). In 1830 he was elected president of the first national black political organization, the National Negro Convention. Allen died in 1831.
744. Noll, op. cit., 139.
745. Richard Henry Lee, letter to Doctor William Shippen, Jr., 2 October 1787, in *Letters*, ed. James Ballagh (New York: Macmillan, 1914), 441. Lee added, "I assure you that confidence in the moderation or benignity of power is not a plant of quick growth in a reflecting bosom. . . ."
746. Lee, letter of 5 October 1787, in *Letters*, 445.
747. Letter of 24 August 1789, in Samuel Adams, *Writings*, ed. Harry Alonzo Cushing (New York: Putnam's, 1908), 4:333. Federal legislation would not be "for federal purposes only as it professes, but in all cases whatsoever," Adams warned: "Such a Government would soon totally annihilate the Sovereignty of the several States so necessary to the Support of the confederate Commonwealth, and sink both in despotism."
748. Ibid. Lee also was troubled with reliance on amendments that by their very nature were add-ons, not integral parts.
749. Letter of 27 September 1789, in Lee, *Letters,* 505.
750. Joseph Gales, *Debates and Proceedings in the Congress of the United States* (Washington, D.C.: Government Printing Office, 1934), 1:451-52.
751. Ibid., 758-59.
752. Ibid.
753. Ibid.
754. *Journal of the First Session* . . . , 70-71, 88.
755. Ibid., 759, 784, 805.
756. Gales, *Debates and Proceedings in the Congress of the United States*, 1:783-84, 796, 948. See also Anson Phelps Stokes, *Church and State in the United States* (New York: Harper & Brothers, 1950), 92-100, and Oliver Perry Chitwood, *Richard Henry Lee, Statesman of the Revolution* (Morgantown: West Virginia University Library, 1967), 187-88.
757. The American form of government, he noted, needed "the Christian religion, as the great basis, on which it must rest for its support and permanence."
758. *Virginia Miscellaneous Records*, Library of Congress, quoted in Chitwood, *Richard Henry Lee, Statesman of the Revolution*, 188.
759. Letter of 13 September 1789, in Lee, *Letters*, 2:500-501.

760. See Gary DeMar, *God and Government* (Brentwood, Tennessee: Wolgemuth & Hyatt, 1989), 1:161.
761. See Federalist 41.
762. James Thomas Flexner, *George Washington and the New Nation* (Boston: Little, Brown, 1969), 245.
763. Fawn Brodie, *Thomas Jefferson: An Intimate History* (New York: Norton, 1974), 321.
764. Letter to John Taylor of Caroline, quoted in Henry Adams, *History of the United States of America during the Administrations of Thomas Jefferson and James Madison*, 9 vols. (New York, 1889-1891), 1:212.
765. James Madison, *Notes of Debates in the Federal Convention of 1787* (Athens, Ohio: Ohio University Press, 1966), June 18, 1787.
766. There is no evidence that Jefferson ever became a theist; late in life he acknowledged that revealed religion was useful in ordering society.
767. Compare, for example, George Washington, *Writings*, ed. John C. Fitzpatrick (Washington, D.C.: Government Printing Office, 1931-44), vols. 19 and 29. Various writers produced stylistic verve, but the substance was Washington's.
768. Monaghan, *John Jay, Defender of Liberty*, 218: Jay entered into theological discussions but tried to avoid them when he was in a severely disadvantageous position; once, when a physician doctoring Jay scoffed at Christ's resurrection, Jay replied, "Sir, I pay you for your medical knowledge and not for your distorted views of the Christian religion!"
769. Benjamin Franklin, *Papers*, ed. Leonard W. Labaree (New Haven: Yale University Press, 1959-), 7:294-95. In 1757 in London, Franklin received a book manuscript from a deist and responded "You yourself may find it easy to live a virtuous Life without the Assistance afforded by Religion, but common folk need it."
770. Willard Randall, *A Little Revenge: Benjamin Franklin and His Son* (Boston: Little, Brown, 1984), 43.
771. Franklin, of course, is the subject of hundreds of biographies and thousands of monographs and essays. Donald H. Meyer tried to pin down "Franklin's Religion" (see his article in Melvin H. Buxbaum, ed., *Critical Essays on Benjamin Franklin* [Boston: Hall, 1987], 147-67) and ended up nailing a jellyfish to the wall. His conclusion was that Franklin "did not have a visionary imagination. Franklin's might be called a graphic imagination, an engineering, manipulative, hands-on approach to the world that could grasp the meaning of smokeless chimneys and improved heating devices, but was impatient with the fabulous, the theophanous, the unworldly." Insofar as Christians, through God's

grace, become interested in that which they cannot physically touch, it appears clear that Franklin, unless the change occured when he was very old, was not touched by that grace.

772. See Page Smith, *John Adams* (Garden City, N.Y.: Doubleday, 1962), 921, for a well-written summary of viciousness: "The guillotine fell with the regularity of a metronome . . . young women whose crime lay in their birth were roasted alive in the Place Dauphine; priests were hacked to pieces on their altars. . . . Young men and women were lashed together in 'Republican marriage,' drowned or smashed by cannon fire, and hurled into open pits. One government followed another; an old terror gave way to a new one, and each new turn of the Revolutionary wheel served only to double the enthusiasm of the American Francophiles."
773. See Flexner, *George Washington: Anguish and Farewell*, 3:389, 392.
774. Proclamation of 30 May 1793, in Philip S. Foner, ed., 64. The proclamation argued that the revolutions "have withdrawn the veil which concealed the dignity and the happiness of the human race, and have taught us, no loner dazzled with adventitious splendor, or awed by antiquated usurpation, to erect the Temple of Liberty on the ruins of Palaces and Thrones."
775. Thomas Fleming, *1776: Year of Illusions* (New York: Norton, 1975), 114.
776. Ibid., 125-26.
777. Smith, *John Adams*, 920.
778. See Herbert M. Morais, *Deism in Eighteenth Century America* (New York: Columbia University Press, 1934), 153-55.
779. Some later came back; John Randolph of Roanoke, Virginia, read Voltaire and Rousseau and then condemned Christianity, but in 1817 he wrote in a letter to Francis Scott Key that he finally had faith in Christ and assurance that his sins were forgiven. (See Henry Adams, *John Randolph* [New York, 1898], 14.)
780. Morais, *Deism in Eighteenth Century America*, 22.
781. E. H. Gillett, *History of the Presbyterian Church* (Philadelphia, 1864), 1:296-98.
782. Morais, *Deism in Eighteenth Century America*, 161-62.
783. For additional detail, see Marvin Olasky, *Central Ideas in the Development of American Journalism* (Hillsdale, N.J.: Lawrence Erlbaum, 1991), 58-60.
784. Jonathan Elliot, ed., *The Debates in the Several State Conventions on the Adoption of the Federal Constitution* (Philadelphia: Lippincott, 1901), 4:543-35. The legislature stated that "the United States[note the plural], at the time of passing the Act concerning Aliens, were threatened with actual invasion; had been driven, by

the unjust and ambitious conduct of the French government, into warlike preparations, expensive and burdensome; and had then, within the bosom of the country, thousands of aliens, who, we doubt not, were ready to cooperate in any external attack." The Sedition Act, according to its backers, was not a dimunition of freedom, because "the genuine liberty of speech and the press is the liberty to utter and publish the truth; but the constitutional right of the citizen to utter and publish the truth is not to be confounded with the licentiousness, in speaking and writing, that is only employed in propagating falsehood and slander." Governors from Pontius Pilate onward, however, have had trouble discerning what the truth is.

785. Resolutions passed by the Kentucky legislature on November 10, 13, 14, and 22, 1798; Elliot, *The Debates in the Several State Conventions on the Adoption of the Federal Constitution*, 4:540, 545.

786. Elliot, *The Debates in the Several State Conventions on the Adoption of the Federal Constitution*, 4:528. The resolutions were passed by the legislature on December 21 and 24, 1798, with wording as follows: "That this Assembly doth explicitly and peremptorily declare, that it views the powers of the federal government as resulting from the compact to which the states are parties, as limited by the plain sense and intention of the instrument constituting that compact; and that, in case of a deliberate, palpable, and dangerous exercise of other powers, not granted by the said compact, the states, who are parties thereto, have the right, and are in duty bound, to interpose, for arresting the progress of the evil, and for maintaining, within their respective limits, the authorities, rights, and liberties, appertaining to them.

"That the General Assembly doth also express its deep regret, that a spirit has, in sundry instances, been manifested by the federal government to enlarge its powers by forced constructions of the constitutional charter which defines them; and that indications have appeared of a design to expound certain general phrases (which, having been copied from the very limited grant of powers in the former Articles of Confederation, were the less liable to be misconstrued) so as to destroy the meaning and effect of the particular enumeration which necessarily explains and limits the general phrases, and so as to consolidate the states, by degrees, into one sovereignty . . . ."

787. Ibid., 530.
788. Ibid., 531.
789. Ibid., 532.
790. Ibid., 534, 536.

791. Ibid., 547.
792. Ibid., 548.
793. "The ultimate right of the parties to the Constitution, to judge whether the compact has been dangerously violated, must extend to violations by one delegated authority as well as by another—by the judiciary as well as by the executive, or the legislature."
794. Elliot, op. cit., 549-50.
795. Elliot, *The Debates in the Several State Conventions on the Adoption of the Federal Constitution*, 4:551. Madison hit hard, noting that those favoring big government were attempting "to expound these phrases, in the Constitution, so as to destroy the effect of the particular enumeration of powers by which it explains and limits them. . . ." He even used words suggesting conspiracy: "a design has been indicated to expound these phrases. . . ."
796. Ibid.
797. Ibid., 553, 567. In words that were almost direct quotations of anti-Federalist concerns, Madison noted that "to consolidate the states into one sovereignty nothing more can be wanted than to supersede their respective sovereignties, in the cases reserved to them, by extending the sovereignty of the United States in all cases of the 'general welfare'—that is to say, to all cases whatever." That was wrong not only in practice but in logic, Madison noted, if the Constitution is analyzed squarely: "A preamble usually contains the general motives or reason for the particular regulations or measures which follow it, and is always understood to be explained and limited by them. In the present instance, a contrary interpretation would have the inadmissable effect of rendering nugatory or improper every part of the Constitution which succeeds the preamble."
798. Ibid.
799. Elliot, *The Debates in the Several State Conventions on the Adoption of the Federal Constitution*, 4:571-72.
800. Ibid., 567.
801. Ibid., 572.
802. Adams, *Writings*, 4:394-95.
803. Nathanael Emmons, *A Sermon preached before [the] governor . . . and House of Representatives . . . May 30, 1798, being the day of General Election* (Boston: Printed for the State, 1798), 21.
804. Ibid., 25.
805. Ibid., 31.
806. Ashbel Green, 34.
807. Ibid., 34-35.
808. James D. Richardson, ed., *A Compilation of the Messages and Papers*

of the Presidents (Washington, 1896), 1:269-70, 284-86. John Adams' position evidently was similar to that of Irving Kristol today: "People need religion. It's a vehicle for a moral tradition. A crucial role. Nothing can take its place."

809. Adams, *Writings*, 4:337.
810. Was Washington a Christian? From his words, we cannot say. Throughout the 1790s his customary language concerning religion was instrumentalist: He did not talk about the truth of Christianity.
811. Washington, *Papers*, 35:229-30. Washington had made a rough draft of what he wanted to say, and Alexander Hamilton (with some input from James Madison) developed it. Once again, Washington worked over Hamilton's material and only proceeded with the ideas that were faithful to his own thinking.
812. Henry, *Life, Corespondence, and Speeches*, 2:631.
813. Ibid., 632. Henry added, "Reader! whoever thou art, remember this; and in thy sphere practise virtue thyself, and encourage it in others."
814. *Gazette of the United States*, quoted in Brodie, *Thomas Jefferson: An Intimate History*, 317.
815. Naemie Emery, *Alexander Hamilton* (New York: Putnam's, 1982), 174; John Adams' letter to Abigail, 9 January 1797.
816. Charles J. Stille, *The Life and Times of John Dickinson* (Philadelphia: Historical Society of Pennsylvania, 1891), 282, 286-87.
817. Anthony Stokes, 138; cited in Bernard Bailyn, *The Origins of American Politics* (New York: Knopf, 1968), 72-73.
818. Lilian Miller, 36-37. Dunmore, again dismissing the power of ideas, wrote to the Earl of Dartmouth in 1774 that "if it had been thought fit to vest all the [patronage] which this government affords in the hands of the governor, I should have had the means of keeping down the attempts of party and faction which have put the public affairs of this colony in the alarming situation in which they actually stand." (See Leonard Labaree, *Royal Government in America* [New Haven: Yale University Press, 1930], 106, and Albert Berry Saye, *New Viewpoints in Georgia History* [Athens: University of Georgia Press, 1943], 116-17.)
819. Bladen's document is reproduced in *William and Mary Quarterly*, (1960): 521-30.
820. William Keith, *Discourse*, quoted in Herbert L. Osgood, *The American Colonies in the Eighteenth Century* (New York: Columbia University Press, 1924-1925), 2:334-35.
821. Ibid.

822. Bolingbroke, *Political Tracts*, 76, cited in Burgh, *Political Disquisitions* (London 1774), 3:111.
823. Burgh, *Political Tracts*, 3:30.
824. Ibid., 29.

Index